Veloce *Classic Reprint* Series

BSA

Motorcycles – the final evolution

Other great books from Veloce Publishing –

A-Z of popular Scooters & Microcars, The (Dan)
Beginner's Guide to Classic Motorcycle Restoration, The (Burns)
BMW Boxer Twins (Henshaw)
BMW Boxer Twins 1970-1996 Bible, The (Falloon)
BMW Café Racers (Cloesen)
BMW Custom Motorcycles (Cloesen)
BMW GS (Henshaw)
BMW Motorcycle Story – second edition, The (Falloon)
Bonjour! Is this Italy? (Turner)
Book of the classic MV Agusta Fours, The (Falloon)
Book of the Ducati Overhead Camshaft Singles, The (Falloon)
British Café Racers (Cloesen)
British Custom Motorcycles (Cloesen)
BSA 350, 441 & 500 Singles (Henshaw)
BSA 500 & 650 Twins (Henshaw)
BSA Bantam (Henshaw)
BSA Bantam Bible, The (Henshaw)
BSA Motorcycles - the final evolution (Jones)
Caring for your bicycle (Henshaw)
Caring for your scooter (Fry)
Drag Bike Racing in Britain (Lee)
Ducati 750 Bible, The (Falloon)
Ducati 860, 900 and Mille Bible (Falloon)
Ducati 916 (Falloon)
Ducati Bevel Twins (Falloon)
Ducati Desmodue Twins (Falloon)
Ducati Desmoquattro Twins - 851, 888, 916, 996, 998, ST4 1988 to 2004 (Falloon)
Ducati Monster Bible, The (Falloon)
Fine Art of the Motorcycle Engine, The (Peirce)
From Crystal Palace to Red Square (Turner)
Funky Mopeds! (Skelton)
Harley-Davidson Big Twins (Henshaw)
Hinckley Triumph triples & fours 750, 900, 955, 1000, 1050, 1200 - 1991-2009 (Henshaw)

Honda CBR FireBlade (Henshaw)
Honda CBR600 Hurricane (Henshaw)
Honda SOHC Fours 1969-1984 (Henshaw)
How to Restore Classic Largeframe Vespa Scooters (Paxton)
How to Restore Classic Off-road Motorcycles (Burns)
How to restore Honda SOHC Fours (Burns)
How to Restore Suzuki 2-Stroke Triples GT350, GT550 & GT750 1971 to 1978 (Burns)
How to Restore Triumph Trident T150/T160 & BSA Rocket III (Rooke)
How your motorcycle works (Henshaw)
Italian Café Racers (Cloesen)
Italian Custom Motorcycles (Cloesen)
Japanese Custom Motorcycles (Cloesen)
Kawasaki Triples (Walker)
Kawasaki W, H & Z - The Big Air-cooled Machines (Long)
Kawasaki Z1 & Z900 (Orritt)
Kawasaki Z1 Story, The (Sheehan)
Lambretta Bible, The (Davies)
Lambretta LI Series Scooters (Sparrow)
Laverda Twins & Triples Bible (Falloon)
Mike the Bike – Again (Macauley)
Moto Guzzi 2-valve big twins (Falloon)
Moto Guzzi Sport & Le Mans Bible, The (Falloon)
Motorcycle Apprentice (Cakebread)
Motorcycle GP Racing in the 1960s (Pereira)
Motorcycle Road & Racing Chassis (Noakes)
Motorcycles (Henshaw)
Motorcycles & Motorcycling in the USSR from 1939 (Turbett)
Norton Commando (Henshaw)
Norton Commando Bible, The (Henshaw)
Off-Road Giants! (Volume 1) (Westlake)
Off-Road Giants! (Volume 2) (Westlake)
Off-Road Giants! (volume 3) (Westlake)

Piaggio Scooters - all modern two-stroke & four-stroke automatic models 1991 to 2016 (Willis)
Racing Classic Motorcycles (Reynolds)
Real Way Round, The (Yates)
RED BARON'S ULTIMATE DUCATI DESMO MANUAL, THE (Cabrera Choclán)
Royal Enfield Bullet (Henshaw)
Save the Triumph Bonneville! – The inside story of the Meriden Workers' Co-op (Rosamond)
Scooter Lifestyle (Grainger)
SCOOTER MANIA! (Jackson)
Slow Burn - The Growth of Superbikes & Superbike racing 1970 to 1988 (Guntrip)
Suzuki Motorcycles - The Classic Two-stroke Era (Long)
Tales of Triumph Motorcycles & the Meriden Factory (Hancox)
Triumph 350 & 500 Twins (Henshaw)
Triumph 350/500 Unit-construction Twins 1957 - 1973 Bible (Henshaw)
Triumph Bonneville (Henshaw)
Triumph Bonneville Bible (59-88), The (Henshaw)
Triumph Bonneville T140 (Paxton)
Triumph Production Testers' Tales (Hancox)
Triumph Speed Twin & Thunderbird Bible (Woolridge)
Triumph Thunderbird, Trophy & Tiger (Henshaw)
Triumph Tiger Cub Bible, The (Estall)
Triumph Trident & BSA Rocket III (Rooke)
Triumph Trophy Bible, The (Woolridge)
Velocette 350 & 500 Singles 1946 to 1970 (Henshaw)
Vespa - The Story of a Cult Classic in Pictures (Uhlig)
Vespa Scooters - Classic 2-stroke models 1960-2008 (Paxton)
Vincent Motorcycles (Guyony)

www.veloce.co.uk

First published in October 2014, this Veloce Classic Reprint published July 2019 by Veloce Publishing Limited, Veloce House, Parkway Farm Business Park, Middle Farm Way, Poundbury, Dorchester, Dorset, DT1 3AR, England. Fax 01305 250479/Tel 01305 260068/e-mail info@veloce.co.uk/web www.veloce.co.uk or www.velocebooks.com. ISBN: 978-1-787115-48-4. UPC: 6-36847-01548-0

BSA

Motorcycles – the final evolution

VELOCE

Brad Jones

Contents

Acknowledgements

As with most books of this nature, the co-operation and generosity of others has been essential in enabling the author to present something that is both authoritative and fresh. In this respect I would firstly like to thank Stephen Mettam, who held the position of BSA Motor Cycle Division Chief Stylist from 1967 to 1971 (and the man largely responsible for the appearance of the 1971 BSA and Triumph motorcycles), for the use of a multitude of period photographs from his personal collection, as well as supplying much information – both factual and anecdotal – that has allowed this book to greatly enlarge upon many topics with an accuracy that can only come from an eye witness.

The extensive BSA archives held by Warwick University have been invaluable in yielding much hitherto unused information, sourced from a number of original documents held within the institution. Likewise, the many photographs supplied by the Vintage Motor Cycle Club have also proved invaluable for both research and presentation purposes.

Photographers Dominique Bresson, Dan Mahony, Geoff James, and Thierry Bouguet, and Mortons Media photographic library made available a number of racing photographs that have greatly enhanced the visual aspect of several pages of the competition chapter.

NVT specialist Steve Sewell (www.bsauk.com) allowed me to use any number of his impressive collection of original BSA component drawings, adding yet another interesting facet to some of the chapters dealing with the motorcycles themselves.

And in America Ed and Arlene McDermott, who became BSA dealers during 1971, have freely provided fascinating and informative insight to how it was at dealer level.

Publisher's note
The contemporary images used within this book are, in some cases, not of the best quality. Nevertheless, because of their importance, they have been included in order to tell the whole story.

Foreword

I am flattered to have been asked to write this foreword, as I was very involved with the design of all of the BSA and Triumph motorcycles bikes built for sale in 1971-2.

Motorbikes are designed for a purpose: the two extremes must be at each end, the working bikes such as those used by the police and ambulance services, and at the other end, bikes used just for fun. On my first two visits to the USA, our most important market, conversations with bike owners confirmed how different were their requirements from those of the riders that I knew in the UK. I met no-one who regarded two wheels and a motor as economy transport. Every one of them used their motorbike for leisure:

"After a long, hot day in the office I ride for an hour in the desert; a six fifty is a great way to unwind.

"I have to get off-road and get away from everything, into the woods.

"I like to be out in the open: little traffic, no stop lights, no-one in my way."

And in answer to my curiosity regarding their wish for those so small fuel tanks:

"It only needs to be big enough to get me to the next hamburger stall."

"I ride hard for half an hour; a gallon is plenty enough."

Author Brad has devoted a lot of space to reactions worldwide, to the 1971 ranges of BSA and Triumph bikes. Anything made before yesterday may be called old. Soon it will be vintage, later it becomes veteran, and one day it will be called historic. The eminent historian Hugh Trevor-Roper has said: "Today, most professional historians 'specialise.' They choose a period, sometimes a very brief period, and within that period they strive, in desperate competition with ever-expanding evidence, to know all the facts." There are facts and there is still a lot of fiction regarding this range of bikes. Brad was still at junior school when these bikes were revealed in 1970; at that time he probably had not yet even noticed motorbikes. Now he loves the brand and owns a lot of models from this range, designed and built to sell in 1971 and 1972, and he has been finding out about them. At this time, about half of the BSAs were sold in the USA, and the rest were exported elsewhere or sold in the UK. Triumph was then owned by BSA, and some bikes were built by BSA and badged Triumph: about 85 per cent of Triumphs were sold in the USA, and the rest exported or sold in the UK. The UK was a small part of the total market.

Someone once said: "History is yesterday's news." And history is not just what happened then, it is what we make of it now. Every year or every century, someone discovers a little more about a particular subject. Four thousand years after, it can be so difficult to tie in the importance of a previously unknown item in the tomb of an Egyptian King: there is little or no contemporaneous evidence, particularly written evidence. Historians still debate when and who was the first to use a fork for eating, and that was only about five hundred years ago.

The bikes on these pages were built within living memory of some of us. Facts have to be easier to find – but are they? It is still a puzzle why someone pulled the plug at the last moment, and still a puzzle why so much money was required, and more, and more. The staff at

Mid-1971 and a press test day at Mallory Park race circuit, with Divisional Chief Stylist Stephen Mettam at speed on a Small Heath-built 250 Triumph Trail Blazer. (Author's archive)

Umberslade Hall are often accused of the downfall of BSA. All of the BSA design and development teams at Small Heath and Redditch, and the teams from Triumph at Meriden were relocated at the Hall. There they took on a big program for updated and entirely new models. The top management at the factories was well aware of any slippage in timing – much of it caused by delayed restructuring or unwillingness on its part – and had about one year's warning. Perhaps we will never know why this famous brand is no longer manufacturing. The factory no longer exists but we still have the last 'historic' magnificent BSAs.

Stephen Mettam
Scarborough,
England

Introduction

On the face of it 1971 promised much for the BSA Motor Cycle Division, though, as it transpired, it was ultimately to be a year of bitter-sweet contrast. On the one hand the 21-strong range of new BSA and Triumph models, ranging from 250cc to 750cc, and collectively known as 'The Power Set,' had been greeted with great enthusiasm by the world's press; in addition to which, racing versions of both brands' machines proved themselves in many of the world's most prestigious races, so often coming away with outright wins, thereby vanquishing the might and financial capital of the flourishing Japanese motorcycle industry.

On the other hand, the same year witnessed a series of events whose consequences were so severe as to see BSA cease manufacturing road motorcycles in 1972, followed by the company being wound up for good in 1973. The repercussions of BSA's unforeseen demise were so far-reaching as to be felt by the two remaining British volume bike manufacturers, namely Triumph and Norton Villiers. Regardless of several half measures over the next few years, as serious contenders in the worldwide market, the writing was clearly on the wall for these two concerns.

Presented within this book is an objective look at all of the 1971 model year motorcycles and related events that took place in and around this so-critical year. All the old – and so very often inaccurate – prejudices have been cast aside to make way for a fresh appraisal using much

archive material and, where unearthed, the actual words that were said at the time by those involved, and not the all-too-frequently twisted interpretations of them, some of which have, over time, grown into overblown and now tottering mythical behemoths.

It is disconcerting indeed to have discovered that some commentators have, over the years, completely contradicted their original opinions of some of the 'Power Set' machines, though it is entirely possible that, in latter years, pressure to conform to the now 'accepted' view may have come into play, such are the levels of emotion on this topic. However, and regardless of motive, this has played its part in portraying a distorted picture to a new generation of BSA and Triumph motorcycle enthusiasts, not to mention falsifying history. Often fuelling this negativity over the past four decades has been the deep and bitter resentment that is still so prevalent in some of the ex-employees from both factories, and in this respect, the Division's Research and Development Centre at Umberslade Hall comes in for a particularly hard time, though, as we shall see, some of what has done the rounds over the years has little actual bearing on the truth.

As the 1960s drew to a close, the Division had at last awoken to the fact that it needed new engine designs to remain competitive in the coming decade, and the 'Power Set' was, with the exception of the all-new 350cc DOHC Twin, intended as something of a stopgap. Umberslade

Hall's engineers were by the start of the 1970s working on, amongst other things, a completely new range of two-stroke engines, ranging from 50cc to 400cc; a 350cc, four-valve DOHC Single, and the continued development of the Division's rotary engine, the potential of which was eventually realised some 20 years later, when it appeared as a race-winning Norton.

The optimism felt by some was illustrated in October 1970, following a week-long visit that took in both factories and Umberslade, when Triumph's US sales team, numbering over 20 members, returned to the States confident for the future. Heading the Group, BSA Company Incorporated Ltd's (BSA Inc) Sales Executive Vice-President, Dave Bird, summed up the reaction of the team thus: "We were particularly interested to see Umberslade and to learn the extent of the test facilities and the future planning programme there. Everyone in the party now realises just how much work is being done, and they are returning with considerable enthusiasm for the 1971 range of machines."

Without doubt some fundamentally poor decisions and actions were implemented at various levels within the Division, not to mention the influencing factors from outside the factory gates which contributed to BSA's financial crash in the summer of 1971. But for the bikes themselves to shoulder so much of the blame, as has often been the case, is for the most part unfair. Despite the American motorcycle press being virtually unanimous in its praise for most aspects of the new models, the only sure-fire test of their sales success (or otherwise) failed to occur, simply because at the peak selling period in the States (BSA's/Triumph's largest market by far) very few machines were actually available in the country, so no-one really knows how successful they would have been: it is from this uncertainty that the negatively biased speculation has been permitted to grow. Ironically, US demand for BSA/Triumph's 1971 models was higher than that of any previous year.

While the bulk of this work naturally concentrates on BSA, because of the intertwined nature of Triumph Motorcycles in the Small Heath company's affairs (due to the commendably rationalised 1971 models, and BSA owning the Meriden-based concern outright), Triumph tends to fade in and out of the picture throughout the book. The latter half of the 1960s was to witness a mutual and counterproductive dislike developing between the two factories, the seeds of which were apparently sown once Triumph's 200cc Tiger Cub had, in the name of

rationalisation, transmogrified into the Bantam Cub in 1966 – in actuality, little more than a BSA Bantam fitted with a Tiger Cub engine. Introduction of the badge-engineered 250cc TR25W two years later would only exacerbate the trend, with both models being assembled at BSAs Small Heath Works from the onset.

Using this book

By the late 1960s, in the interest of secrecy all new motorcycle developments had been allocated an anonymous-sounding project number (ie P25, P30, etc), and these numbers are referred to extensively throughout this book. Each project number loosely encompasses the model's engine type, and, where necessary, bridges both marques, though there are contradictions within this framework – the relevant listings are given here for reference. Triumph model types are always preceded by the letter T.

Number	Model
P22	K2 Ariel 3 – 50cc
P25	D18 Bantam – 175cc
P30	E35 Fury, T35 Bandit – 350cc
P34	B25/B50 Gold Star/Victor T25 Blazer/Trailblazer – 250cc/500cc
P36	T100 Daytona/Trophy – 500cc
P39	A65 Thunderbolt/Lightning/Firebird Scrambler/TR6 Tiger/Trophy T120 Bonneville – 650cc
P40	A75 Rocket 3/T150 Trident – 750cc
P40/13	A75 Vetter Chopper/TRX75 Hurricane – 750cc

There were, in essence, two separate markets in which both factories operated – the USA, known at the time as 'export,' and 'home and general export' (home/gen-ex), denoting the UK and rest of the world. In the interests of clarity, all references to USA models within this book are referred to as US-spec or USA-spec.

Throughout the book references are made to Armoury Road, Small Heath, and Meriden. The first two denote BSA's factory, and the latter Triumph's factory.

With regard to motorcycles built at Small Heath, where build and dispatch dates are listed, accepted wisdom dictates that the 'date built' column represents just that. However, there is an equal likelihood that this actually refers to the date each machine entered the factory's dispatch department.

More information on the subjects covered in this book can be found at www.bsa1971.com.

Chapter 1

Small Heath Works, subsidiary companies and reorganisation

The beginning

Founded as the Birmingham Small Arms Company in 1861 by a consortium of gunsmiths, it was a further 49 years before motorcycles were manufactured at the Small Heath Works, though the company had diversified into bicycle components from 1879, and complete bicycles by the early 1880s. The original factory building had been completed by 1862, though only its front block was to survive until demolition during the mid-1970s, the other three sides being destroyed during the Second World War. The complex grew in size with an assortment of buildings being erected over the years, until the final significant construction was completed in 1916. This last building was an enormous, four-storey, three-part linked block that became the 'face' of the Small Heath Works; more so once three large letters spelling 'BSA' were mounted on the end of each of the three sections during the 1950s, though it did undergo some major alterations

The earliest known photograph of the Small Heath works, dated 1867. Following the Second World War, only the front block on the left remained intact. (Author's archive)

due to wartime bomb damage. The block – throughout its life unofficially referred to as the 'new building' – had much of its capacity utilised for engine building and testing, and motorcycle assembly until 1970, as well as housing the drawing offices and main enamel shop, to name but a few departments. The purpose-built street leading to the main entrance was named Armoury Road for obvious reasons, and formed part of the postal address.

The company was able to make and machine many components to finished product on-site, with workshops capable of aluminium casting, chrome plating, etc, as well as its multiple machine shops and the big forge works.

Satellite works

A smaller factory, Waverley works, sited the other side of the Moore Street Terminus railway line that ran parallel to Armoury Road, had been home to Motoplas, BSA's motorcycle accessories company, as well as the service department throughout the 1950s and much of the 1960s.

A further armaments factory in Montgomery Street, whose south-eastern entrance was literally opposite Armoury Road, was also to house various engineering departments in later years once gun-making had ceased.

A fourth factory, some 12 miles (19km) distant at Redditch, had been built by BSA in 1938, and following the cessation of war, was to manufacture the 'S' series Sunbeam motorcycles, after having taken over that company in 1943. The engine of BSA's ubiquitous two-stroke Bantam was also assembled at Redditch, since the model's introduction in 1948, transferring to Small Heath in 1970. During the late 1960s the factory was also home to some of the smaller BSA group engineering subsidiaries.

The early 1950s again saw BSA expand its motorcycling interests by buying out both Triumph and Ariel Motors, though the latter concern would be extinct as a motorcycle manufacturer by 1967, having already moved production to Armoury Road in 1963. Significantly aiding Triumph's future prospects was its brand new factory built in countryside near to Meriden village in 1942, the previous premises in Coventry having succumbed to aerial bombardment during 1940. While some machinery was salvaged, much of Meriden's machine shops had been fitted out with new equipment, making them a favourable acquisition. Triumph continued to prosper, with the vast majority of its bikes being sold in the USA, where they consistently held a higher profile than those of BSA. Even after the BSA crash of 1971, Triumph managed, after a fashion, to retain its individuality as a manufacturer until its eventual demise in 1983.

To date

The much vaunted 'family' image at Small Heath was indeed fact, and not something borne of a peep through rose-tinted glasses, and, in general, manifested itself in two different ways. It was not uncommon for successive and current generations of families to be employed 'at the BSA' simultaneously, and the many works outings, social clubs, sports teams, Christmas parties and charity events all helped to foster a community feeling. Outside of the factory BSA's voluntary Recreation Association regularly organised benefits for local groups, such as pensioners and orphans. Additional to this, each month the Board of Directors allocated varying sums of money to go to charities deemed worthy. To keep the whole group informed of current inter-group developments, an in-house monthly newspaper was also issued.

By the end of the 1960s, a fair proportion of the 3500 production-orientated workforce was made up of West Indian and Asian immigrants. There were no major racial problems within the works, which, considering the times, probably says a lot about how the company was run at shop floor level. In stark contrast, the Meriden works was populated by a predominantly white workforce, coupled with poor racial tolerance.

Parent company – Board of Directors

The Board of the Birmingham Small Arms Company Ltd was, by February 1970, made up of eight directors, some with big profiles within the company, such as Chairman Eric Turner, who had been there since 1960, and the relative newcomer (1967), Managing Director Lionel Jofeh. Most of the other members were to remain relatively anonymous to the group's large workforce, though all were also board members of various other group companies.

Pictured in the 1950s, in the foreground is the 'new' building, while at the other extremity is the only remaining part of the original 1862 building. (Author's archive)

(From left) Chairman Eric Turner, Managing Director Lionel Jofeh, and Finance Director Laurie Beeson. Once Jofeh had been appointed, Beeson was dissuaded from involving himself with certain aspects of the Motor Cycle Division accounts. (Courtesy VMCC)

In general, the Board met monthly (interspersed occasionally with stock transfer committees, attended by the Chairman and Finance Director only), to deal with the group's expenditure, takeover bids, property leasing, high level appointments, and public donations etc. Bi-monthly Managing Director's reports of the group's subsidiary companies were discussed, with any action deemed necessary being sanctioned.

As with most large corporations, a private minutes book existed which had a very restricted circulation, probably only for the eyes of executive and non-executive directors: not really surprising as it often contained sensitive agenda such as directors' remuneration, high profile dismissals, controversial reports, etc.

While the transfer committees were held at Small Heath, the Board Meetings took place at BSA House in London, a building leased by BSA since the 1950s. Standing on a corner of St James Street in the borough of Westminster, the six-storey premises initially comprised showrooms on the ground and first floors, where BSA group products were often displayed up until the latter part of 1971. Directors and – where known – their prime business interest were –

Eric Turner, CBE	Group Chairman
Laurie Beeson	Administration & Finance Director
R Danielson, MBE	Metal Components Division
John Hatch	Lazard Bros & Co Ltd
Lionel Jofeh, OBE	Divisional Managing Director
Samuel Roberts, CBE	G A Harvey & Co Ltd
John Rowe	Birtley Engineering
Harry West	Nuclear Power Group Ltd

In addition to the Directors, Company Secretary Graham Niven was also in attendance at all Board Meetings.

Group companies
During the period covered by this book the BSA group's engineering empire consisted of several divisions, most comprising a number of companies, the majority of which BSA owned outright. The group's structure was thus –

Motor Cycle Division
BSA Motorcycles Ltd
BSA Motoplas Ltd
Triumph Engineering Company Ltd

USA
Birmingham Small Arms Company Incorporated

Research establishments
Group Research Centre
Motor Cycle Division Research Establishment

Metal components
BSA Sintered Components Ltd
Belford Sintered Metals Ltd
BSA Metal Powders Ltd
BSA Precision Castings Ltd
BSA Monochrome Ltd
BSA Foundries Ltd
BSA Alycast Ltd

Coal preparation & material handling
Birtley Engineering Ltd

Birtley Manufacturing Ltd

General engineering
BSA Guns Ltd
BSA Allvin Ltd
BSA Redditch Ltd
BSA Carbodies Ltd
Ucan Products Ltd

Central heating
Harford-Unical Ltd

Non-motorcycling
The central heating company, based at Montgomery Street and known as BSA Harford until December 1970, dealt, in the main, with the development, assembly and distribution of oil-fired domestic heating boilers and radiators, at one stage leasing a fleet of sign written trucks to a road distribution company for this purpose. In August 1970, the company formed a partnership with British Petroleum and Shell-Mex which, by the end of the year, witnessed record levels of production and sales in the UK and a change of name to Harford-Unical Ltd.

Chesterfield's Birtley Engineering had a primary interest in supplying specialised plant to the UK coal mining industry, and even though, in 1969, it managed to win a prestigious contract in Canada, whereby it designed and supervised the setting up of a completely new mining complex, the slowly shrinking UK industry forced the company to diversify a little.

The first significant step into pastures new was heralded in 1970 by the GPO awarding Birtley a £350,000 contract for the fit-out of a new, partially automated sorting office in Leicester, followed shortly afterward by Birtley supplying 180 weir gates to Romania: a deal worth £100,000. The diversification policy also saw the company's Durham-based manufacturing works fabricate its own designs of steel, glass fibre and teak up-and-over garage doors. While under the control of BSA, Birtley remained a profitable company.

The divisional title of 'General Engineering' covered the Small Heath Works-located operations, including gun manufacture, the Allvin vending machine company (a recently acquired shareholding), Carbodies – the Coventry-based builder of the iconic Metropolitan London taxi (using its own bodyshell on a British Leyland-supplied chassis, and with BL engine), Ucan – specialised in fixings for the construction industry (in early 1971 the Surrey company expanded its interests into the profitable DIY market by buying out London-based S Greenman Ltd), plus the Redditch factory which, by 1970, had become

something of a white elephant, now only housing various small parts of the Metal Components Division, such as Precision Castings and Monochrome. Falling under the Metal Components umbrella, the latter was a highly technical outfit, specialising in precision-hard chromium plating on items such as cylinder bores and industrial hydraulic and pneumatic rams of up to 30ft (9.12m) in length. However, due to a drop off in orders, the decision was made to close the company in April 1971.

In contrast, towards the end of 1969, the Tipton-based BSA foundry was showing such promise in what was a swiftly expanding market that the BSA parent board agreed to sanction £500,000 for a totally new seven acre

By the end of the 1960s several of the group's metal components companies were regularly exhibiting at many of Europe's big trade fairs. (Courtesy VMCC)

(28,328sq m) plant to be built at Darlington (although within six months the cost had spiralled to £750,000). Both plants' main work was now in the area of 'shell moulding:' a casting process whereby the use of a silicon-coated sand (zircon) enabled better results in accuracy and productivity rates. Aided by the implementation of modern automated systems, a reduction in workforce numbers was also achieved.

Sintered Components, and the recently acquired Belford Sintered Metals, located in the north east in County Durham, were undoubtedly the pride of the Metal Components Division, using the most modern equipment and know-how in sintering technology. In brief, the process of sintering involves making components (ie car door lock mechanisms, sprockets, oil pumps, etc) that would normally be time-consuming to machine from a casting, by compressing a combination of metal powders at extremely high pressure, followed by a hardening process via a special furnace. The finished component is

Leaders in powder metallurgy

BSA SINTERED COMPONENTS LTD

dimensionally very accurate and strong. During 1969, the two companies held a one third share of the UK market.

Sintered Components moved from BSA's Montgomery Street premises to Waverley Works during 1968, leaving Metal Powders as sole occupier. The move was timed to coincide with that of Sintered Component's Somerset subsidiary – SMC Sterling – to the same premises, though, at the last minute, many key members of the workforce opted out of the previously agreed transfer to Waverley, resulting in a larger than planned loss of output. This necessitated BSA having to fill the vacancies locally, and was the cause of the only fluctuation in profit in recent years: another successful company within the BSA group.

Alycast was acquired by BSA in early summer 1970, previously supplying the Motor Cycle Division with components such as alloy wheel hubs for some years. Specialising in aluminium die casting, the Telford New Town works was subsequently extended in late spring 1971 to (ironically) meet the demands of the Motor Cycle Division.

Although all of the Metal Components companies returned good trading figures for 1970 – despite the many industrial disputes throughout the UK at the time – as with most group companies whose products were closely tied to the motorcycle business, 1971 proved a poor year financially for Alycast.

Whilst not listed in the group's portfolio, BSA had a significant investment in Alfred Herbert, a machine tool company largely allied to the motor industry, and it, too, also endured a rather poor 1971, due to a drop in demand for its products.

Group research establishment

Sited in the Kitt's Green area of Birmingham, the Group Research Centre was a science-based department that specialised in fields such as metallurgy and electronics, the results of which could benefit any group company. In 1970, as part of the BSA group's expansion for the future, new laboratories were built on to the existing building, doubling the size of the centre. At the time, the centre was being run by D A Oliver, CBE, under the title of Director of Research, before he retired in May 1971 and was succeeded by H C Child.

Motoplas

BSA launched its motorcycle accessory company, Motoplas, in the 1950s, which was initially housed at Waverley Works, then Armoury Road until autumn 1970, when it finally moved to Montgomery Street. Its products always centred around windshields, rear view mirrors, crash bars, and the like, though many more diverse products were developed over the years, and by the late 1960s Motoplas catered for most other brands of motorcycles as well. The contact for interested dealers was Motoplas Sales Manager S Fitzmaurice, who retained his office at Armoury Road after the department's move.

Troubled times

Having already won the Queen's Award to Industry for Export in 1967 and 1968, at this point it is worthwhile explaining the financial problems that BSA faced as it approached the 1970s. By mid-1969, having published the interim stockholders' report, the company openly admitted that things were not quite as they should be. For the first time in the decade the half-yearly profits were substantially lower than the previous year's, the deficit being a massive £650,000, and the following six months were to tell the same tale. The explanations were genuine enough, though, ranging from increased raw materials and labour costs, a drop in profits from two of the group's subsidiary companies, the unforeseen problems that came

Caron Gardner greatly enhancing the Motoplas accessories stand at the Olympia Show of January 1971. The well kitted out BSA A65 wears several of the company's products. (Courtesy VMCC)

out of re-siting another (Sintered/SMC), and a drop off of BSA and Triumph motorcycle sales in the USA, which was by far the Motor Cycle Division's largest market.

The increasing presence of competitive Japanese motorcycles in the States was one reason for this; lower than expected sales of the new 750cc, three-cylinder bikes (due not to their performance – they were the fastest production bikes in the world at the time – but because of their rather ugly styling) another, and the growing difficulty potential customers were experiencing trying to obtain hire purchase yet another, thereby favouring the smaller and cheaper machines imported in abundance by the likes of Honda Yamaha and Suzuki. These and an incorrect market forecast which predicted overall US bike sales would fall in 1970 (sales figures actually dramatically increased!) resulted in the redundancy of 550 production-linked employees in August 1969.

BSA group Chairman Eric Turner offered the following account of the problems – '

"Since devaluation some 18 months ago, costs have been rising rapidly throughout British industry. The only ways in which these extra costs can be recovered are through greater volume of production, thus spreading fixed costs over larger numbers, through increased productivity or efficiency, or by increasing selling prices. This year, as was said in the interim statement, our sales will be less than we expected, improvements in productivity have been more modest, and, because 80 per cent of our output is exported, there is precious little chance of passing on increased costs to the customer. In these circumstances, the extra costs we have had to bear are bound to result in reduced profit margins.

"The main items are inevitably materials and labour. In addition to rises in the cost of raw materials, a number of our component suppliers have also felt it necessary to put up their prices to us. Labour costs have been rising rapidly, as have many other expenses, such as National Insurance, rates, transport, postage: in fact, virtually all of the hundreds of items of expense in any manufacturing organisation. In these circumstances, it becomes more than ever vital to reduce manufacturing costs by better production engineering and by improved design. Our activities at Umberslade, the Motor Cycle Division's research and development centre, have a direct bearing on both these areas.

"During the last few years we have built up our sales in the USA to such an extent that the majority of the more powerful machines sold are either BSA or Triumph. We still have the majority of the business, but the introduction of two or three large capacity machines during the last couple of months or so was bound to reduce our market share to some extent. Although we did not know when these models would be introduced, we expected that they would come sooner or later, and this is why we have been working for quite a long time on new models in the medium to small capacity classes."

August brought further anguish for the company when BSA shares nose-dived after the stock exchange learned of a supposed cash shortage within the group, with a loss in share value estimated at several million pounds. Eric Turner again spoke publicly, strongly dismissing the rumours, and going so far as to suggest that an ex-BSA employee may have been at the root of the scaremongering. In essence, BSAs brokers backed Turner's claim by stating that the financial rumours were largely based on gambling of a 'spiv' nature. The collective reassurances worked, and by the end of the following day's trading, the share price had returned to the pre-crisis level of 10s10½d.

Far from being complacent, however, the efforts of both manufacturers' general export sales departments resulted in new orders from fresh markets. Triumph's Export Sales Executive, John Wilding, made an extensive 15-country tour of South and Central America, returning with over £90,000 worth of immediate orders, while a similar visit to the Middle East bore fruit with the sale of a number of Triumph's famous 650cc 'Saint' police bikes to Kuwait for the first time. Not to be outdone, on a visit to Africa, BSA's Assistant Export Manager, Peter Glover, managed to increase sales of the A50/A65 'Police Special' and the company's 250cc Fleetstar, with new orders emanating from the Ivory Coast, Kenya, Lesotho, and Tanzania. Several countries in some of BSA's traditional Middle Eastern and Caribbean markets also placed new orders during the second part of the year.

So 1970 was a year of missed opportunity. As soon as signs that demand for motorcycles in the US were, in fact, on the up (1970s figures were actually to become the highest to date), the division increased motorcycle production as quickly as possible, though – not surprisingly – it ultimately failed to match 1969's total. Demand in the States for the division's bikes was high, and the stock of machines there was soon exhausted, leaving exasperated dealers crying out for replacements. The aesthetic problems of the 750 Triples had been partially resolved with Triumph's T150 receiving a face-lift similar to that of the T120 Bonneville, thus greatly enhancing appearance, and, at a stroke, banishing all sales resistance.

Hampering BSA's efforts to supply enough bikes was the huge production-oriented re-organisation at Armoury Road, which had commenced early in the year, compounded by a two-month strike by electrical components supplier Lucas, and industrial disputes at Britain's dockyards.

Even though the group's total profit was marginally down on that of 1969, this was largely due to re-jigging of the works, the associated closure of Redditch, and wholesale changes to the US setup (the latter operation accounting for in excess of £330,000), all of which were carried out as future investment policies. Additionally, BSA's bank overdraft had also been reduced from 1969's level. However, these two financially poor years – coupled with recent production capacity investment expenditure – left the company with smaller cash reserves than was desirable: at the very least a financially stable 1971 was essential.

Infrastructure investment
The first significant productivity-linked modifications

undertaken at Small Heath Works relevant to this book occurred in 1965, when a multitude of new equipment was purchased and installed – quickly enabling production figures to double – under the initiation of Harry Sturgeon, who had succeeded Edward Turner as Managing Director the previous year. Conclusion of this phase took place two years later when a computer-controlled Fisher & Ludlow conveyor system, that ran from overhead tracks and fed the assembly lines with components via containers, had also been installed. The combined cost of these two investments was an enormous £850,000.

By the end of the decade the 1971 season had been marked by BSA as the start of a new era, both in terms of product and output, and a reorganisation of the plant took place in 1970 in an effort to increase efficiency. Undertaken by the group's Manufacturing Services Department, and under way by March, the intention was to obviate, where possible, unproductive operations in the manufacture of parts and sub-assemblies, as well as refine the after-build procedures each motorcycle went through after being wheeled off the assembly line. To achieve this, the initial phase saw many storage and component production areas re-sited to minimise unnecessary movement of materials around the huge factory complex. All the raw materials were now to be delivered to the 'new' end of Small Heath, accessed from the adjacent Golden Hillock Road, and work their way through the factory to a marshalling yard sited in the older buildings, arriving as finished sub-assemblies such as frames, engines, forks, etc. It was here that the computer-controlled parts bins were loaded and despatched to the assembly lines, now located in the old Spares Department building, No 64 shop. The cost of resiting and rewiring the conveyor system alone amounted to a staggering £33,000. This reshuffle saw 'Spares' taking up residence in the Montgomery Street premises only a few years previously vacated by Sintered Components.

It wasn't only the engineering departments that were involved in these changes either, as the Planning, Administration and Buying departments also found themselves relocated. The final phase of the planned reorganisation terminated in October, the schedule having been carefully planned around the production of the new models which, in the event, were to be delayed until the end of the year in any case.

With the virtual closure of BSA's 47-acre (190,202sq m) Redditch factory as part of the reorganisation plan, approximately 400 machine tools migrated to Armoury Road, the transportation costs for which amounting to £7000.

Also involved in the changes was General Engineering

Guns at Armoury Road. In this regard a further £113,000 was allocated for many of the necessary building and structural alterations: for example, re-siting of several furnaces. Another 400 or so ex-Redditch machine tools were also allocated to this division; transport costs this time being around £8000. Unsurprisingly, some of the initial costings were subject to change, as unforeseen problems materialised and extra equipment was found to be necessary.

Total finance required for this phase of reorganisation

A windowless portal in the 'new building' awaits the ascent of one of the many relocated machine tools. (Courtesy University of Warwick Library)

– truly an enormous undertaking – was in the region of £175,000. Besides utilising much of BSA's commendably compliant workforce, led by Works Manager Alistair Cave, approximately 350 personnel from external contractors, consultants and agencies were also engaged.

The following are broken down examples of expenditure –

Rearrangement of frame section	£2000
Installation of existing rolling roads	£25,000
100-line board extension to internal telephone exchange	£6218
Transfer of enamel shop	£10,000
30cwt goods lift	£4250
Redecoration costs	£6450

Additional to the above was ongoing replacement of worn out machinery, and the purchase of new equipment necessary for building the new models (which, in some cases, required different machining techniques), and in order to meet the planned increase in production. Total

expenditure for this investment exceeded £1.5 million, and, again, examples are given of how the funds were spent –

Percussion screw press and ancillary equipment	£65,000
Heat treatment equipment and facilities	£77,325
Diamond turning lathe for pistons	£7060
6 special purpose automatic drilling machines	£25,000

The factory's already over-burdened heating system was significantly improved with the installation of an additional boiler. With the steady increase in personnel since the existing equipment had been commissioned, and the recent influx from Redditch (all Redditch employees had been offered posts at Small Heath), the plant's management pressed the Board for an upgrade during the reorganisation as the system could no longer cope with the demand placed upon it. With the current boilers constantly working to 100 per cent capacity during the winter, they were still almost 20 per cent short of the required output, and when a breakdown occurred, the whole system had to be shut down for repair work. In addition, general maintenance work could only be carried out during a short period in the early evenings. The new boiler alleviated these problems, and provided back-up for the first time, but at a cost of in excess of £30,000.

Once the reorganisation had been completed, it was calculated that 100,000 motorcycles per annum could be built, 25,000 more than was previously possible. On top of this figure was a planned yearly output of 25,000 Ariel 3 trikes.

Although never able to achieve anything like the production capacity of Small Heath, Triumph's smaller and more modern Meriden factory also benefited from over £120,000 worth of new machinery in 1970 alone, and during early spring 1971, in the interest of increased production, something in the region of 200 existing machine tools were relocated as part of the same programme.

Quality control

With the reorganisation complete, once the bikes left the assembly line, they descended to the basement via a lift, where they were first subjected to a run on the new 'rolling road' installation before undergoing several basic checks; only then being either packed, or, if for overseas shipment, crated.

It was in this department that, as part of a drive for improved quality control, a new process called 'quality audit' was introduced. This involved randomly picking a motorcycle from the first batch of a new production run and checking that it had been correctly packed, or crated, and that all external controls functioned correctly. The machine was then subjected to a 200-mile (321.8km) run on public roads, before being taken to the Motor Industry Research Association (MIRA) test circuit where rigorous speed and braking tests were carried out.

Upon returning to the works the engine was stripped and the parts inspected by engineers from departments such as Production, Planning, Design, and Inspection. Any faults found or improvements deemed worthwhile were reported to the respective department, where they were acted upon immediately. The machine was then rebuilt, incorporating any improvements/parts found necessary, and sent around Small Heath's own circuit several times as a final test. To verify that any changes implemented achieved the expected results, a machine from the final week's production of the same batch underwent the same rigours.

The process proved such a success that BSA Inc in America was able to terminate the 'quality check programme' previously carried out by dealers to ensure the machines they sold were as they should be.

Recruitment

An employee requirement forecast for motorcycle production, calculated very carefully to coincide with the start of the 1971 model build programme during mid-1970, was to become largely redundant as events unfolded. With production theoretically peaking during October with 550 examples of the P34 and 400 P39s; 64 P40s in November, and 550 of the ever errant P30 in April 1971, the delay experienced in all models actually reaching the assembly lines left the schedule in tatters.

To compound the recruitment problems, somewhat incomprehensibly Small Heath had failed to fill its skilled labour vacancies in time, even though several months' leeway had inadvertently been gained in this respect. By spring 1971, this was seriously affecting component supply, prompting Lionel Jofeh to cite it as a major factor in the current production delays.

Even P22 figures were all at sea, as for a period in autumn 1970 this was virtually the only model being built, with much of 1971's allocation produced in this period; again, eroding track worker estimates.

As part of the reorganisation, many departments were realigned, and with this came a multitude of new appointments. Since March 1969, over 40 managerial changes at works and divisional level were made, many of which came from outside the motorcycle industry, as areas such as Marketing and Warehousing were comparatively new to the Midlands motorcycling sector, and specialist knowledge was deemed necessary.

At this time, overseeing Divisional Engineering was Meriden-based Bert Hopwood, while at Armoury Road,

day-to-day running of the factory was still managed by the capable and forthright Al Cave, whose title of General Works Manager by now encompassed the duties of the recently-vacated Services Director post, following John Balder's departure during 1969.

As 1971 dawned, key departments at Armoury Road were organised as follows –

Manufacturing

Kenneth Strangward	Divisional Manufacturing Director
E J Dutton	Divisional Manufacturing Facilities
G T Davies	Divisional Manufacturing Processes Manager
Norman Shearer	Director Manufacturing Services Dept
G D Fearon	Manufacturing Data & Records Manager

Forge

Kenneth Allen	Manufacturing Manager
D Seaman	Deputy Manufacturing Manager

Pre-Production

Henry Vale	Engine Build & Test Production Manager

Quality Control

Vic Grey	Divisional Quality Manager
Jack Roberts	Quality Manager

Technical Service & Repair

Frank Adderley	Service Manager

Purchasing

L A Smith	Divisional Purchase Director

Costing

E G R Jones	Divisional Budget & Cost Controller
R Brown	Divisional Financial Procedures & Systems Manager
V D Smith	Engineering Cost Controller
Ken Peck	Forward Cost Estimating Manager

Warehousing & Despatch

John Henderson	Divisional Warehousing & Despatch Controller
Geoff Heath	Shipping Manager

Marketing

Peter Deverall	Divisional Marketing Director
John Jardine	Divisional Marketing Manager
F Marsden	Divisional Market Research Manager

Product Planning

F F R Clarke	Divisional Director
John Dumeresque	Divisional Overseas Planning

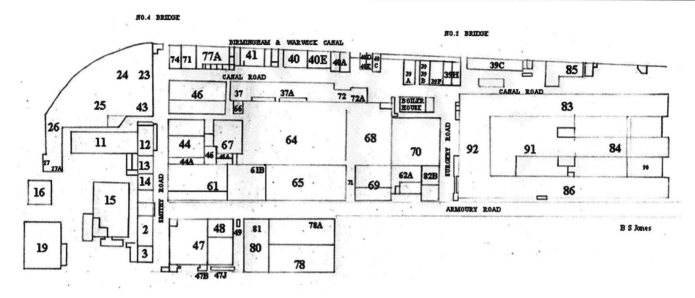

Small Heath plant layout following the reorganisation. The production area had moved from the 'new' building, far right, into 64 shop, the assembly lines now fed from the marshalling stores situated in the adjacent 68 shop. Both quality control and despatch departments were housed in the basement directly below 64 shop. (Author's archive)

Special Projects

Kenneth Walker	Divisional Manager

Publicity

Reg Dancer	Publicity Relations Officer
David Lloyd	Divisional Press Officer

Advertising

John Flexman	Divisional Advertising Manager
Peter Hotchkiss	Assistant Advertising Manager

Sales

John Harrison	UK Sales Manager
Ivor Davies	Deputy UK Sales Manager
Wilf Harrison	General Export Manager
Peter Glover	Assistant Export Manager
Norman Vanhouse	UK Fleet Sales Manager

Personnel

Gwyn James	Group Personnel Director
D V Young	Personnel Manager
P J Hill	Deputy Personnel Manager

Metallurgy

Stuart Abercrombie	Chief Metallurgist

Services

D Macdonald	Management Services Manager

Whilst clearly not Armoury Road appointments, because of the overlap in interests, it is also worthwhile listing here the principal posts for the research and development centre at Umberslade Hall –

Mike Nedham	Divisional Chief Engineer
Dr Stephan Bauer	Divisional Technical Director
Alan Sargent	Engineering Manager
Stephen Mettam	Chief Stylist
Ernie Webster (BSA) & Brian Jones (Triumph)	Chief Designers
Michael Martin	Chief Project Manager
Colin Saunders	Technical Services Manager
E Mosedale	Divisional Quality Engineer

Once Deputy Managing Director and Engineering Director Bert Hopwood had relinquished his position in summer 1970, Mike Nedham became responsible for all engineering matters, extending to both Armoury Road and Meriden Works, and in effect placing him as number three in the BSA Motor Cycle Division.

Containerisation

A new, more efficient and cost-effective transportation system was implemented for the major overseas markets (USA, Canada, Scandinavia, West Europe, Australia), utilising the then relatively new to Britain concept of containerisation, via the freightliner road/rail system that had been introduced as part of the 'Beeching' railway rationalisation plan in 1965.

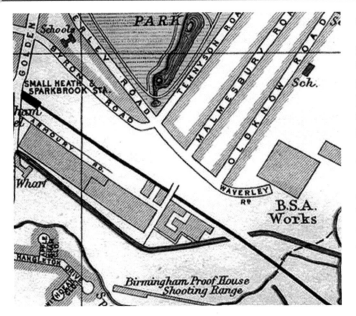

Waverley Road works on the right – a stone's throw from BSA's main factory buildings, centre left. (Author's archive)

BSA's nearby Waverley Road Works, situated northeast of the factory, was chosen as the 'shipping station,' the group's Board of Directors sanctioning the sum of £33,992 in October 1970 for the building's conversion and implementation of the necessary infrastructure. This, in the main, involved clearance of the existing works, which occupied 250,000 sq ft (23,225sq m) of floor space, and for many years housed the BSA Service Department, and Sintered Components since 1968. The alterations required the building of four loading bays suitable for the containers, each of which was 40ft (12.24m) long, and capable of holding approximately 44 crated motorcycles. In January 1971 the Board was asked for a further £16,065 for continued expenditure, which was forthcoming.

All machines earmarked for export from both Meriden and Small Heath Works were delivered to Waverley by lorry already crated, and, upon arrival, were sorted according to final destination. All of the relevant paperwork, such as packing lists, consignment and shipping notes, and invoices, was now produced on one machine specially designed for the purpose.

Once loaded the containers were road hauled to either the assigned dockyard or, alternatively, Birmingham's Landor Street freightliner depot, some two miles (3.2km) distant, for further transit by rail to Southampton Docks, from where loads destined for the USA and Canada sailed. All North American shipments were handled by the American container company Seatrain, with whom BSA had negotiated an exclusive contract.

By January 1971, a regular flow of containers were leaving Waverley on a weekly basis, all destined for the States, and initially carrying Small Heath's B25 and T25 250cc models, which were the first of the new bikes to be manufactured. By May, once both factories had been able to put all of their respective models into production (with the exception of the DOHC 350s), the flow of export machines was sufficiently impressive for BSA to hold a press conference, which, not surprisingly, coincided with the Division's largest shipment to date.

Two trains, laden with approximately 1400 America-bound motorcycles between them, were to leave Landor Street for Southampton Docks on subsequent days: 20 containers on the day of the conference, Tuesday, June 8, and the remainder the day after. Hauled by a 2580hp British Rail Class 47 locomotive, Tuesday's train carried a special nameboard: 'BSA Triumph Export Special.'

The conference was attended by the key men involved in the joint venture: namely, the division's Shipping and Despatch Manager, John Henderson, BSA Shipping

A loaded Seatrain container leaving Waverley Road for the Landor Street freight terminal. (Courtesy University of Warwick Library)

Manager Geoff Heath, and Seatrain's UK Marketing Director, Ralph Picariello.

Members of the press were shown around the depot, as well as given a trip up to Landor Street, where they witnessed the containers being loaded on to freightliner flats. For those who were interested – or whose expense budget was generous enough – continuing the journey to the train's destination at Southampton Docks was rewarded with proof of the division's commitment and dependency on the US market. Here, the containers were loaded onto the gas turbined powered ship, *GTS Oceanliner*, the world's fastest container ship at the time, whose maiden voyage had only taken place two-and-a-half months previously.

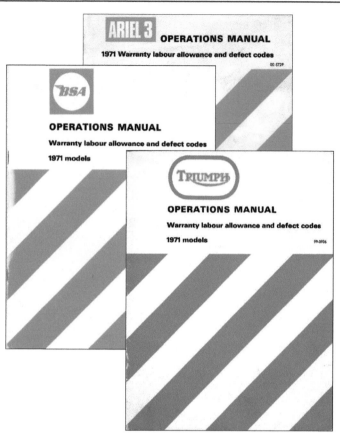

The three operations manuals that covered warranty work for all 1971 models. (Author's archive)

The first of the two freightliners prior to leaving Landor Street terminal for Southampton.
(Courtesy University of Warwick Library)

UK dealers

Whilst American dealers experienced many changes in sales and service procedures as a result of the restructuring of BSA's US organisation as 1971 approached, very little changed for their home market counterparts, with arrangements between factory and customers remaining the same. Two topics of note, however, were the revised system for BSA/Triumph warranty work, and the Personal Export scheme.

Commencing in 1971, while the three month warranty period for parts and labour remained the same, a revised dealer reimbursement system was introduced which, from

March 1, 1971, incorporated a work rate of £1.60 per hour, and operated in conjunction with the new Warranty Operations Manual introduced for each marque. The time allowance code – now broken down into hours and minutes – was to be entered on the new claim forms, rather than the actual hours and cost of parts, as had previously been the case, due to all warranty costings being processed by computer. Not only did the new, fixed, hourly rate generally benefit dealers, but where a bike displayed a second fault, the revised forms made an allowance for this possibility, thereby greatly reducing time spent on paperwork.

Personal export

Since July 1967, via a scheme known as Personal Export, Britain's motorcycle manufacturers were, in agreement with Her Majesty's Custom and Excise, able to offer foreign tourists new motorcycles at a considerably lower price than listed in their own country of origin. To qualify for the scheme – and avoid the extraordinarily high purchase tax that all British-built motor vehicles were saddled with (the rate of which was 36⅔ per cent by

One of several ads from UK dealers that appeared in American magazines during 1971. (Author's archive)

Purchased through the Personal Export scheme, American Charles Engberg collects his new, 1971 BSA A65 Lightning from Elite Motors. (Courtesy Charles Engberg)

1971, equating to a massive additional £148 on the retail price of the top-of-the-range BSA Rocket 3) – the potential buyer had only to reside outside of the UK, and collect the pre-paid bike in person. During the first year of the scheme, some dealers abused the system, presumably by selling to UK residents without charging the purchase tax, and this was brought to the attention of HM Customs, which made BSA liable for the unpaid taxation. Certainly, by 1969, all bikes earmarked for the scheme were pre-registered in Birmingham.

With US citizens the most affluent at the time, the scheme was generally aimed Stateside, and advertisements by several of the larger British bike dealers were regularly placed in American magazines prior to the start of each sales season, and continuing through to early summer. For 1971, potential American BSA/Triumph customers were able to save 30-40 per cent on showroom prices back home: not surprisingly, it was a popular option for many.

Initially adversely affecting the year's personal export sales figures was the relative lack of bikes in the UK as the summer began. Ironically, even though all but the P30 was in full production by May, the majority of output was rushed to the USA to alleviate the dearth of BSA and Triumph motorcycles there, which meant that customers sometimes had to settle for either the previous year's model or, worse still, buy a different marque!

Despite this – and as further proof of the popularity of the Power Set models – the month of August saw 267 BSA and Triumph motorcycles sold through the scheme: a considerable improvement over the same month the previous year, which had accounted for 152 bikes.

Umberslade Hall

Universally slated nowadays for all the ills that led to the demise of BSA, the R&D Centre located at the stately residence Umberslade Hall near Hockley Heath, undoubtedly made good sense at the time. This pooling of the division's resources in terms of each factory's design staff, development engineers, etc, had been instigated by Managing Director Lionel Jofeh's predecessor, Harry Sturgeon, shortly before his premature death in 1967.

After having already surveyed several potential premises by April, Jofeh had plumped for Umberslade, a mansion built at the end of the 17th century. Although, on the face of it, a rather unsuitable building for the intended purpose, a large extension housing a combined machine and workshop was soon built onto the southern side of the house, partially enveloping a series of single-storey extensions that gave way to two floors as the ground level sloped away to the rear, added over the years to provide ample facilities for the experimental and development work.

Of three storeys and internally featuring much wood panelling, the majority of the hall's first and second floors were used as offices by staff engaged on important design projects, such as the new rotary and four-cylinder engines, with many of the larger rooms divided up to provide additional office space.

A separate apartment on the first floor was occupied by the incumbent caretaker and his wife, who stayed on

once BSA had leased the premises, and, besides their normal caretaking duties, also ran the in-house dyeline printer. There was a further, non-motorcycle area within the building, used as an office by one of the family who owned the house and his secretary for the purpose of estate management, which, at the time, included two lakes, lawns, woodland and livestock within its 15 acres (60,702sq m), and organisation of the hall's upkeep.

All of the ground floor rooms featured high ceilings, and internal walls of nearly four feet (1.22m) thick, resulting in many doorways requiring two doors: one each side of the wall. The former ballroom – which sat centrally and to the front of the building – was utilised as the drawing office, with a small, mainly glass, cubicle erected in one corner in which the chief draftsman resided.

Within two months of taking up residency, the large entrance hall behind the drawing office that had, until then, been the domain of the receptionist, was also partitioned off, again to create further offices; even the stationery

Photographed in 1970, the circa 1700-built Umberslade Hall was leased in early 1967 by BSA. (Author's archive)

Top: The enormous workshop extension at the southern end of Umberslade Hall, as it nears completion. Bottom: The ballroom was utilised as the Centre's drawing office – space was always at a premium. (Author's archive)

December 1970 – the busy workshop with a number of test bikes receiving attention. (Author's archive)

cupboard doubled up as the computer link room for the Maths Group.

The conservatory situated at the northern end of the building became the Styling Department's office, with workshops located in the basement. Also sited beneath ground level were several more areas containing, for example, frame and brake testing rigs, as well as an engine dynamometer.

The following amusing anecdote from Chief Stylist Stephen Mettam well illustrates one of the building's aspects –

"The main conference room had two doorways: one from the hall and one from a corridor. For convenience, the one opening onto the corridor had its corridor door removed, leaving the internal one. The one to the hall was not used, so the cleaners parked a vacuum cleaner in this big 'cupboard.' No other staff ever used it – until the receptionist realized this was a conveniently close place to hang her coat out of sight.

"Late one afternoon a bunch of us were meeting in the conference room. At 5 o'clock the receptionist went from the hall into this 'cupboard,' closed the door and, in the dark, removed her skirt to put on her trousers (she rode a scooter). Our meeting finished and one member not familiar with Umberslade stood up with his papers and opened what he thought was the door through which he had entered, to be met by a loud scream. We all looked up at this poor girl standing there, horrified, in her knickers."

Give a dog a bad name

Much of the negative comment written about Umberslade Hall over the last four decades or so has gained such momentum that failing to include detrimental comment in modern works is, it would seem, almost a crime. Many apochryphal tales have been inflated out of all proportion; in all probability at the time out of anger and an understandable though misplaced bitterness at the total collapse of BSA, but later for no better reason than it was deemed fashionable to pour scorn on the centre, making it – along with the models that emerged from it – a scapegoat. As well as the design and development of motorcycles, in fact, the centre also carried out experimental work for BSA guns, and the group's tool and fixings subsidiary, Ucan.

Housing 270 staff at its peak, there were, without doubt, personnel problems at the Hall, which often stemmed from resentment between the various factions that had been transferred from either the Small Heath, Meriden and Redditch factories, and the many engineers who had previously worked in the British aircraft industry (although a hugely overlooked fact here is that these numbered around 60 only; less than a quarter of the workforce). In hindsight – and with regard to the latter contingent – integrating this number of personnel from an alien industry undoubtedly caused additional antagonism, which could have been avoided had a larger proportion of Umberslade's staff been recruited from within the motorcycle industry. However, to explain why the diversification of employees was considered necessary, when questioned about how BSA was to meet the ever increasing competition and stringent technical requirements to obtain the critical import licences, Umberslade boss Mike Nedham said –

"This is why we have had to recruit new people with special knowledge: only by pooling motorcycle knowledge with that of newly imported specialists can we hope to design and develop products that will be competitive in world markets."

Regrettably, the marque loyalty so prevalent amongst previous employees of both BSA and Triumph became a barrier to progress, manifested by a distinct, non-pooling of resources. The depth of this division was well illustrated by the lunchtime football matches played on the R&D Centre's immaculately-kept front lawn: although friendly, the teams were always BSA versus Triumph.

Much has been made of the influx of design engineers previously employed by aero companies such as Vickers Armstrong and Rolls-Royce, and the apparent resultant detrimental effect on the design and development of new motorcycles. Some aspects of these criticisms undoubtedly hold water; the rather different cultures of the aircraft and motorcycle industries initially problematic in terms of professional and personal clashes. However, it is interesting to note that of the six arguably most

important positions at Umberslade, only two came directly from this source: the top man at Umberslade, Divisional Chief Engineer Mike Nedham, and Engineering Manager Alan Sargent. Nedham had initially held a senior position at Westland Helicopters before moving on to Rolls-Royce Aero Engines. By virtue of an inter-aero company takeover, Sargent found himself working for Nedham, after recent engagement on engine fitment work for the supersonic airliner Concorde. Both men had strong motorcycling backgrounds, with Nedham at one stage working at the Scott Motor Cycle factory. By the time of his BSA appointment, Nedham was also extraordinarily well connected to some aspects of the motorcycle world, as Mettam explains –

"When we needed a top rider for a '3,' someone mentioned Agostini. At Meriden or Small Heath there would have been enough racing guys to ask, but at Umberslade we had few. Mike knew I was a keen GP follower so I was called to his office, and the conversation went like this:

Mike: What do you know about Agostini, have you heard of him?

Me: Very good, second perhaps to Hailwood. I have watched him race in the Isle of Man. Giacomo holds the record there for the fastest lap on a single, a Works 250 Benelli; better lap time than even any Manx Norton. He is under exclusive contract to race MV Agusta.

"As I spoke, Mike fumbled in a desk drawer until he found a notebook. Calling his secretary he handed her the open notebook, saying 'Call this number, [****] will probably answer; tell her I want to speak to Count Agusta, no-one else. If he is not there, ask when he will be. Stephen, don't leave.'

"Very soon he was through: they were obviously on Christian name terms and very familiar. Mike told him what he was with BSA and asked if we could borrow Agostini. They compared diary dates and that was that. I cannot remember now races we were short of a rider for: someone like Cooper or Pickrell must have been injured."

Of the remaining four posts, Technical Director Dr Stephan Bauer had been recruited for one from Norton Motors, where he had designed the revolutionary and award-winning Isolastic frame for the Norton Commando, though admittedly the Swiss-born physicist had also been at Rolls-Royce prior to his Norton engagement. Brian Jones (who initially held the post of Production Engineer), and Ernie Webster from Triumph and BSA became joint Chief Designers; Chief Project Manager was Michael Martin (brother of BSA Competition Shop boss Brian), and the man responsible for the appearance of the new machines – Stephen Mettam – had, shortly before being engaged by Triumph, been at the UK's leading design house, Ogle. Another keen rider, Mettam also raced a BSA Bantam 125, and an Ariel Arrow-engined 250 in the early 1960s.

Regardless of the many promising experimental projects undertaken at Umberslade – several of which were, over time, cancelled by Small Heath's Board of Directors – the centre is now only associated with the redesigned and rationalised BSA and Triumph models built for the 1971 selling season, and somewhat predictably, related events which led to the financial crisis that summer.

Such developments as the racing fairing that was fitted to the 1971 Daytona 200 winning and dominating 750 BSA/Triumph Triples rarely get a mention. The fairing had been designed by Umberslade engineers, who used a wind tunnel for air flow development work (commonplace within the aircraft industry since the early 1950s), resulting in a three-piece fairing that achieved a drag factor decrease of 5 per cent over the previous year's version.

New logo

It was during the restyling period that the logo used for BSA tank badges since the mid-1940s found itself being considered for change. The new E35 and A65 fuel tanks were to feature angled styling stripes in the vicinity of the badges, and while this looked fine on the right-hand side, on the left, the angles of the badge and stripe were opposing. It was suggested that the logo's trademark wing be abolished, and the angle of the left-hand badge reversed so that it would be at ease with the striping, resulting in separate left- and right-hand badges rather than an identical pair. Some appropriate decals were made up, but Mettam was not impressed by the idea, and managed to reach the compromise seen here, which still eliminated the problem of conflicting angles. A pair

Proposed tank decal and one of the prototype E35/A65 tank badges. In the event neither was adopted. (Author's archive)

of chromium-plated cast brass badges were made up from the drawings, although by the time that the Styling Department received them, the idea had already been vetoed from higher up. The design was used on an early styling mock-up of P30, albeit made of card, but these badges were never actually fitted to anything, and are thought to be the only pair in existence.

How high?

By far the commonest criticism levelled at the R&D Centre concerns the 'notorious' oil-containing frame designed for the BSA and Triumph 650cc Twins, designated P39, and its resulting seat height which, over the years, elicited comment about a rider needing to be a giant at least 6ft 6-inches (1.97m) tall in order to be able to ride the bike. So, was this true? Once again, things were not quite as these overblown myths suggest, although all of the 1971 oil-in-frame (o-i-f) 650 models do have a higher seat than previous twin-cylinder models.

The Triumph P39 frame, identical to BSA's version in all respects, bar the engine mounting lugs. (Author's archive)

Triumph's three P39 Twins – TR6, TR6C and T120 – are quoted by many period road tests as having a seat height of 34½-inches (87.6cm) – excessive, indeed, especially when compared with their BSA counterparts which could manage only 32½-inches (82.5cm) with exactly the same size frame!

Upon closer inspection it would appear that the 650 Triumphs were more usually fitted with excessively padded seats, which accounted for the extra two inches. 1971's Trident and the little-altered 500cc Trophy and Daytona models wore seats of the same proportions as 1970 bikes, and continued to use their existing frames: hence no disenchantment with these in that respect.

In what was, in all probability, a realisation of the increased seat height, exaggerated by the nose of the saddle being a little wider than on previous machines, BSA chamfered the edges of its seat, in a partially successful attempt to minimise this effect.

A cursory glance by even the layman reveals where

the problem lies: the seat rails were just too high, and this was relatively easily rectified for the 1972 model year, along with the fitting of slimmer seats for the Triumphs, whose padding was now more in-line with that used in 1970.

To put this into context, it's worth noting that, at 32½-inches (82.5cm), the seat is only half an inch taller than BSA's 1970 A65s, and both of that year's 750cc Triples, all of which featured a 32-inch (81.3cm) seat. A return to 1970 levels of seat padding and shorter rear damper units were the first shortcuts taken before the seat rails were actually lowered satisfactorily, though this left the seats with their low noses looking a little awkward. Official announcement about the altered frames came early in December 1971, with the declaration that all bikes from February 1972 would have the lower seating position.

Besides the slightly higher seat level, the P39-framed bikes entered production with reduced oil capacity: the deficit over the previous year's machines being one pint (1.125 litres), though the brochures actually quoted capacity as five pints (2.8 litres) rather than four (2.25 litres). The volume inside the oil tank had been sufficient enough for the correct quantity of lubricant, but problems with hot oil frothing on its return to the frame prompted Meriden's engineers to move the filler cap from behind the steering head to the back of the top tube under the seat nose, the returning oil now apparently running

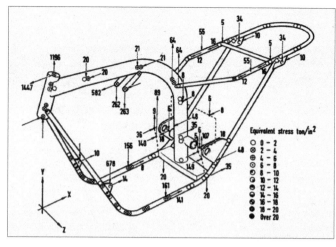

New technology for the Motor Cycle Division: a computer stress prediction diagram for the P39 frame. (Author's archive)

down from the top of the tube after exiting a return pipe positioned towards the front of the top tube; whereupon it had cooled sufficiently. Yet certainly on 1971 models, a glance into the re-sited filler cap reveals that the return pipe simply dumps the hot lubricant on top of the reservoir of oil in the rear vertical tube.

More mysterious still is that the division's then Deputy Managing Director, Bert Hopwood, stated that the reason the filler cap was moved was purely because of

Stephen Mettam speaking in early 1971 on the function of the Styling Department –

"The description of Stylist has so far only been used in the automotive industry. In other industries they are usually known as industrial designers. Our job is to make the motorcycle look a whole machine rather than a collection of individual parts. Heath Robinson contraptions may be great fun, but not many of us would want to use them in our daily lives.

"Over recent years there have been a number of mechanical changes that have required modifications and new components, and there has been a tendency to simply bolt them on in the most convenient place. If, in addition to being highly functional, the machine looks good and is in keeping with modern trends, it is obviously likely to attract more customers. Quite often it makes no difference to the working of the machine whatever the relationship of the individual parts to each other. But it can make a great deal of difference to the total appearance.

"In a nutshell, what we are out to do is to remove the

Chief Stylist Stephen Mettam some years prior to his BSA appointment, aboard his racing 125 Bantam. The stylised initials logo on the tank would accompany many of his later drawings. (Author's archive)

Model-maker Rodney Humphries, nearing completion of a wooden P30 mock-up engine unit. (Author's archive)

An unused decal designed for 1972's Triumph TR6C. (Author's archive)

bits and pieces image that has come to be associated with motorcycles.

"We have a head start in this field over our biggest competitor, the Japanese. Because we are a small industry – in comparison with the Japanese 'giants' – it is possible, for one thing, to provide our motorcycles with a better finish. It need cost no more to do a good design than a bad one, but it does cost slightly more in production to achieve the good looks which can attract the customer.

"We have tried to keep a family image for each marque; we have to keep the difference between BSA and Triumph but, at the same time, make the different things match up with the common parts to blend them into a whole.

"Market research has shown us that the first reason for anyone buying a particular model is its looks, and that is why the decision was made to set up this department. Their job is to decide what is needed to

make the motorcycle work; our job is to make the whole thing look attractive without losing any performance or ease of servicing qualities.

"Marketing tell us what kind of bike they want and the bike that comes off the production line must look right for the particular job it has to do. For instance, there is a big difference between a road machine and a motocross machine, although the basic parts are much the same.

"It is essential that we think in three-dimensional terms, because an object may look quite right from one angle but quite different from another. After discussion right at the start of a design with the engineering designers we make sketches and drawings, which are again discussed and modified before models are made.

"Everything has to be modelled before acceptance, and it is usual to make several different models in the course of getting the whole machine to look right, and, at the same time, be acceptable from an engineering point of view."

The popular, American-built Trackmaster flat-track racing frame and swinging arm, both similar in detail to the P39 versions. (Author's archive)

In the Styling Department office with Stephen Mettam, and seated, Alf Judd. (Author's archive)

worries that some owners may have mistaken it for the adjacent fuel filler cap. Whichever version is correct – or maybe even both? – the admittedly smaller-engined o-i-f 250/500cc P34 models suffered neither frothing or, as far as is known, any reported incidents of mistaken identification of caps.

Communication, though, had clearly failed between the frame designers and Meriden, because when the factory tried to put its T120 engine into the frame, it simply would not fit! Much time was wasted in trying to rectify the problem, though this did eventually, by virtue of a redesigned rocker box, result in a much improved method of tappet adjustment on the motor. Predictably, Umberslade's engineers have since shouldered all the blame for this, which is presumably where the problem initially lay, but an obvious question is how on earth did Triumph employees at Umberslade fail to liaise with the factory? Part of the answer, surprisingly, lies in the fact that these 'ex' Meriden men were now themselves considered outsiders, with relations suffering accordingly.

Even more disturbing are allegations from Meriden white collar workers that the higher echelons of the division did not actually want the Triumph version of the P39 to be manufactured at all; hence the problems. Paranoia or fact? We shall probably never know ...

The frame was, in some ways, revolutionary for BSA in that it was the first production item designed with the aid of a 'Honeywell' stress computer programme, enabling accurate calculations of stress loadings that would occur at various points of the frame. The two major benefits of computer-aided designs were that development time was drastically cut, with the frames being virtually the finished item straight off the drawing board, and the creation of a structure carrying the minimum weight, due to heavier gauge steel tube or a gusset plate being used only where required.

At the subsequent destruction test sessions at MIRA, the frames were found to last up to five times longer than the previous year's, whilst also being several pounds lighter.

Finally, it is interesting to note that, during 1970, the American specialist motorcycle frame designer

Trackmaster offered an extremely popular, nickel-plated oil bearing frame/swinging arm for BSA and Triumph flat track racing bikes, which bore an uncanny resemblance to the Umberslade items; so much so that it is almost inconceivable that some form of collusion did not occur between the two companies. The oil filler cap was sited just aft of the steering head, too!

Asked about the early stages of frame design, Stephen Mettam gave the following illuminating account –

"A new project was usually the entire bike. There must have been very detailed engineering requirements which would eventually become a specification. I worked alongside the engineers, and one of us could lead the other. The o-i-f 650 frame came out of the Styling Department. Noise regulations were getting tighter. You can attenuate the exhaust sound, but when that is pretty good, those DB meters get to hear the suck. Just purse your lips and breathe in swiftly. Who would have thought that breathing was so noisy? Engineers needed bigger plenum chambers and bigger air filters: there just wasn't enough space in a frame. We were pushed but didn't want big lumps; frame tubes were where inlet boxes needed to be.

"I'm not a structural engineer, but I suggested that one big tube might offer a much more rigid bottom bracket swinging arm mount, and provide space where we needed it. Sums confirmed this; we obtained some three inch (7.5cm) steel tube, shaped the bent part from jeluton (wood), slipped onto it the vertical and top tube, and made up a wood welding jig to weld all the other joins. My model shop worked fast: it was aerosol-sprayed silver, all the cycle parts and a 650 engine fitted, and we had a full-size, non-working model – sold!

"I cannot remember which brand motor was first but we quickly built another. That whole range of frames for both brands did not start with frame designers. Blame the air filter for the new bikes. This conveniently coincided with choosing next year's colours so everything was changed. Too much was happening, and alongside this was the 350 range and the rotary-engined Single and Twin. That was a super smooth bike to ride."

Mouldings

Fibreglass mouldings for fairings, leg shields, and panniers, etc, for road-going motorcycles also largely became the domain of the Styling Department; the work usually being carried out on behalf of BSA's accessories company, Motoplas, which went on to market most of the products. By the late 1960s, Motoplas offered four motorcycle windscreens – the Tri-Point, Tri-Point Mk II, and the Tri-Yorker – all of which were simply sheets of moulded transparent Perspex, and, for the latter, a more substantial two-part handlebar fairing.

While developing a similar but more modern handlebar fairing for the UK's police force, it soon became clear that offering this to all BSA and Triumph customers made good sense, as it had been specifically designed for the new range of bikes, all of which featured semi-high, wide handlebars and direction indicators. While the Mk II Tri-Point had already been modified to enable use on the Indicator models, Umberslade's new, two-part fairing was made up of a fibreglass apron that offered protection to the entire handlebar width, with a curved Perspex screen bolted to its top edge in the usual manner. Overall, its mounting was substantially more rigid than on earlier designs, and while the previous two handlebar fixing points were retained, an additional pair of sturdy, adjustable brackets were fixed to the underside of the fork top nuts, resulting in a stylish, flex-free fairing.

Al Cave's PA, Chris Strachan, aboard Centre hack A65L, fitted with the Alf Judd-designed, two-part fairing.
(Author's archive)

1971 Fleetstar

BSA's police and fleet-user bike, a slightly de-tuned B25 Fleetstar, was scheduled for a production run of an o-i-f version late in 1971, and the Styling Department was given the task of designing or adapting the necessary ancillary equipment. The new handlebar fairing was an obvious contender, as were the Umberslade-designed, quickly detachable, tough ABS plastic panniers which, mounted on steel tube framework, offered a certain amount of protection for both bike and rider in the event of a spill. Unlike the current leg shields available from Motoplas, which simply formed a rounded shield approximately 18-inches (45.7cm) in length, two new, substantially longer shields were designed which gave a far greater degree of rain protection. While both types hugged the contours of the three-gallon (13.5-litre) fuel tank fitted as standard to all Fleetstars, one was also actually moulded around the front of the primary chaincase before sloping back over the rider's boot, and then assuming an upward direction, with a similarly designed shield for the right-hand side of the motorcycle. Lower fixing points for the two types were direct onto a specially fabricated set of crash bars, the lower mounting of which made use of the front engine mounting frame lug, whilst the second version's top fixing attached to the underside of the tank (these crash bars were also fabricated for the P39 and P40 models). However, neither the leg shields nor the pannier system made it into production because of enforced expenditure cuts in the summer, and the Fleetstar – when it appeared in November – had to make do with existing equipment.

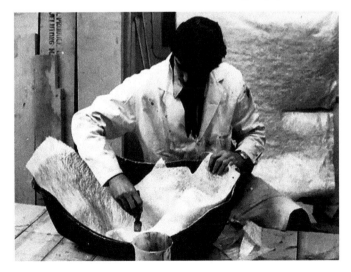

The Styling Department's apprentice, Paul Hayward, applying resin to fibreglass sheeting.
(Author's archive)

Projected ancillary equipment for the 1971 B25 Police Fleetstar, parked at the rear of Umberslade Hall. Note the Smiths chronometric speedometer: a requirement on most UK police models in the interest of accuracy. (Author's archive)

The finished prototype radio/pannier console fitted to a P39 Triumph. (Author's archive)

Police: Stop!

Following an enquiry from the relevant police body, and after consultation with BSA's UK fleet Sales Manager, Norman Vanhouse, the Styling Department proceeded to design and build a prototype radio/pannier unit that was to house the very fragile, valve-operated police radios in a virtually vibration-free cocoon. The unit was an efficient, all-in-one console with number plate, indicators, rear lamp and 'Police: Stop!' lamp incorporated in the same moulding. Final tests found that valve life had been enhanced by around 500 per cent.

Despite the prototype's success the project was doomed for two rather bizarre reasons. Firstly, the technical departments of the UK's constabularies (around 40) each insisted upon minor but different detail changes before even considering accepting the unit (there was no single department within the police force that had the power to decide on an overall specification). Secondly, every constabulary bloody-mindedly refused to accept responsibility for any radio malfunctions, instead, expecting BSA to pick up the tab.

This was not the first time that the UK's police force had flexed its collective muscles: several years previously one constabulary refused point-blank to accept the relatively new A65 model which had superseded the pre-unit A10 in 1962. Not wishing to lose the order, BSA acquiesced and obligingly built up the required number of A10s from spares!

Against the clock

By the end of 1969, Divisional Chief Engineering Director Bert Hopwood, who was, in effect, subordinate only to Eric Turner and Lionel Jofeh, had become concerned about the progress being made with the redesign of several bikes, and, in particular, he was justifiably alarmed at the number of new component parts approved for manufacture, seemingly without the usual procedure of pre-assembly and quality checks: a legacy of trying to alter so many existing machines from the two ranges, which, at this juncture, had all become motorcycles over 250cc, as well as the new DOHC 350s and the almost ready for production Ariel 3. Mettam sometimes came across drawings he had apparently approved, although he was quick to spot a forged signature on these documents, and, where possible, acted accordingly, but this does demonstrate the pressure experienced as deadlines drew closer.

In spite of accusations of poor productivity from Umberslade's engineering staff, an inescapable fact is that, by spring 1970, the August deadline had become totally unrealistic, and with the benefit of hindsight it was realised that steps to postpone either part of the new range, or wait until the following year to introduce these machines, would have largely averted the 1971 crisis. However, to have done this would have meant

that so much of what had already been put in place at vast expense would have been subject to cancellation, with many subsequent financial penalties being incurred: presumably, it was considered a worthwhile gamble to press on regardless.

The R&D Centre finally closed in January 1972, signalled by Mike Nedham's departure, though the first reduction in staff had occurred in July 1971, when 56 employees were made redundant in the first wave of job cuts instigated after the group's financial predicament was made public. By November that year, staff numbers had been further reduced to 83, and in the final weeks just a handful of employees were retained to service the remaining test equipment.

The front lawn at Umberslade in early autumn 1969. The seven machines, some featuring wooden parts, are (from left to right front row): Triumph US P39, BSA P30 and BSA US P39. Nestling in the background: Triumph USA P40, prototype Monkey Bike, Triumph home/general export P40, and BSA Bantam Bushman.
(Author's archive)

Chapter 3

Colours and photo sessions

1970 for 1971

By the beginning of April 1970, the division's Styling Department had finalised all of the colour schemes that the 1971 range of BSA and Triumphs were to carry in both the USA and home and general export markets. Of the 13 colours selected, only one failed to make it into production: the striking, white-painted American version

of the BSA A75 Rocket 3. Rather late in the day, but before the November US launch date, the colour was cancelled, the bike now to be finished in red; the same as the home and general export versions. The decision, in all probability, emanated from the Sales Department which, regardless of any market research findings to the contrary, always insisted at this time on the top-of-the-range model being red.

Dove grey

BSA model frames were to be painted in a dull silver colour that mimicked the finish of the titanium frames that the works motocross machines had used for a time. This was in accordance with a directive from the American sales team, which desperately wished to reverse BSA's declining image. Mettam had wanted BSA models to become style leaders, and undoubtedly the silver-coloured frames would have considerably emphasised the aesthetic qualities of the newly-designed motorcycles.

But something happened during the procurement stage, when BSA Works Manager Al Cave – ignoring the Styling Department's directive – stepped in and, on his own initiative, ordered a job lot of ex-army dove grey paint at a knockdown price. By the time that Mettam discovered the unauthorised change, it was apparently too late to cancel proceedings. He insisted that the BSA frames should revert to the traditional black finish, but to

Pressure from BSA's Sales Department led to this bold colour scheme for the A75 being abandoned. (Author's archive)

no avail – wheels had been set in motion and the frames were destined to be dipped into vats of dove grey paint.

While in no way attempting to denigrate Al Cave's character (very much a 'man of the people,' and consequently – and crucially – popular at shop floor level), more than one colleague has since openly criticised some of his rather unorthodox actions. As production deadlines for the new bikes drew ever nearer, Cave tried to persuade the Styling Department to incorporate some readily available, 1970 model year components into the totally new designs, though this was rejected out of hand by Mettam. In connection with this, in private Cave had unashamedly leant on his young PA, Chris Strachan, to change the minutes of some meetings in favour of his own proposals, in order to 'legitimately' push them through! Though this was an extremely dubious move, and serious enough to warrant disciplinary action, it is generally recognised that, however misguided, it was done with the aim of keeping production running and not for any personal reason or gain. Little known is the fact that Al Cave was quite well connected, in that his wife was the daughter of Eric Turner's predecessor, Jack Sangster, a name revered in recent BSA and Triumph history.

For the cycle parts, with the exception of flamboyant red and blue (well established BSA colours), and excluding the aforementioned white, four new colours were introduced and named by Stephen Mettam as bronze, sterling moss, plum crazy, and Chinese yellow. The first two were for the A65FS/L and A65T 650cc Twins respectively; plum crazy was for the two E35 350cc Twins, while Chinese yellow was intended for the A50 500cc Twin that, at this stage, was still intended as part of the 1971 range.

It was much the same situation for Triumph, with spring gold, olympic flame, and pacific blue being used in recent years. New colours were the 250cc T25 models' tangerine (initially named bloody red but changed due to concern about causing offence), and the 650cc T120's tiger gold and jealous green, used on the pair of 350cc T35 DOHC Twins. All colours – with the exception of bloody red/tangerine – were either metallic or polychromatic (more than one colour), the former having anodised metal flakes suspended in the paint itself, and the latter being sprayed over a base coat of silver or gold, both formats creating an attractive, sparkly effect in sunlight.

Although the colours and mudguard striping details were now to remain unchanged, the petrol tank designs for BSA's large capacity Twins were originally to have either one, two or three styling lines, and four 'laser'

stripes for Triumph's 750cc T150 and the US-spec T120. Unfortunately, no photographs of these designs appear to exist.

In the studio

In early summer the bikes were photographed at Small Heath's photo studio for the new season's brochures, though several machines were clearly built up using non-production parts, notably the petrol tanks for the P30 and P34, which had neither fuel taps nor bosses in which to screw them. The road-going P34 was also fitted with a side panel that had to be extensively modified before being fit for production, and all examples of the new 8-inch (20.3cm) TLS front brake used brake plates and levers that were clearly prototype parts.

Taken from the US brochure 'The Power and the Glory,' BSA's bronze A65 Lightning. (Author's archive)

The results of this photo session were primarily for American brochure use, although most of the photographs also found their way into the two less than flamboyant foldout home and general export BSA and Triumph brochures which featured black and white images throughout.

Two bikes shot especially for this market were the BSA B25SS and Triumph T25SS, both of which featured the 8-inch (20.3cm) front brake, rather than the 6-inch (15.2cm) trail/motocross version fitted to equivalent US models. Some of the photographs, presumably of the same machines, were shot from a slightly different angle, though it is not clear whether or not these were from the

Although all of the Power and Glory brochure bikes appear to have been touched in to an extent, colours remained the same with the exception of those of the A75 (bottom right); this is the very same photograph as it appears at the beginning of this chapter. (Author's archive)

same session. Rather strange was the omission of the home and general export blue B25SS, which, even when printed in black and white, would have been noticeable, as the fuel tank was devoid of striping.

On location
The same period saw three BSA location photo shoots taking place: one on tarmac; the other two off-road. The M6 motorway provided the venue for the 'road' shoot, which took place on a private service station slip road used by staff to access the site. Several bikes were photographed, although, as is often the case, only one shot from the session was ever used: that of the A65 Firebird Scrambler piloted by Stephen Mettam.

Triumph's 'Think Big' brochure, prepared by Small Heath's Advertising Department, featured these cropped shots throughout, in an attempt to give a dramatic, in-your-face feel to the bikes. (Author's archive)

BSA model	1971 colours	Triumph model	1971 colours
B25SS	Flamboyant red/black striping	T25SS	Tangerine/black flash
B25SS	Flamboyant blue	T25T	Tangerine/black flash
B25T	Polished aluminium/black striping	T35R	Jealous green/black flashes
E35R	Plum crazy/white striping	T35SS	Jealous green/black flashes
E35SS	Plum crazy/white striping	T100R	Olympic flame/black scallop
B50SS	Flamboyant red/black striping	T100C	Olympic flame/black scallop
B50T	Polished aluminium/black striping	TR6R	Pacific blue/white double scallop
B50MX	Polished aluminium/black striping	TR6C	Pacific blue/white double scallop
A65T	Sterling Moss/white bottom	T120R	Tiger gold/black double scallop

A65L	Bronze/white bottom	T150	Spring gold/black double scallop
A65FS	Bronze/white bottom	T150 USA	Black/white double scallop
A75R	Firecracker red/chrome		

Some of the schemes varied slightly on home and general export models, and, where they did, are dealt with within the text. Listed colour schemes apply to the petrol tanks.

The home/general export Tiger Gold Triumph Bonneville photographed in early 1971. (Author's archive)

While at the M6 shoot, the BSA entourage had a run-in with the station's assistant manager, who rather tersely ordered them to clear off as they were on private property! A trip to the service station manager's office with the officious gentleman soon restored the status quo, as BSA had already obtained permission to use the road.

A second location shoot also proved eventful, this time with the police turning up and enquiring about ownership of the bikes, by all accounts suspecting they were stolen. The venue this time was the Clent Hills situated to the east of Birmingham, which had taken more than a week to locate, with Mettam visiting potential hills in his 'breathed on' Mini, accompanied by two Americans – the Art Director and photographer – hired by BSA Inc. Reflecting upon Mettam's driving style after one of these excursions, one of the two exclaimed "I'd recommend Stephen to anyone to show them around, but I'd never buy a second hand car from him!"

Two photographs were subsequently used as part of the resultant American 'off-road' brochure 'The British Are Coming.' Interestingly, several of the riders featured on the cover were from the Styling Department, and positively identified are model-maker Rodney Humphries riding a B25SS, and also pictured astride the same machine inside the brochure (albeit badged as a B50), and the department's boss on the same Firebird he had ridden at the service station shoot.

The third session featured off-road bikes exclusively and took place in a wooded area south-east of Redditch near Studley. Sadly, nothing from the resulting films was ever used.

It's worth pointing out that when the Advertising Department selected photographs to be used in brochures, advertisements, press photos, etc (usually slide-mounted), those that were rejected were there and then unceremoniously thrown into the waste paper bin.

Whether any location shoots for the ten Triumph models took place is not clear, but certainly nothing dating from this period for 1971 ever appeared. The only link, albeit tenuous, with any off-road activities is the cover of the USA 'Hit The Trail Big' T25 brochure, which features an obscure shot from the Clent Hills session.

As an interim measure for the official UK launch of the range in November, a series of location photographs were taken with just a handful of bikes. Sessions with both marques' P30s occurred (see Chapter 5), as well as BSA's B25SS and A65L which all appeared as black and white images, along with a single photo of two Triumph Twins – the TR6 Trophy and T120 Bonneville. Divisional personnel appearing in some of these were Press Officer David Lloyd and, once again, Stephen Mettam.

With 1971 approaching a now much delayed programme of photo sessions for the home and general export publicity material was put into motion. Within the first six weeks of 1971, examples of most bikes in the range were taken up to the Porthmadog area of North Wales where photo shoots at the nearby William Clough Ellis 'Mediterranean' designed town of Portmeirion, Black Rock Sands, and surrounding areas took place. The time of year was far from ideal, but with many of the new machines now at last leaving the assembly lines at both factories, publicity material was eagerly awaited by BSA's Advertising Department and dealers alike. Most of the photographs used depict blue skies or beautiful atmospheric lighting conditions, courtesy of the sun either rising or setting, belying the fact that in some shots the surrounding landscape was snow-laden, complete with accompanying bitter wind keeping temperatures around the freezing mark: pity the brave bikini- and swimming trunk-clad models! It appears that probably eight models in all were hired for the assignments – male and female – plus Triumph's ubiquitous

One of the few flamboyant blue BSA B25SSs built, on the beach with Triumph's Percy Tait riding a US-spec Triumph T120 Bonneville. Both photographs are from the Black Rock Sands photo shoot. (Author's archive)

test rider and racer, Percy Tait, who handled many of the action shots. Two of the professional models have been identified as David Osbourne and Karen Young, the latter having already appeared in several BSA press photos the previous autumn.

While all of the BSA machines were fitted with the smaller, US-spec petrol tanks, only Triumph's TR6R and T120R wore the larger home and general export versions (though a small-tanked Bonneville was also present), in what was a further indication of the disarray the division found itself in whilst playing catch-up in order to make the 1971 season. The TR6's 4-gallon tank featured a broad white centre stripe which the T120 echoed in black, along with a black tank bottom. While retaining their 1970 3-gallon fuel tanks, the two virtually unchanged 500cc T100 Triumph Twins differed from US-spec by virtue of the Trophy's tank now appearing without painted scallops, and the Daytona featuring a broad black band running along its tank side.

A further shoot took place at an unknown race circuit, where Percy Tait was captured riding the 750cc Triples of both marques, though apart from a small advertisement placed in the programmes of the Easter Anglo-American Match Race Series, the BSA photographs remained unused. One more mystery location, an airfield, was used, resulting in a red A75 Rocket 3, supplanting the more anonymous image from Black Rock Sands on most of the forthcoming publicity material.

During the same period the entire range – with the exception of the B50MX – visited the Small Heath studios once again, but this time featuring production-ready machines with only the P34 B50's horn still to undergo

Following the North Wales photo shoot, each model is thought to have come away with its own colour poster: these generally destined for dealer and exhibition use. (Author's archive)

a change of position, and the large bore chain case-mounted engine breather pipe yet to be introduced.

In the main, the 1971 photographic material appeared as either adverts in motorcycle papers and magazines around the world, or were part of a series of A4 colour brochure sheets, totalling 17 in all. Once again, the uncertainty surrounding the home and general export blue B25SS was evident on the relevant brochure: while a blue home market spec version graced the front, the rear portrayed a US-spec SS: ie red with a 6-inch (15.2cm) front brake. By the time that these brochures were issued, the blue option had not been a production model for two months: a total of only about 146 were built.

Four more of these brochures were almost certainly put together and probably printed for the four P30 models, though none was ever released. At least two of these bikes had been present at the Portmeirion shoot. Most of the brochures were also reproduced as dealer-only posters, although in this respect the Rocket 3 example reverted to the photograph from Black Rock Sands.

In addition to these brochure-destined photo shoots, a further joint BSA/Triumph 'tarmac' session for the four 650cc Twins also took place early in July, with some of the resulting images appearing as adverts in the UK and European motorcycle press during August. These were still 1971-spec models, fitted out with all the appropriate home and general export parts, the BSAs now having reverted to black frames from dove grey during May, midway through production.

1971 for 1972

During May 1971, all of the proposed 1972 model year BSAs and Triumphs for the US market were photographed at Small Heath's photographic studios. The new colours for both marques followed an identical theme to that used on the 1971 models, with just the basic colours themselves changed. All frames were now black.

In one of a series of now revered magazine articles published in 1998, Stephen Mettam revealed how he and BSA/Triumph Marketing Director Peter Deverall disagreed over the new colour proposals. With Deverall being his superior, Mettam found it difficult to override the Marketing Director's colour choices, so after consulting Umberslade Hall's boss, Mike Nedham, he had bikes finished in both paint schemes, one each side of the machine, or in some cases, two identical bikes carrying the different colours.

The proposed colour scheme of flambordeaux, polished aluminium and white – and a black frame – for 1972's B50T Victor 500. (Author's archive)

Shot in summer 1971, this was the last promotional activity for the 1971 home/general export bikes. This model is a 650 Thunderbolt. (Author's archive)

Six projected colour schemes for BSA's 1972 US models. Top right is the P30 Fury, which, along with the SS version, was the only bike to retain its 1971 colours, black frame excepted. (Author's archive)

This was in preparation for a viewing by some of BSA's top brass, including Chairman Eric Turner and Managing Director Lionel Jofeh, who in each case came down in favour of the stylist, thus vindicating the professional's judgement over that of the enthusiastic Deverall.

As it transpired, very few of the colours that these bikes wore ever made it into production, as a direct result of the uncertainty and panic that had overcome many of those in decision-making positions within the division once BSA's financial problems became clear, manifesting itself as an irrational distrust of any decisions made under the direction of the recently disposed Peter Thornton, BSA/Triumph top man in the USA until his June dismissal.

The 1972 colours had actually been chosen by Mettam, following discussions with BSA Inc's Product Planning Director, Tony Salisbury, and an American automotive consultancy company in early 1971. However, largely because of Salisbury's links with Thornton, most of these colours were summarily dropped.

BSA	Proposed	In production	Triumph	Proposed	In production
B25SS	Candykist White stripe	Cancelled	T25SS	Yellow fever Black flash	Cancelled
B25T	Sunrise Polished aluminium stripe	Cancelled	T25T	Yellow fever Black flash	Cancelled
E35R	Plum crazy White stripe	Cancelled	T35R	Jealous green Black flashes	Cancelled
E35SS	Plum crazy White stripe	Cancelled	T35SS	Jealous green Black flashes	Cancelled
B50SS	Hi-violet	Hi-violet	T100R	Vermillion	Cherry

Model			Model		
	White stripe			Black flash	White flash
B50T	Flambordeaux	Hi-violet stripe	T100C	Vermillion	Cancelled
	Polished aluminium stripe	Polished aluminium tank		Black flash	
B50MX	Flambordeaux	Hi-violet	TR6	(Bronze variation)	Polychromatic
	Polished aluminium stripe	Polished aluminium tank		Black double scallop	Blue/white double scallop
A65T	Etruscan Bronze	Etruscan Bronze	TR6C	(Bronze variation)	Polychromatic
	White bottom			Black double scallop	Blue/white double scallop
A65L	Vedoro (?)	Firebird red	T120	(Bronze variation)	Tiger Gold
	White bottom			Black double scallop	White double scallop
A70	(Dark bronze)		T120 750	(Bronze variation)	Cancelled
	White bottom			Black double scallop	
A75	Burgundy	Burgundy	T150	Black	Regal purple
	Chrome	Chrome		Gold double scallop	White double scallop

Listed above are the paint names, where known, of the original colour proposals and those that actually came off the production line from August 1971. Most of the machines retained their striping, with only BSA's A65 models and the B50SS appearing with fuel tanks finished entirely in a solid colour. Of the 200 A70 models built, most were finished as the 1972-spec Lightning, with the black frames that had been phased in around early May. The 750 T120 was postponed until the following season, and some home and general export bikes featured slight variations of colour schemes.

As with BSA, Triumph's two P30 Twins also held on to the previous year's colour schemes. Few of these new colours were to make any official listing, and most paint names have been lost as a result. (Author's archive)

The US bikes were always dealt with first as a matter of course; the short but vital selling season dictating that publicity material be ready far earlier than for all the other markets. When the BSA and Triumph home and general export range was photographed in early July, the job was handled by an outside firm, rather than in-house as was usual practice. The reason for this – on the face of it odd – decision was that the division's own photographer has suffered an unexpected and fatal heart attack shortly before shooting was to commence. Because of the short notice and tight deadlines involved, and importance of the assignment, the existing, less experienced staff of three were not considered up to the job. At this time, some in the upper echelons of the division already knew that stormy weather was just around the corner, and that unnecessary risks were, where possible, to be avoided, hence the contract being entrusted to the Birmingham photographic partnership of Morland Braithwaite.

The bikes (including the non-catalogued but still available to this market BSA B50T and B50MX) began to arrive at Morland's on July 10, and continued doing so for the next 19 days, though the BSA 750cc Twin only appeared at the beginning of September. One anomaly here is that the bikes were all fitted with the shorter American market front mudguards – in all likelihood these were, in fact, US-spec bikes that had simply received a fuel tank swap for the session.

Mettam was present at all of these sessions, ensuring that the correct side panel decals were fitted to each bike. Whilst there, incidentally, he borrowed a 35mm camera, which he set up next to the studio photographer's and simultaneously photographed each model for his own personal reference. By the time the resulting brochures were released, the 650 and 750 machines featured matt black front brake plates, and for BSA black rear lamp brackets, following some studio retouching of the original photographs.

BSA

Model	No	Dept. entry	Despatch
B50SS	DE10583	–	15.7.71
B50T	DE10404	–	15.7.71
B50MX	–	–	–
A65T	HE11898	–	15.7.71
A65L	GE10881	–	15.7.71
A70L	HE01171	1.9.71	10.9.71
A75R	EE00509	–	10.7.71

Triumph

Model	No	Dept. entry	Despatch
T100R	23363	20.5.71	25.7.71
TR6	29728	8.7.71	29.7.71
TR6C	–	–	–
T120R	30496	13.7.71	19.7.71
T120 750	30496	–	29.7.71
T150	–	–	–

Detailed in this table are the models and their engine/frame numbers, where known, as well as the dates that the bikes left their respective factories for Morland Braithwaite's studios in south Birmingham.

On location (again)

Several of the earlier painted bikes for the US market were involved in location shoots, the Twin and three-cylinder models being shot at Hednesford Raceway by American photographer Antonio Antonetti, while the 500cc BSA B50MX and T took part in an off-road session in woods close by.

As photographed, the fuel tank of this B50 Victor Trail originally featured a polished aluminium stripe and flambordeaux body. (Author's archive)

Stephen Mettam piloting a 1972-spec T25T whilst on an undated, late spring photo shoot at Cannock Chase. (Author's archive)

One of the B50T shots later appeared in a 1972 brochure, still wearing its proposed colours, albeit reversed and now featuring flambordeaux rather than polished aluminium striping. By August, flambordeaux had changed in name to hi-violet, though it is generally thought that the two colours are the same; the issue being further confused by lighting conditions changing the hue of the colours considerably. In the absence of written evidence, it is impossible to be conclusive on this.

At this shoot a B50MX was also photographed, though none of the resulting slides appears to have survived, at least not in the public domain. Mettam was in attendance – as he was for all photo shoots linked to the American market – and, aboard the 500MX, followed the same route as the B50T pilot, only to veer into a hollow, just out of sight on the published photograph, and ending up colliding with a tree at the bottom of the incline, damaging both handlebars and brake lever.

By studying the B50T photograph here it seems unlikely that it was shot much later than April 1971, and possibly earlier, as the surrounding trees are largely bereft of fresh foliage, and the low weak sun lights the bike perfectly. Additionally, by late May, the tank scheme reversal had taken place, thereby supporting this estimated date.

Several photographs from the Hednesford session in May were also used in American BSA and Triumph brochures for 1972, and, again, most were retouched to the revised colours and designs in an art studio, although the results are not too convincing and rather obvious. Machines attending the session were BSA's 650cc Thunderbolt and Lightning, and the 750cc Rocket 3, and for Triumph, its two 650s, the Trophy and Bonneville, and 750cc Trident. Only BSA's Rocket 3 escaped the artist's airbrush, its burgundy paint colour and overall scheme avoiding being binned.

Confirmation of these dates comes in the form of an internal BSA paint code list, which includes 13 colours/schemes (many of which were obviously intended for projected 1972 bikes), all dated April 28, 1971, which ties in with the off-road 'action' photo shoots mentioned previously.

The same document – after dealing with a handful of June-dated T/E35 colours – then lists 27 further colours/schemes, all dated July 13, 1971. Once again, many of these can be applied to the current models, including the soon to be deleted 250cc bikes, and, more significantly, they were by and large those that went into production for the 1972 model year, so were the final approved colour schemes.

Location shoots for the BSA home and general export models, whose number after July had been whittled down to four, are likely to have taken place post-May, as they all feature in their individual and respective brochures with genuine paintwork. The North Wales beach resort Black Rock Sands appears to have been used once again, though during the summer this time.

Making up these brochures were shots from the Morland Braithwaite sessions, as well as images of each bike wearing a small, US-spec fuel tank listed as an option. From this it would appear that all of the machines from the BSA and Triumph ranges were again

Triumph T120 and BSA A75. These Hednesford photographs were actually shot by Antonio Antonetti while riding pillion backward on another bike, strapped to Stephen Mettam, the bike's pilot. (Author's archive)

Pit lane posturing and hairy chests from three of the division's top works riders ensured an element of authenticity for this final Triumph location shoot of 1971. (Courtesy Suffolk branch of the TOMCC)

photographed for the US market, the resulting images appearing in two black and white, dealer-only brochures; it is from these sessions that the small tanked photos would have been sourced. The studio in question is unknown, but in all probability it was Morland Braithwaite's again. It is feasible that these were the same home and general export machines but with items such as fuel tanks, handlebars, and, in the case of the B50MX, side panels, changed, in which case it would perhaps explain why the home and general export brochure bikes wore the short American mudguards.

Likewise, two further location shoots for Triumph's home market bikes, also now numbering four only, took place at a similar time, though, unfortunately, the exact locations remain unknown. It is known that one of the shoots was held at a race track, possibly Mallory Park, where some of the 1972 bikes appeared alongside an A75 and two T150 production racers and a T35R Bandit. Rather than hiring models, factory racers Percy Tait, Paul Smart and Ray Pickrell stood in, making a convincing job of it. Colours remained the same as for US models, though the P36, P39 and P40s were finished as the five Triumphs in the dealer brochure, featuring a revised paint scheme on the fuel tanks that, in the event, did not reach the production line, and is a further indication of the uncertainty surrounding the 1972 colours. A T150 finished with this scheme did the rounds in the States as a press test bike, and is thought to have been the same machine photographed at the race circuit session. The cover shot, as with its BSA equivalent, was taken from the 1970 La Quinta launch, though with the fuel tank touched-in to match those inside the brochure. In common with BSA, each Triumph model received its own fold-out brochure featuring photographs sourced from these sessions.

Mystery colour
Even though the 1972 range of BSAs carried the colour schemes which appeared in the 1972 brochures, an unlisted and unnamed colour did seem to find its way onto some 1972 model year machines. While still apparently being either metallic or more likely polychromatic in format, the colour itself was a pinky red, as seen on the A65 on this page in a photo taken in the USA in either 1972 or early 1973.

It was not only on the 650 Twins that the colour appeared, however, as something very similar has in recent years been seen on some American-sourced B50 cycle parts that had clearly never been fitted to a motorcycle.

Amal proposal
A rather offbeat series of colour proposals appeared in the shape of painted carburettors. Carburettor manufacturer

The unlisted colour that mysteriously found its way onto some 1972 BSA models. (Author's archive)

Dating from around 1970, these 'coloured' Amal carburettors were passed over by the styling team. (Author's archive)

Amal, on its own initiative, sent four of its concentric carburettors finished in black, gold, silver and white to Umberslade's Styling Department, as a suggestion to the Motor Cycle Division. None was ever adopted, though some of the black-painted B50MX works engines already had black-painted carburettors for the purpose of heat dissipation.

The two brochures at top are dealer only, their purpose being to allow a preview of the coming season's bikes at the earliest opportunity, while the two full colour ones below were for general distribution. (Author's archive)

Chapter 4

P22 – Here it is, whatever *it* is

Preconceptions

As with so many of the BSA Motor Cycle Division's activities and products of the era, the Ariel 3 has, and still does, come in for much criticism, usually in the form of cheap jibes and largely inaccurate comments, born of poor or negligible research, generally aimed at the concept of the trike and little else. The fact that it failed to reach its forecast annual sales figures of 25,000 has given the green light to its many detractors, who consistently use the same old tired clichés. Perhaps it's just too easy to swim with the tide ...

Certain motorcycle journals that heaped much praise upon the trike at its launch and in subsequent tests, unashamedly performed 180-degree turns once BSA was on the rocks just over a year later, totally and unprofessionally contradicting their previous views.

Here, though, as with the following three chapters, we look at the machines and accompanying events without hindrance from past preconceptions, and provide a fresh look via the many press reports of the day and original documentation.

Courtesy of BSA/Triumph Chief Stylist Stephen Mettam – whose team was given the task of transforming the inventor's rather basic prototype into an attractive, practical and saleable machine – we can present an eyewitness account on the Ariel 3's development. The Ariel 3 initially displayed several minor faults upon introduction, which, by the end of 1970, had been effectively dealt with, although, as Mettam points out, BSA had undoubtedly made one poor decision which would haunt the three-wheeler throughout its life, and alienate many of its intended customers.

The cover of the 1970 fold-out Ariel 3 brochure carrying one of two slogans used for the Trike's launch. (Author's archive)

Start me up

By opting to use the Dutch-manufactured Laura Anker 50cc, two-stroke engine, BSA had a motor that, although reliable and proven by utilisation in several mopeds of different brands, when cold, often required a fair amount of pedalling before firing up. Period road tests from motorcycle magazines consistently awarded top marks to most aspects of the trike, with its ingenuity, nippy acceleration, good braking, and handling precision coming in for particular praise – but not its starting!

Launch

The Ariel 3 was announced to the world on Thursday, June 11, 1970 at London's Royal Festival Hall, at what was a very 'hands-on' press conference. Inside the building, BSA Group Managing Director Lionel Jofeh addressed over 200 assembled journalists and celebrities. Pertinent to his speech were the following comments –

"We think that our sales in the first full year will exceed 25,000 machines worth over £2½ million" … "We are not simply looking at the existing moped market. The Ariel 3 is a means of expanding into a new and much bigger market. It is estimated that over four million people go to work by public transport; in addition, there are 15 million car license holders – and all those licenses cover mopeds." And finally …. "We feel the Ariel 3 is one of the most exciting developments to come out of Birmingham since the Mini."

So BSA certainly couldn't be accused of not thinking big in its outlook for the moped's prospects. Mr Jofeh went on to say that, even though the trike was envisaged for the UK only at present, it was foreseeable that overseas sales were possible.

Following the introductory speech, and armed with the obligatory press kits, the guests then made their way outside onto the Festival Hall's terrace. Here, an oval circuit had been coned out, where, prior to being let loose on the new machines (finished in either orange, pacific blue or everglade green), somewhere in the region of 14 'Ariel 3 Girls' completed a number of demonstration laps. Along with the journalists, several personalities also gave the trikes a try out, among them Tony Hicks of the pop group The Hollies, BBC radio presenter Jack De Manio, and a trio of Lords: Montague, Harlech, and Strathcarron.

BSA had also provided four Ariel 3 technicians from the factory, easily identifiable by their white lab coats, to answer any technical queries the guests wished to pose.

The response from the press was all that could have been wished for, with widespread editorial coverage across the British Isles; the then current national newspaper strike apparently having little effect on

Ready, steady, GO! – the Ariel 3 girls about to set off on demonstration laps, while BSA management and press look on. (Courtesy University of Warwick Library)

publicising the launch. By the beginning of October, BSA's Press Office had gathered more than 200 favourable reports and features from almost every category of newspaper within Britain: dailies, Sundays, local, financial, technical, etc. A direct result of this and the publicity campaign launched three weeks later on July 1 was an overwhelming request for catalogues: one day alone the Small Heath Advertising Department received a staggering 3200 letters requesting Ariel 3 literature.

Shortly after the Festival Hall event, three dealer conferences were held: one in Blackpool, one in London, and the third in the Midlands at Wilshaw's Belfry Inn. Organised by current UK Divisional Sales Manager John Hickson, these once again featured test sessions and the Ariel 3 girls, as well as lavish promotional displays. The dealers were to largely echo the opinion of Britain's journalists, and were reported as being unanimous in opinion that the trike was a winner.

The 'face' of the Ariel 3 was the model and actress Caron Gardner, who had completed three photo shoots prior to the June launch; these being poolside at Northampton's Overstone Solarium Hotel, at the adjacent lake, and at a small fairground. Several of the photographs were used in the press kit, along with an official press release and a salesman's guide.

What the press said –

"A revolutionary form of transport which, if successful, could well and truly put the moped on the map in Britain ... enormous potential in the UK." – Two Wheeler Dealer

"It is a runabout fun machine on three wheels ... almost insultingly simple to drive." – The Times

"A family supertrike." – Sunderland Echo

"Slick in city traffic, the revolutionary Ariel 3 is easy to ride and the answer to parking problems." – Morning Advertiser

"Most unorthodox passenger machine to be produced by a British motorcycle factory for years ..." – Motor Cycle and Cycle Trader

"After a spin on BSA's new Ariel 3, a three-wheel moped, during last week's heat wave, I thought my days of commuting by public transport were at long last over. "
– Investors Chronical & Stock Exchange Gazette

"It's the latest thing in fun travel."
– The Cambridge Daily News

"Britain has chalked up a first with a three-wheeled moped."
– The Scotsman

"In no sense is the Ariel 3 a gimmick, it is a soundly engineered machine with many excellent features." – Engineering

"The machine's strong points are its stability and simplicity, plus its economy." – The Birmingham Post

"It is obviously going to have a tremendous appeal for the economy-minded who are nervous of riding a two-wheeled machine."
– The Daily Mirror

"It's incredible the way the rear end hugs the road. You tend to forget the Ariel has two wheels at the back, though you can play tricks on it you'd never get away with on a moped. " – Motor Cycle

"At first I could not believe that it would lean like a two-wheeler, but it did just that." – Birmingham Mail

"It's the answer to every housewife's nightmare – a motorised shopping basket. – The Sun

"In love again – with a three-wheeled moped."
– The Morning Star

Promotion

The year-long promotional programme was allocated a £70,000 spend, and although in many areas it followed conventional approaches such as posters, brochures, newspaper ads, and even some promotional films, the emphasis was firmly placed upon public demonstrations, which were achieved in two ways. Firstly, teams of two Ariel 3 girls toured Britain during July and August, visiting over 70 towns and cities, arriving in Ford Transit vans containing a number of the three-wheelers.

As well as the publicity that these demonstrations received, the sign written vans were very evident up and down the country. Each side of the vehicle was emblazoned with 'The Ariel 3 Girls Are Coming To You,' along with a picture of the machine underneath. Additionally, the girls were kitted out in specially designed outfits, comprising patent leather ankle boots, coloured slacks with black side stripe, and black 'Ariel 3' badged PVC tabards worn over a white blouson, topped by an orange and white 'Corker' style crash helmet. Several high profile appearances of the Ariel 3 girls on television news and feature programmes during the summer generated further free promotion.

The second aspect of the promotional campaign involved appearances at fêtes and carnivals, with the trikes again ridden by celebrities. Two of the most noteworthy of these events were held at Kent's Brands Hatch racing circuit, where Lotus Cars boss Colin Chapman and Austrian Formula 1 racing driver Jochen Rindt had some fun riding a pair of 3s, and in Bournemouth during August when comedian Joe Baker and Radio Two disc jockey Pete Murray bought Ariel 3s to use as runabouts while performing at the Pier Theatre, also

Ariel 3 girl Caron Gardner. All but the two fairground photographs were shot at Northampton's Overstone Hotel. The location of the fairground, sadly, remains a mystery. None of the six images was used in the publicity campaign, and are seen here for the first time. (Courtesy VMCC)

riding them in a town centre parade over the Bank Holiday weekend. BSA – not slow to capitalise on another publicity coup – sent Field Sales Manager Fred Green to the coast to officially hand over the machines in front of the press.

The final event of the summer campaign was a charity carnival held at Battersea Pleasure Gardens, where BSA's celebrities this time were two female vocalists, Olivia Newton-John of pop group Toomorrow, and Cindy Kent from the pop/folk group The Settlers, who performed on the day, and David Jacobs, another Radio Two DJ. Incidentally, The Settlers were also hired for a one-off lunchtime performance at the Small Heath Works canteen in October, followed by a press photo session with some current BSA models and several Ariel 3s.

The same month was to see an unscheduled publicity opportunity in the form of fund raising week for the Muscular Dystrophy charity. BSA Export Manager Wilf Harrison, a committee member of a Midlands branch of the MD Group, offered a fleet of nine Ariels, ridden by the Ariel 3 girls, as well as the help of his wife and that of his assistant, Peter Glover, for the charity's letter delivery service.

An unknown speedway track was host to another

A further shot from the 1970 brochure emphasising the fun and carefree image that BSA's Advertising Department projected for the moped's promotion. (Author's archive)

publicity event that, whilst hosting an international meeting, had Ariel 3s taking part in a parade, and raced later in the evening by some of the speedway riders.

Finally, and for further publicity purposes, two BSA apprentices – Robert Tillotson and Patrick Tomkinson (son of endurance racer Mike Tomkinson) – made a trip to Barcelona for the 1970 Montjuic Park 24 hour race on a pair of Ariels. Making a round trip of 2000 miles all told, the duo camped en route, carrying all necessary equipment aboard the trikes.

Two slogans accompanied the birth of the three-wheeled moped, along with a large, fold-out brochure/poster combination. The poster proper and an A4-sized black and white, double-sided leaflet used the same artwork, albeit in a different arrangement. The slogans? 'It's not a bike, it's not a car, but it's fun' and 'Here it is, whatever *it* is.'

At the same time BSA accessories subsidiary Motoplas issued a double-sided leaflet illustrating many after sales goodies, such as a tinted windscreen and a groovy 'Ariel 3' transfer for the leading sides of the luggage moulding. As a sign of the times, prices were given in both pounds, shillings and pence, as well as the new decimal currency that was to be introduced in the British Isles in February 1971.

Cindy Kent, David Jacobs, and Olivia Newton-John at Battersea Park in September. (Author's archive)

Teething troubles
By the end of the year BSA had sent out several service sheets to dealers, detailing minor modifications that were to be carried out on early machines. Most importantly was a revised, larger sparkplug gap, introduced due to some plugs shorting out, plus two other measures that would, in some cases, reduce starting problems: elimination of the

sediment trap loop in the fuel pipe, which was sometimes causing air locks, and ensuring that the small, Encawi carburettor was not in contact with the chain guard – where this occurred, the fuel mix became weak, due to the carburettor failing to sit in the required vertical position.

1971 promotion campaign
For 1971 a new, smaller brochure was prepared, the photo shoot for this taking place during February, although many images from the previous brochure were still retained. The cover was styled on a large-sized poster that carried a new slogan: 'Ariel 3 lets you laugh all the way to the shops.'

April saw the Ariel 3 girls mobilised once again for a new campaign covering England and Wales. 78 distributors had been given the task of appointing 1000 new dealers between them, and the eight girls, working in teams of two and again equipped with the Transit vans, had the task of collecting two machines from a distributor and visiting the

Cover artwork of 1971's Ariel 3 brochure. (Author's archive)

dealers chosen by him, where they demonstrated the trike. If successful, one machine was left as an immediate test vehicle, with the relevant distributor then forwarding more stock forthwith. Where considered viable, public demos were carried out in relevant towns or cities.

Other aspects of the campaign included Ariel 3s as competition prizes, with the National Coal Board's in-house newspaper, *Coal News*, giving away four examples, while international detergent conglomerate Procter & Gamble donated over 100 trikes in conjunction with its Fairy Liquid and Ariel Powder product promotion.

Birmingham's New Street Station shopping precinct was the venue for an Ariel 3 stand that was in operation for two weeks, supported by local BSA dealers Vale Onslow and Frank Cope; several trikes were available to test ride in a special arena.

The upmarket shoe retailer Russell & Bromley used Ariel 3s in a publicity campaign for its newly-opened Leeds branch, where 8000 promotional carrier bags were delivered around the area by the trikes. The shop also displayed a machine within the store, supplied by local dealer Watson Cairnes, which reciprocated by carrying a Russell & Bromley window display on its premises.

Rallies in Sheffield, Doncaster and Rotherham, the Biggin Hill International Air Fair, the Lord Mayor of Birmingham's parade, and several of Chipperfield's Safari Parks all saw Ariel 3s in service.

Finally, a Jersey-based company, Hirabike, took delivery of a fleet of twelve 3s for use as hire bikes by the island's thriving holiday trade, and six machines were also shipped to Bermuda for a similar enterprise.

Chief Stylist Stephen Mettam on the development and marketing of P22 –

"In the mid-1960s George Wallace designed a three-wheeled bike. The two back wheels were on a common axle, like a car. The front wheel and forks, and the front half of the frame and pedals pivoted from the vertical plane, just like any two-wheeled bike as you corner it. The chain twisted as the bike leaned over but did not mind too much. Raleigh were briefly interested but did not buy the idea. George fitted a small motor and offered the machine to BSA. They bought it.

"Bruce LeMarquand, who had experience and success merchandising consumer goods, was appointed by the BSA Group to control concept, marketing, and sales of this product. BSA wanted a new product to compete in the fast-growing moped marketplace, and grab back some of the declining scooter market. A design brief was raised for this product, and, amongst various requirements, was that it should be aimed at females; that it should be able to carry the shopping, and that it might even be parked in the kitchen and not look out of place next to the cooker or the washing machine – if she had one: washing machines were not so common in 1967.

"In the latter half of 1967 as an industrial designer I was appointed Chief Stylist by Engineering Director Bert Hopwood, to look after the appearance design of all BSA and Triumph motorcycles. I joined the company at about the same time as Bruce, and was detailed to look after the appearance design and ergonomics of Trixie. Its official listing as a design project was P22, but before it was ever named Ariel 3, all of us at BSA called it Trixie: the name seemed so appropriate. Steve Wilsher in the Styling Department, produced some very 1960s art nouveau-style decals for the sides of the fuel tank on the shopping

By the summer, so successful was the Jersey hire scheme that Hirabike set up a similar operation in London, and as an endorsement of the Ariel's revolutionary design and appearance, the company was quoted as saying: "With a new service such as this, we also wanted a new design. We wanted a product which was new and sufficiently attractive to generate interest in itself, as much as in the service we are offering."

However, as the seriousness of BSA's financial problems became common knowledge by the end of the summer, the trike was openly lambasted as a 'white elephant' due to its failure to achieve forecast sales, and once production had finally ceased the following year, the floundering BSA was faced with having to sell off an estimated 50,000 of the now-redundant Laura Anker engines at a considerable loss. As the months rolled on,

moves to shift complete machines included incentives such as a year's supply of petrol with every trike sold, and free servicing for those existing owners who could persuade a friend to purchase a new Ariel 3.

Undoubtedly the most unlikely of the many publicity events staged to promote the revolutionary Trike. (Courtesy VMCC)

platform at the back; it may even have been Steve who conceived the name Trixie. Whichever advertising agency got the job did some research, and was proud to discover that a very early British automobile was a three-wheeled Ariel, and expected everyone to appreciate the continuity – and although BSA owned the name Ariel, not many at BSA wanted to call our Trixie the Ariel 3! This Trike was always referred to as a bike. Trixie was NOT intended to be a bike; it was NOT to look like a bike or a moped. The early concepts had no exposed nuts or cables, nothing to make it look like a bike: it was perhaps closer to a motor scooter. The original George Wallis motorised working model had a catch operated by a lever on the handlebars to keep the front half vertical when parked. Once the rider was on board the catch was released. Some riders tried to pedal off then release – that did not work. It has been stated elsewhere that George inserted a torsion bar between front and back. This is not so. The design engineers at BSA fitted two torsion bars to George's original model, so that when the rider dismounted, the front half stayed almost upright. The two torsion bars were fighting each other and not strong enough to keep it vertical when parked, and not strong enough to make the rider aware that they were even there – just right!

"Some engineers at BSA were keen to use spoked wheels; I wanted more solid wheels. My arm was twisted to design chunky spoked wheels but the pressed steel spoked ones fitted to the rear axle soon distorted, so I was permitted to use design experience gained at Dunlop's Rim & Wheel factory, and my first idea of car-type wheels were the ones used. Trixie's frame is pressed steel and contains the steering head, chain, torsion bars and pivot

for the rear two-wheel bogie.

"The development machines used a BSA 50cc, two-stroke motor designed by John Hobday. John was probably not with the company when it began manufacture of the Bantam in 1947, but he had for years developed and enlarged the Bantam engines, and had designed some very reliable small stationary engines for use with pumps and generators. John's Trixie motor was wonderful; you could not even turn it over without it starting. Starting the bike was so easy, you just got on and began pedalling and the motor started immediately. It had a sprag clutch so it just ticked over by itself when stopped at traffic lights.

"At the last moment before production, at about one year before launch of Trixie, when money was being committed for tooling, someone decided that the factory was too busy and finances too stretched with the other new bikes that were being planned, so it was decided to use a Dutch Anker Laura moped motor. This was a big mistake. It was fast enough at about 25mph, but was a devil to start. You needed to pedal for several yards before it fired, which was not so easy for the lightweight mums it was aimed at. This weakness was so obvious at public promotions, which had been organised more like a fashion show with a dance routine. A troupe of youngish girls built like fashion models lined up with dead engines and pedalled off together to start their routine. This would have been so easy with Hobday engines, but the Lauras were so slow to start that the line was broken, and the expressions on the riders' faces did not inspire confidence in the machine. The original BSA sprag clutch was inserted between this motor and the final drive so that part was okay. It was easy to ride – the two back wheels plus motor plus tank plus shopping in the basket strapped to the platform were one unit riding firmly on the road. The only weight you were aware of was the front half of the bike, and the torsion bars held up that part so it felt even lighter than a pushbike to ride.

"Working at the research establishment at Umberslade Hall, if I knew I needed to be at Small Heath the next day, I left the car at Umberslade and rode an Ariel home. Driving in with all the rush hour traffic, cars were not much faster, and at the traffic lights I crept forward continuously beside cars or between lanes, determined to not put a foot down, and this I usually achieved. I enjoyed it for short journeys.

"One problem for me at BSA was getting the design staff there to appreciate the usefulness of plastics. The Ariel had moulded plastic legshields and plastic sidecovers at the rear. It took a lot of persistence on my part to achieve this. Plastic was a dirty word: they knew only of the expensive drape-formed windshields that Motoplas made or unreliable and prone to leaking glassfibre fuel tanks. They tried every way to avoid the use of plastics on the Ariel 3. Weight and durability were my main considerations, but BSA design engineers preferred sheet steel. In comparison, tool costs were similar, manufacturing cost was similar. When it came to assembly, the fitting of plastics had a slight advantage. What decided it was finishing cost – plastic needs no painting. Painting at BSA was an expensive additional cost, sometimes as much as the part itself. In use the great advantage was durability, if you bashed it, it flicked back, no need to replace it or suffer ugly dents, and Trixie did not rattle like the Ariel Leader.

"As soon as Bruce LeMarquand knew that the release of the Ariel 3 would be delayed a year, he said 'I have done my job, I have nothing more to do for a year, so I will go and run the family brewery in the Channel Islands, they have been asking me to go there for years, I just wanted to do something more interesting.'

"The BSA sales team used the outlets they knew – bike dealers – this was a pity. Bruce had intended that it would be sold by supermarkets and hardware stores, servicing might have been a problem but he wanted it to be marketed like any other 'white goods,' it was not a motorbike. He expected sales of 50,000 plus per annum. It would be good now in the 21st century, electric powered, with a three-phase brushless motor and Li-ion cells.

"At around launch time, bike reviewers should NOT have commented: we needed reviews in Womans Own or Good Housekeeping, more than in bike magazines. It is a pity it was ever offered for test to bike magazines. It was not a motorbike, it was an economy means of transport for the not-yet-two-car household. Marketing feedback from customers – who were mostly 30-plus something females – was favourable, but it sold only about 8000 a year via the motorbike dealers. Good for sales of a bike, but not what was intended, it is a pity that Bruce's plans were not followed."

Above: The inventor's prototype ridden by *Motor Cycle* journalist Vic Willoughby in the early 1970s.
Left: Probably the first example built using production parts. Note the spoked wheels Mettam mentions, and also the 'P22' decal, the Trike's development code. (Author's archive)

Chapter 5

P25 Bantam

Negative continuity

By 1971, the single cylinder, 13bhp, 175cc, two-stroke D175 Bantam made an awkward bed partner to the flamboyantly-styled 'Power Set' range that was unveiled late in 1970. While absent from the extravagant launch, it did feature in the full range brochure of the same period. Launched in the late 1940s following BSA's

175 cm³ Bantam

Small bike – *big* escape – that's BSA's Bantam. Lets you escape to the hills; to the beach; to the river; to the trail. Lets you escape the headaches, too. The tax and insurance headaches; the running cost headaches. Your BSA Bantam cuts the *cost* of escape all along the line, yet still gives you all the BSA reliability and advanced design that are built into the big BSA competition models. 175 cm³ engine gives maximum efficiency. Competition tested hydraulically damped front forks. Speed styled petrol tank. Dual seat in foam rubber with passenger safety strap. The BSA Bantam is the big-hearted bike.

1971 Bantam. By the start of the new decade the descriptive copy that emanated from BSA's Advertising Department was rather more exciting than the bike's appearance. (Author's archive)

acquisition from German manufacturer DKW of the then 125cc engine, as part of the victor's war reparations, the Bantam had become the first bike that many novice riders encountered, and consequently often sowed the seeds of brand loyalty.

Development

By the end of the 1960s, after having already been hiked to 150cc the previous decade, the 100mpg+ two-stroke was looking a little old-fashioned, though sales were still good with both public and fleet users, notwithstanding the in-house competition it faced in 1968 from BSA's own 250cc, B25 Fleetstar with regard to the latter bracket of customers.

Its increasingly staid image and modest performance figures had prompted Umberslade Hall – under the direction of Chief Project Manager Michael Martin – to work on an uprated and more modern-looking version which, had it come to fruition, would have been christened D18. The power output of this development is not known, but using the 20bhp obtained from BSA's petroleum-running motocross Bantam of the period as the ultimate figure, it is not unreasonable to suggest that 15 to 16bhp could have been achieved from a road-going version. Significantly aiding development work was BSA-sponsored Dr Gordon Blair of Queen's University Belfast, where research work on two-stroke induction flow characteristics and exhaust expansion systems, in conjunction with Michael Martin, was achieving useful results.

The experimental work was tied into a complete range of new, two-stroke engines being developed at Umberslade, with capacities ranging from 50cc to 400cc.

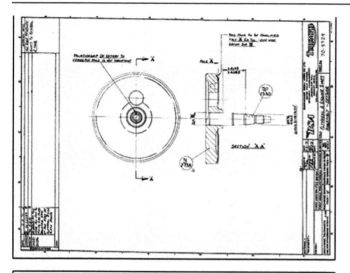

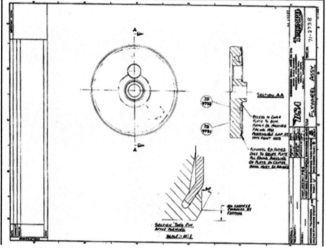

Crankshaft details dating from March 1971. The bottom drawing shows the packing disc fitted to the flywheels to increase crankcase pressure: part of the P25's power upgrade. (Courtesy Steve Sewell/SRS)

Ultimately, the projects were all cancelled, which was a shame, because the D18 was to have had an alloy barrel and new cylinder head, both of which would have featured a revised cooling fin pattern, affording the engine unit a much needed face-lift in line with contemporary Spanish and Japanese two-strokes, as aesthetic qualities are as important to impressionable learners as performance. BSA engineers had already designed an automatic positive lubrication system that would have dispensed with the antiquated and messy petroil operation, and it is certain that this would have been part of the D18's specification.

The timeframe of the projected D18 is unclear, though cancellation of work-in-hand was, in all probability, a direct result of the dire financial situation that unfolded in

1971. Hard details of how the D18 would have appeared are also lost, but a peek at the direction styling may have taken is provided by the lone drawing seen on p55. A full-size model mock-up was made, but before it could be photographed the engineer responsible took it home with him the day he received his redundancy notice.

Umberslade also built two prototype Trials Bantams in or around 1970/1971, which made use of a specially-fabricated frame hosting an o-i-f-type alloy Victor fuel tank, forks and front hub, but as far as is known these never competed in any events and were purely for evaluation purposes.

So, as not quite part of the Power Set, the D175 began the 1971 season with virtually the same engine specification it'd had for the previous two years, when it received its last upgrade of reworked crankshaft and crankcases, and a centrally-mounted sparkplug that had significantly contributed to its current power rating. For 1971 the transmission gear teeth were strengthened and the kick starter underwent changes in the interest of improved clearance, while both frame and footrests benefited from being strengthened, and different rear shock absorbers and seat padding were intended to improve ride.

Colour schemes were also carried over from the previous year, although early in 1970, the D175 had been allocated a dove grey frame in keeping with the rest of the redesigned BSA models. However, this idea fell by the wayside, and the 1971 Bantam appeared still wearing a black frame, and either polychromatic aircraft blue, flamboyant red or black tin-ware. Excepting its inclusion in the Big Escape Brochure, publicity was zero, and, short of seeing it in a BSA showroom, there was little evidence that the Bantam still existed as a production machine.

Bushman

The trail-orientated Bantam Bushman originally introduced in 1967 was initially intended to continue into 1971 with the same modifications as the D175. As well as altered gearing, a pair of 17-inch (43.2cm) wheels replaced the previous 18-inch (45.7cm) rear and 19-inch (48.25cm) front, and there was a new paint scheme.

Up until the birth of the B25T/B50T Victor Trail series, the Bushman had been BSA's only serious off-road machine, introduced in response to calls for something of this ilk from continents such as Africa and Australia, where large and rugged areas of livestock grazing land were the norm.

That it was cancelled for 1971 was not really surprising, given the new and more exotic models that were coming, but doing this meant that potential customers – assuming they were still to buy a BSA – would have to pay more for the 250cc, four-stroke Victor which, whilst a fine off-road machine, had moved away from the relative simplicity of the two-stroke system. Those who wished to continue with the small capacity, lightweight two-stroke configuration would, of course, have been spoilt for choice, with most of the world's motorcycle manufacturers offering similar machinery, and BSA therefore losing out.

Last orders

Following up on the 220 slightly detuned fleet spec Bantams delivered in early autumn 1970, the GPO placed a further order for 400 bikes, plus accessory equipment, in October, the contract being worth £69,000, and solidly illustrating that the rather archaic-looking utility two-stroke could still draw in big money. This was, however, to be the last fleet order, and, on 6th June 1971 the Bantam was discontinued after 23 years of continuous production.

15 SEC

— R. H. Slee —

The shape of things to come ... perhaps. A two-stroke proposal from 1971. (Author's archive)

Shot in autumn 1969, had the Bushman made it into 1971, it would have been finished in Etruscan bronze, a colour that finally featured on BSA's 1972 A65 Thunderbolt. (Author's archive)

Chapter 6

P30 – 350CC DOHC Twin

Misconceptions

In common with most of the 1971 BSA/Triumph range, a fair amount of inaccurate reporting has, over the years, generated many throwaway clichés about the P30-coded BSA E35 Fury and Triumph T35 Bandit, fuelled largely by the eleventh hour cancellation of all four versions of the bike.

Two major criticisms often bandied about are that the P30 came too late, and was, in any case, no match for its competitor in America, the Honda CB350 Twin. The first point is partly correct, as had it been introduced several years earlier, Honda may not have been able to run away with so much of the market for this capacity class, but to write it off as 'too late' in 1971 is not right, and in the main attributable to hindsight. In 1971 America, mid-capacity motorcycles were still selling in very high numbers.

As for performance, it's well known that the Edward Turner-designed prototype, which had been developed and built at BSA's Redditch factory, was a remarkably swift machine, having achieved 104mph (167kmh) on the MIRA test circuit. This was largely due to the lightweight nature of the machine – including the engine, which featured some poorly-designed and overly-pared components that broke all too frequently: the main culprits the crankshaft and valves. Whilst re-housing the original motor in a more suitable frame, and adopting new forks (necessary, anyway, as the prototype's items were prone to break) created little in the way of headaches, a major problem lay in the work required to produce a reliable engine.

Much redesign work was carried out at Meriden under Bert Hopwood and Doug Hele, resulting in an engine

that bore little resemblance to Turner's original. Once the motor had been turned over to Umberslade Hall, ex-AMC Development Engineer Jack Williams (father of racer Peter) worked on reinstating some of the power lost during the radical redesign, his time spent largely on the cylinder head. In this he was assisted for the best part of six months by a young American TriCor employee, Tom

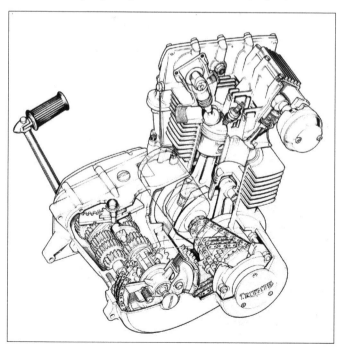

One of several promotional line drawings issued in November 1970. (Author's archive)

(Courtesy VMCC)

Divisional Chief Engineer Mike Nedham on the 350 engine in 1970 –

"A major feature of the new 350cc DOHC engine is the 180-degree crank. The engine is designed for high rotational speeds, where the balance advantage of a 180-degree crank is significant.

"The arguments in favour of two camshafts instead of one are considerable. In a high performance motor cycle engine, it is necessary to place the valves at an angle.

"For this reason, you need two camshafts if you are to achieve the accurate control of valve behaviour which can come from the use of overhead camshafts.

"This also means that you get a more open head design, and the cooling of the head between the valves is much easier.

"In the new engine, the drive to the camshaft is by chain. With a gear drive, the problem of growth of centre line with aluminium barrels and heads creates too much of a noise problem, and one cannot happily use a toothed belt drive, as the width of belt required is an embarrassment in an across-the-frame motorcycle engine.

"Again, for much the same reason as with the camshaft drive, the primary drive retains a relatively conventional duplex chain.

"With accurate alignment of sprockets and adequate tensioning, high speed drives by chain are a very satisfactory solution."

Gunn, who had been transferred to Umberslade as part of his engineering training. Eventual power output was down from that of the prototype, but not as much as so often has been claimed over the years.

How fast?
Today, the scarcity of running examples (estimates vary from 12 to around 20 original factory bikes) has meant that owners and journalists, when granted a test ride, have rarely ridden the machines in anger, let alone getting anywhere near the power plant's 9000rpm peak power limit. Therefore, they have usually had to rely on little more than folklore in summing up the ultimate performance and potential marketplace prospects of the bikes.

However, one of these original-build bikes – a T35R now residing in Australia – has at last dispelled the performance myth. The owner, not afraid of showing his Bandit the cane, claimed that Honda's CB350 was no match in terms of power, and, less surprisingly, handling. Featured in a motorcycle magazine, the test rider was able to confirm the Bandit's Honda-beating performance

without reservation – not at all the same as the usual opinion so often aired over the decades since BSA's demise.

Origins
Designed during the mid-1960s by BSA's ex-Managing Director, Edward Turner, while in retirement, and anticipating future US laws concerning a left side gear change, once accepted for development, it quickly became apparent that very little of the original P30 engine would remain unmodified once the many flaws had been engineered out. Bert Hopwood has stated that it would have been as well to start afresh with a new design, but Turner's apparent influence and stature with some Board members was presumably too strong to dismiss. Reluctantly, Hopwood agreed to undertake the necessary work to enable the engine to reach production.

By the time Meriden had completed the redesign work, which included a new crankshaft, crankcases, camshaft drive train and all castings, the unit was far removed from the prototype.

The first full-size P30 'model' carrying a host of well-disguised wooden parts, and finished in candy apple blue. (Author's archive)

Rebirth

When the Styling Department was given P30 to work on in 1968, it was still intended to utilise a single downtube frame similar in configuration to that used on Turner's prototype, and a dummy bike was built up around a similar frame, fitted with many wooden parts, such as fuel tank, silencers, engine and wheel hubs (the latter having drilled alloy rings attached to enable spokes to be fitted) all of which was the work of the department's two model-makers Rodney Humphries and Stanley Tranter. The fork yokes were fabricated from sheet steel. This early model was photographed wearing proposed fuel tanks and decals for both BSA and Triumph versions, and from these photos it can be seen that experiments with pressed steel swinging arms were being carried out, a similar arrangement appearing on some of the P39 prototypes.

The frame was a specially fabricated one-off that Stephen Mettam had managed to divert to his department for engine clearance checks upon arrival at Umberslade Hall. However, once the wooden engine unit was offered up, it soon became abundantly clear that it was not going to fit. After some deliberation with the engineers, Mettam was eventually permitted to remove the obstructing bracket with a hacksaw! This became academic, though, as certainly by September 1969, frame builder Rob North had been commissioned to build a totally new duplex frame similar to one designed for the forthcoming BSA/Triumph works racing triples. Once this had been introduced, the project began to evolve into something far more purposeful-looking,

the now necessarily redesigned side panels the crucial factor here, and responsible for the disappearance of the prototype's bulky mid-rift look. Not only did the frame pave the way for the lean and compact P30 which graced 1971 brochures, but, with its racing pedigree, it also guaranteed a fine-handling motorcycle.

Because the whole of the bike was totally new, Mettam was able to work in unison with the engineers who, where possible, willingly accommodated his ideas concerning the external appearance of the engine. Said Mettam –

"The chain drive to the camshafts was originally between the cylinders. The engineers moved it to the timing side of the crankcase and tried very hard to disguise its presence. As soon as I discovered this I requested that I be much more involved with the engine design. I removed the (pseudo) cooling fins and designed a BSA and a Triumph cam box cover. They had wished to hide the cam box because it was not a feature we were accustomed to seeing. I was more than keen to emphasise to the world that we had twin overhead camshafts. They had a broad symmetrical cam chain case, which covered the whole bank of fins. I requested that it be cast to follow the form of the chain – lopsided because of the slipper tensioner – a super identifying feature. I wanted a new, unique character, rather than follow the thirty-year-old features of both brands, smothered by time and not recognised by any young bikers.

"The design engineers were – as never before – willing to listen to my reasons for where components should be located. If it still worked and was convenient to manufacture, they would move it for me.

"Items that had to be there could be featured or hidden, and in either case might need to be moved. The starter motor and the oil filter were moved a few times before we were all happy. Some compromises are beneficial to all parties."

What's in a name?

Both marques were early on given pretty lacklustre-sounding names, with Triumph's 'Tiger 90' firmly planting the new bike in the past. 'Apollo' for the BSA – although bang-up-to-date (the recent Apollo moon landings) didn't really cut the mustard, either.

By March 1970, Fury and Bandit monikers were firmly in place, as were the bikes' type designations, E35 and T35, although only shortly beforehand, 'XT35' had been applied to the high exhaust-piped Triumph.

Anyone playing around with the two names will appreciate that BSA Bandit and Triumph Fury roll off the tongue far more easily, and a story citing a typing error as

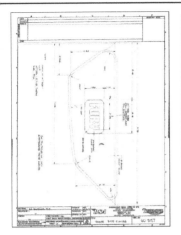  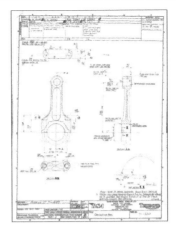 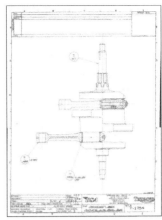

Component drawings illustrating decals for side panels and fuel tank, con-rod and crankshaft details. (Courtesy Steve Sewell/SRS)

Autumn 1969, and the first duplex-framed P30 seen in both road and SS guises. The frame wears the dull silver paint that Mettam had intended to be used on the entire BSA range for 1971. (Author's archive)

Early 1970, and most production shapes are here, with just the headlamp stays, instrument binnacles, dual seat and rear lamp housing to be modified. (Author's archive)

the reason for the resultant reversal has done the rounds for many years, though without confirmation.

Rolling

Intended to be offered with an optional electric start version, it was during 1970 that development P30s took to the roads, although exactly when is not clear, but certainly by May.

However, even as 1971 approached, breakdowns were not uncommon, and one such occurrence was when a P30 test rider called in at Birmingham BSA dealer Vale Onslow only to find that, upon leaving, he was unable to coax the engine into life. Making a call from a nearby telephone box, a works van quickly appeared and whisked away the stricken bike from the gaze of any curious onlookers. Another, more poignant, occasion occurred as late as December 1970, concerning two influential American journalists, who had been invited to Britain primarily to ride and report on the new 350s. As one of the Transatlantic guests circulated Silverstone racetrack on the Triumph T35R provided, the engine suddenly died, but, rather than investigating the problem, the bike was again immediately loaded into a works van and driven back to Meriden. The problem turned out to be a minor contact breaker fault, but, understandably, the incident was embarrassing enough without conducting a potentially damaging post mortem under the noses of the two visitors. This event well illustrates that BSA had its back to the wall as regards production dates, which had already been rescheduled twice.

However, the two P30s ridden by the American duo –

What the press said –

"Aesthetically the overall power plant is a thing of beauty. It's sophisticated and hairy all at the same time, instead of being a group of castings and pieces of machined metal pieces. It takes on almost art-like qualities and it looks as though somebody has lifted out a Grand Prix engine and installed it in a roadster chassis.

"For a motorcycle that sells in the area of $900 it is a lot of machine for the money. It's got a lot of performance … the motorcycle will run at 90mph all day long.

"The bike has all the earmarks of being a winner. It looks good, sounds sporty, handles and has an adequate amount of power for most situations." – Bob Braverman, Cycle Guide

"When the whip was applied, it reacted smartly … The Fury, at the time of our test, lacked the tractor-like lugging power of its Japanese contemporary when the revs dipped low … the low end was strong enough to bring the front end up, but my impression that a little more mid-range torque was needed was confirmed by the factory men, and I'm fairly sure it'll be there by the time you swing aboard … Conversely, up near the top end, the Fury is happy as a lark when rolling 80-85mph. Imagine a five-speed 350 with a 90mph forth gear! … Because of this happy mood when the revs are up, the Fury feels completely at home in the company of big 750cc roadsters. You've a treat in store." – Bob Greene, Motorcycle Sport Quarterly & Hot Rod.

one of each marque and tested on public roads, as well as the racing circuit – became the basis of magazine articles in the States, and while it must be remembered that the bikes were still, in essence, pre-production machines, the comments – mostly relating to the engine and its performance – offer the nearest available thing to a period road test, and, as such, are valuable impressions.

P30 publicity campaign

The general public first became aware of the four new 350cc models during November 1970, following the launch of 1971's BSA/Triumph range of bikes at London's Royal

December 1970, and one of the P30s that US press men Greene and Braverman rode. Standing right is Tony Lomas of Triumph's Development Department. (Author's archive)

Lancaster Hotel. Available there was an abundance of black and white press photographs, both studio and location, plus technical information contained within the various brochures and folders which accompanied the presentation.

The location photo shoots took place very close to the launch date – that for Triumph's T35SS during the first week of November, and BSA's E35R session at around the same time – both machines bereft of internal engine components. For the promotion of several of the new BSAs, the division's Press Officer, David Lloyd, had hired actress and model Karen Young as the glamour girl, and for her E35 session a wooded area was selected somewhere in Warwickshire. The actual location remains a mystery, although it was not in the grounds of Umberslade Hall, as has been claimed. Two photographs from the shoot were selected for press and promotional purposes: one with the rather alluring Miss Young leaning over the bike, and a second in the company of Stephen Mettam, who, understandably, has been mistaken for David Lloyd, entirely due to his having borrowed the jacket that the

latter wore in several other related press photos (Mettam has his back to the camera).

With fewer models in the range, and perhaps because the 350 originated from 'Mr Triumph' himself, the Press Office pushed Triumph's T35 strongly, issuing seven photographs featuring TV actress Carol Cleveland in the company of Triumph's Experimental Department employee and Coventry speedway rider Tony Lomas. Posing with an SS version in the vast grounds of the R&D Centre, the cold afternoon shoot attracted various curious onlookers, from the outwardly gazing faces of staff pressed against Umberslade's windows, to a herd of Friesian cows who persisted in upsetting proceedings, despite being chased away repeatedly.

The studio photographs that featured in 1971's BSA and Triumph brochures ('The Power and the Glory' and 'Think Big' respectively), were produced in-house at BSA's Small Heath studio during early summer, 1970, though – in common with several other machines featured – the P30s were not quite to production specification.

Autumn 1970, and the BSA press photo that was shortly to appear in journals around the world. (Author's archive)

Who's the prettiest? Carol Cleveland and Triumph's T35SS tie for first place. (Author's archive)

The first proposed T35 side panel decal for 1972.
(Author's archive)

The next P30 event was a photo shoot in either January or February of 1971 in North Wales. Of the theoretical eight promotional items emanating from these shoots (four double-sided A4 brochures and four posters), only two have subsequently been seen publicly; once again, courtesy of the division's Chief Stylist, Stephen Mettam. Although thousands of posters were apparently printed, most were destroyed prior to distribution, with Mettam, thankfully, snatching a couple from the first print run. The A4 sheets were intended for home and general export markets, while the posters may have possibly been distributed worldwide as nothing was printed specifically for the States.

With the 1971 ad campaign under way, by spring the bikes for 1972 were being prepared for the brochures, though the four 350s received no immediately obvious changes. Colours remained the same, save for a reversion of frame colour to the more traditional black for the BSA, and the Triumphs appearing with a new side panel decal depicting a Mexican Tiger Bandit-type figure. This latter feature was cancelled, however, as the machine's target market, the USA, had a relatively high Hispanic population, and authorities there were very wary of potential legal action by a Spanish-American organisation with a history of vigorously opposing anything it deemed derogatory about Mexicans living in the States – including cartoon Tiger Bandits!

The four bikes were all photographed during May (see Chapter 3), the only significant differences from 1971 pre-production models being a slightly modified dual seat, a headstock bracing plate, and the SS version's exhaust systems, which now appeared to comprise two separate silencers, rather than the previous integrated unit.

As far as location work went, only the road versions were photographed with Triumph's T35 present at both a home and general export racetrack shoot, and on a visit to the countryside, in all likelihood North Wales once again. These were held during the summer, and it is interesting to note that the Bandit's side panel had, by this time, reverted to the 1971 version. The E35 Fury was probably alongside the rest of the home and general export BSAs at Black Rock Sands, and from these final photo shoots, two brochures managed to reach the proof stage, though it is thought unlikely that any were ever actually printed.

One publication that did appear – not strictly promotional, but proof of a certain amount of intent – was the 1972 E35 parts list book, albeit carrying the same part number as 1971's edition. Inside, although still cataloguing parts such as the SS's high level exhaust system, only the E35R was listed with electric start, and available to both the USA and home and general export markets. Had production commenced, the first machine was intended to carry the date code and serial number NG00101 E35RE, indicating a planned build date of October 1971. Someone was trying ...

However, by June 1971 BSA had begun to disperse some of the pre-production bikes (ten of each marque had apparently been built at Armoury Road six months earlier in January) with one Fury going to a West German dealer, and a further example – along with a Bandit – sent to dealers in New Zealand and Australia respectively. Whether this was for promotional purposes or something more sinister is not clear, but, in any case, was shortly to become irrelevant.

Cancellation

Much has been written over the years about the reasons for cancellation of the P30s – some of which has come from the pens of divisional personnel – to such a degree that, to someone unfamiliar with the convoluted tale, many aspects of the bikes would appear to have been catastrophic from start to finish, for a variety of reasons. Poor power output is mentioned as just one aspect in the smokescreen of untruths and rumours surrounding the bike's failure to reach the production line.

Following advice to cease all P30 work from BSA's auditors, Cooper Bros, in late July, a high level meeting was held four weeks later, at which the pros and cons of pushing on with the bikes to production, or cutting losses and junking the whole programme were debated. Within three weeks

One of the Bandit's last assignments, summer of 1971's North Wales photo shoot. Note that the side panel decal has reverted to the previous design. (Courtesy Suffolk branch of the TOMCC)

Divisional Chief Stylist Stephen Mettam remains sceptical of many of the reasons publicly given in later years about why the plug was pulled. Although being made redundant in September 1971 as part of the summer cuts (implemented once BSA's financial crisis had been made public), he had kept in touch with several former colleagues employed at Meriden and Small Heath, none of whom agreed with the explanations given at the time. More recently, the apparent upward spiralling retail price has been cited as the ultimate reason behind the P30's non-appearance, although, again, Mettam still believes to this day that the decision was a political one, and that someone 'big' did not want the Fury and Bandit to happen. Food for thought.

Final word

BSA's board of directors had opted for total cancellation, although the decision was to remain under wraps and never publicly disclosed. Development work, however, continued until October. Works Manager Al Cave has subsequently stated that this decision entailed the scrapping of enough components to build around 2000 P30s.

As a result of some incautious talk from a factory export representative that reached the Australian media, BSA announced in November 1971 that the P30 had been "put aside," but "not scrapped," although it "could not be put into production for 1972," with BSA's severe financial problems cited as the reason. This appears to have been the last public word on the subject, as, regrettably, BSA failed to regain the stability and finance necessary to make the bike production-viable.

Exactly how many of these posters were printed is open to question. How many survive is a little easier to quantify – very few. E35SS and T35R versions would, presumably, have also been prepared. (Author's archive)

Chapter 7

P34, P36, P39, P40

Introduction

Unlike P22 and P30, which were totally new machines, P34, P39 and P40 utilised existing power plants, albeit updated in some key areas, and are therefore able to be dealt with within the same chapter. In common with P30, these three largely shared the same wheel hubs, front forks, handlebar switch consoles, front and rear lamp units, mudguards, etc, with only a few minor detail differences.

Presented within this chapter are excerpts (in general relating to aspects that have hitherto attracted much criticism) from several period road tests, and although the space they take up may, to some readers, seem a little excessive, they are deemed necessary in order to set the record straight: ie that the 1971 bikes were not universally condemned upon introduction, as those new to these machines could be forgiven for thinking.

Conical catastrophe?

The new wheels were centred around three sizes of conical hubs: a 7-inch (17.8cm) rear, and either a 6-inch (15.2cm) or 8-inch (20.3cm) front, depending on model. Within these sat single leading shoe brakes for the two smaller hubs, and a twin leading shoe unit complete with massive air scoop for the larger one. The effectiveness of the 8-inch (20.3cm) twin leading shoe brake is today almost always condemned out of hand, such is the strength of its bad reputation, but is this warranted? There is no doubt that performance varies from bike to bike – sometimes excellent, sometimes poor, sometimes prone to fade – which does at least indicate that, fundamentally, the brake is a good one.

A 250cc P34 prototype with an early cast brake plate, cast lever arms, and makeshift plate anchor bracket clipped to the fork leg. (Author's archive)

Its problem can usually be traced to one of adjustment, which is relatively frequently required to maintain the brake at optimum working level, and something that should have been ironed out during development by the implementation of an automatic system. Because of this, BSA was forced to send out service bulletins worldwide to dealers reiterating the correct adjustment procedure.

Except where the 460lb (209kg) Triples were concerned, most – if not all – road tests of the period praised the brake highly, and this is particularly significant in the USA, where some magazines ran their test bikes on racetracks and drag strips giving no quarter. Regarding the Triples, it was generally acknowledged that any production 8-inch (20.3cm) twin leading shoe brake would be hard pushed to cope with the speed and weight of the Rocket 3 and Trident, and why the two bikes were not fitted with a disc brake is a valid question.

Typical of magazine test reports of the era is the following comment from the American publication *Motorcycle World*, which, when testing BSA's A65 Lightning, offered "The brakes are as good as we've ever seen on a bike, and far better than most of the cars around you, so watch out behind you."

Changes were few once the design had been finally approved. The brake first entered production with a rubber gaiter fitted between the two brake arms, which, by February 1971, had been superseded by a spring, whose purpose was to ensure that the cable remained seated within the brake arm abutments. Around the same time – and somewhat inexplicably – these brake arms were replaced with shorter, less effective, examples, thereby increasing the pressure required on the handlebar-mounted brake lever. The 250cc P34s were the only production models fitted with the longer brake arms.

The new, lightweight front forks were a vast improvement over what had gone before, in terms of both style and function, now giving 6¾-inch (17.1cm) of well damped movement and pivoting on tapered roller bearings. The right-hand slider was produced in two forms: those destined for the P34 had two brake plate attachment lugs as part of the casting, one for each size of brake, while P30, P39 and P40 sliders were equipped with the 8-inch (20.3cm) lug only.

Upon introduction, some of the forks began to weep oil early in their lives, leading BSA to redesign the double-lipped stanchion/slider seal. The problem was eliminated by the bare metal outer face of the seal being coated in neoprene, now properly sealing it against the aluminium slider that it sat in. The new seals only became available towards the end of 1971.

For 1972 the rib running down the outside of each slider was removed (this rib was not a styling whim, but was, in fact, present as part of the casting process). In addition, the sliders were now also polished, further enhancing fork appearance.

Cycle parts

Mudguards across the range were similar in appearance, the rears generally differing in size to suit the different frame dimensions, while the road-going fronts fell into two categories – home and general export and USA – the former six inches (15.2cm) longer, enabling fitment of the legally-required UK front number plate, and providing a little more in the way of wet weather protection. These guards, mounted on wire stays, had different radiuses to allow fitment to either the 18-inch (45.7cm) or 19-inch (48.25cm) front wheel. The one anomaly here is the P40's guard which, in order to accommodate its fat 4.10-inch x 19-inch (10.4cm x 48.25cm) Dunlop K81 front tyre, had mounting stays which splayed outward from the guard before resuming normal positioning.

While the short US guards were without problem, the longer home and general export versions had a habit of splitting around the front stay area, caused by oscillation of the extended guard. This only became a problem on UK bikes once the law requiring fitment of front registration number plates changed, and owners began removing what was, in essence, an effective stiffener.

By spring 1972, concerns about potential fork twisting induced by heavy braking prompted BSA to introduce a bracing kit for existing mudguards, while adding a pair of vertical wire stays during the manufacture of new guards.

The four off-road bikes wore a specially-fabricated, high level front guard mounted on the underside of the bottom fork yoke, in conjunction with a sturdy sprung bracket. Both guards on the P34 B50MX were made of stainless steel.

Headlamp sizes were a flat-backed 7-inch (17.8cm) for P39 and P40 models, with the semi-off-road A65FS and TR6C using the same 6-inch (15.2cm) version as was fitted to the P30 and P34, though the former shell was

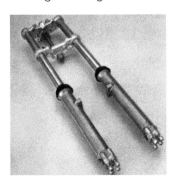

Similar in design and operation to the Italian Cerianis, BSA's new forks contributed greatly to the updated look of the 'Power Set' bikes. (Author's archive)

finished in silver paint rather than chrome. All were rubber-mounted on wire brackets of the same diameter as the mudguard stays, and hung off the fork yokes, lending the lamp area a much lighter and uncluttered look.

Ahead of its time? While initially often attracting negative comments, by 1976, Yamaha's XT500 wore a similar and more obtrusive system with little complaint. (Author's archive)

Silencing levels, exhaust and induction, on most machines was significantly improved. In general, the Twins and Triples featured a pair of long and sleek reverse cone megaphone silencers, while the Singles had their own large lozenge-shaped box silencers, both types reducing decibels to a far more acceptable level than had previous designs. The exceptions were, as with headlamps, the two off-road 650s – the Firebird Scrambler and Trophy – which continued to use 1970 specification silencers. Understandably, BSA's B50MX, whose only area of interest was racing, wasn't included in the exercise.

Induction noise had also been successfully reduced, with all but the P40 featuring a plenum chamber for the new, larger air filters: adoption of the o-i-f systems on P34 and P39 models allowing a generous amount of space for this.

The new indicators and handlebar console switches were designed by Stephen Mettam whilst he was still based at Meriden, even though Lucas was responsible for their manufacture. Mettam recalls that his finished console design used smooth, rounded switch buttons, and how he was dismayed when Lucas changed the design to the rather angular items that found their way into production.

The final noteworthy feature of these models is the adoption of fork top nut mounted instrument brackets, carrying two sizes of speedometer/tachometer in new, anti-vibration rubber cups. The smaller 60mm dials were fitted to the 250SS P34 and the P30, while the rest of the range was graced with the more familiar 80mm dials. This method of instrument mounting also significantly contributed to the clean front end appearance of the redesigned models.

All of the power plants employed in the new motorcycles, with the exception of the B50 which in some ways was a new engine, underwent few changes from 1970, and are described in the relevant model section.

P34 (250/500cc OHV Single)

The five P34s, comprising the BSA B25SS and T, B50SS, T and MX, and the badge-engineered Triumph T25SS and T models (all built at Small Heath) were divided into two basic categories – road and off-road, though SS models were designed to be able to cope with limited off-road conditions, hence the sump guard bash plates, high level exhaust system, and generous ground clearance.

The bikes they replaced – the B25 Starfire and B44 Shooting Star – had also been semi-off-road for the USA market: the 250 by way of a high level exhaust system, and more so the B44, by virtue of its Victor Enduro version, featuring a similar exhaust layout and aluminium fuel tank. While the Enduro was a fair attempt, its off-road prowess was, like the lower-powered B25, compromised by too much weight, something which the new P34 models admirably addressed by the liberal use of lightweight alloys for wheel hubs, fork yokes and sliders, and handlebar control levers. For Triumph, the TR25W had been a trail bike from inception (the W denoting woods), equipped with a high level exhaust system and sump bash plate, but, of course, always suffering the same weight penalties as the near-identical B25.

Market research in the USA identified that most motorcycles were bought purely for leisure purposes, trail riding in particular becoming increasingly popular, and, with this in mind, the four-stroke Singles were styled accordingly. All seven versions used the same frame, a near-carbon copy of the oil bearing examples used by the works scramblers, though largely fabricated from .090-inch (2.286mm) walled tube, rather than the more expensive thinner Reynolds 531 tubing. The frames of the six SS/T models were adorned with various brackets for attaching ancillaries such as exhaust mufflers, electrics box, tool tray, etc. Not surprisingly, the frame was superbly taut in all types of use, and, aided by the competition shop-derived forks, was hard to fault.

One small concern here, though, was in the area of oil cooling – derived from the position of the engine oil feed take-off point – which, theoretically, left the portion of oil that lay in the tube under the seat nose out of the flow direction, thereby failing to circulate all of the oil around the engine. While not an issue on the MXs – or, for that matter, any of the bikes if they were ridden vigorously enough – where the inertia generated by hard braking and acceleration tends to mix the oil somewhat anyway, fast summertime motorway riding can cause the oil to run a little hotter than is desirable, though few, if any, engine failures have actually been attributed to this.

Early maladies included a left-hand side panel that was both difficult to fit and remove, due to the close

B25SS and B50SS Gold Stars – the short front mudguards and the 250's 6-inch (15cm) brake make these two models US spec. (Author's archive)

T25T Trail Blazer and B50T Victor Trail – the Trail models used the same cycle parts for all markets. (Author's archive)

proximity of the two-panel locating pegs to the air filter plenum chamber. This was remedied in two stages: firstly, during late 1970, the pegs were shortened, which eased, but didn't completely resolve, the problem, and then, in around March 1971, a dimple pressed into the chamber's outer rim adjacent to the more troublesome lower peg finally put the problem to bed.

Until redesigned, the megaphone end of the MX was prone to making contact with the rear wheel spokes when the rear suspension was fully compressed.

Some items, such as the aluminium alloy electrics box mountings and horn position, underwent three changes in all, the initial problem presumably caused by having only the slightly smaller cylinder head/barrelled B44 unit available for clearance checks rather than a B50 engine.

The five BSAs wore three different, two-gallon fuel tanks, all very similar in design but with subtle differences. The 250 and 500cc SS models were fitted with steel tanks featuring an offset twist filler cap, while off-road B25/B50T/B50MXs were fabricated from aluminium, had a central, flip-up filler cap, and were slightly more angular. The MX version, although significantly slimmer in order to reduce capacity to one gallon, used the same pressings, though with a thinner centre section. The two Triumph tanks again differed: the

two-gallon SS, whilst maintaining similar proportions to its BSA equivalent, was, in fact, quite different fore and aft, with the aluminium T version remaining identical, bar fuel cap positions, both of which mirrored the BSA's. Additional to these was a three-gallon steel tank (offset twist filler cap) available on request for all home and general export SS bikes, although, rather inconveniently, fitment of this necessitated a shorter dual seat.

The exit pipe of the box silencers was directly in line with the rear right-hand indicator, the resultant heat and vibration giving it a hard life, as well as leaving it stained with oil and carbon after a short while. The remedy was simply a modified exit pipe that now directed dirty gasses away from the bike, and first found on some 1972 machines.

Power plants
The 250cc engine received some very worthwhile improvements, making the unit the best of the C25/B25 series by far. Its light alloy con-rod had a history of breaking, leading to the introduction of a new rod with a larger shoulder section, which, in turn, led to the crankshaft having to be machined accordingly to accept the rod's greater width, therefore affecting inter-changeability with earlier engines.

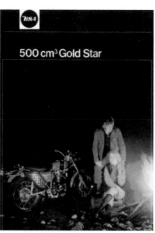

Four of the P34 single-sided brochures released for the home and general export market in April 1971. All cover shots were sourced from the photo shoots in North Wales a few months previously. (Author's archive)

Big end bearing life, the B25's other Achilles heel, was also considerably improved by the fitting of a new, three-stud-mounted, cast iron-bodied oil pump, which eliminated the danger of body warping that, over time, the previous zinc alloy pumps were susceptible to, with the attendant loss of oil pressure – vital for shell type bearings which rely on a film of oil between them and the crankshaft journal. Additionally, fitting a paper element oil filter in the return line greatly improved oil cleanliness, and the big end's prospects.

Both cylinder barrel and cylinder head received larger mating surfaces and gaskets, with the rocker box mounting studs increased in size. The final change of note was the fitting of a thrust washer between the clutch chain wheel and its mounting flange, signalling an end to the chain wheel's wear problems. These clutches also use a flangeless clutch hub, which permits an extra plate to be fitted.

The only obvious external change to these 'SS'

What the press said –

B50SS Gold Star
"For [motorway] work of that nature, the posture is rather too upright, with insufficient weight taken on the wrists and ankles.

"Direction indicators are a novelty on a British-made machine, and the Lucas equipment proved entirely satisfactory ... On first acquaintance the operating switch, incorporating the front brake control, appeared to be stiff in action. However, this was not noticeable once the bike was under way, and the switch could easily be retrieved to the mid-position without over-running.

"The brake is the latest 8 inch diameter, twin leading-shoe pattern, and produced rapid retardation without the sudden effect of its predecessor.

"The bike looks really light, too, with the exposed stanchions of the new front fork ... and ultra-short mudguards adding to the overall impression. But in rain the front mini-guard gave the entire engine gear unit a bath.

"BSA has set out to offer a model reasonably at home in two environments. In that, it has achieved success." – Motor Cycle (UK)

B25SS Gold Star (US spec)
"In handling, steering, economy and braking, the 250 scores well in a competitive capacity class, and our test revealed no glaring omissions on a machine that has obviously been designed to give good all-round performance.

"Wide handlebars and smooth controls made traffic work trouble-free. Brisk acceleration appeared even on moderate throttle openings, and swift, sure braking was the rule.

"The slim head-on aspect showed how well the designers have thought out the 250.

"Although it lacks some of the sophistication of some other 250s, the BSA promises to be running

engines, as they are generally known, was the 3-inch (7.5 mm) wide rear mounting lug. This was also a feature on the 499cc B50 engines, which, internally, had an extremely robust, three-bearing bottom-end incorporated into what was essentially the same crankcase as the B44's, and even though the con-rod was also the B44 item, it was now mounted on needle roller bearings rather than rollers. A similar cast iron oil pump with different internal gears, when some of its rivals have stopped forever.

"With its attractive red, off-white and chrome finish, the BSA looks set to be a big hit with riders who want a willing mount with ample reserves of power."
– Motor Cycle News (UK)

B50SS Gold Star

"The latest offering from BSA is a worthy example of the breed. It's an attractive machine, with a combination of modern and traditional styling that is pleasing to the eye.

"The front brake features an air scoop for better internal cooling, to minimize fading under repeated use. It does the job ... we gave it hard use to minimise the tendency to rely too much on compression deceleration ... the brakes showed no tendency to fade or grab ... [and] seemed to improve throughout the day, never giving the rider any cause for concern.

"The gas tank is rather small for a touring machine, but it has a pleasing shape and a nice red and black color combination.

"With the narrow cases and ample ground clearance,this 500 single has still more cornering potential to be realized.

"The general reaction to the looks [of the silencer] were negative, and this will probably be the most common criticism of the machine.

"The BSA Gold Star rates very high on an overall index of quality, design and performance."
– Cycle Guide (USA)

T25T Trailblazer

"For cowtrailing the Trailblazer is hard to beat because the bike is so easy to ride ... the Trailblazer handles very well in spite of its heft. As it is now, the bike's stability is uncanny. If 40 pounds or so were removed, this machine would be a real campaigner ... One can spend literally hours in the saddle without ill effect.

"In spite of the shoebox muffler, lines are taut and trim. The bike is a super-fun trail machine."
– Popular Cycling (USA)

and clutch modifications the same as for the 250s, were implemented, as was a new engine breathing system which rendered redundant the camshaft-mounted timed breather. The crankcase now breathed directly into the primary chaincase, and exited this via a large-bore pipe that terminated behind the right-hand side panel. Both P34 engine types received a mid-season gear change adjuster, thought to have been introduced in April 1971.

P36 (500cc OHV Twin)

P36 encompassed the 500cc Triumph T100R Daytona and T100C Trophy models, which, for some reason, were built virtually unchanged from 1970's specification, though journalists present at the November 1970 range launch in the US were assured they would be updated for the 1972 model year. The only new cycle parts used were the rear lamp housing, silencers (though, as with the TR6C, the T100C retained the previous year's items), indicators, and handlebar console switches. For home and general export bikes, a convoluted plenum chamber, visible on the exterior of the bike due to the lack of underseat space, further marred appearance.

Engine changes were restricted to larger section con-rods, a drop in compression ratio from 9.75:1 to 9:1, and a revised method of tappet adjustment in line with that of the 650cc Triumph Twin.

The virtually unchanged T100R Daytona, still burdened with its heavyweight wheel hubs and front forks. (Author's archive)

Regardless of over 40 years of subsequent journalistic comment implying that this was how all Triumph Twins should have looked, the press of the day roundly condemned the bikes as old-fashioned in comparison with the updated models. They may have been selling well in 1970, but five or ten years later? Certainly not in the same volume. Offering the largely unchanged Daytona and Trophy alongside more modern-engined machines in the same range would have been feasible up to a point, in order to fill a niche in the market. But to suggest that all Triumph Twins should have remained cosmetically untouched is nonsense, and BSA's US marketing team knew this only too well.

P39 (650cc OHV Twin)

This still is probably the most talked about of the new machines, due entirely to its oil bearing frame, which has been the subject of so much debate/criticism over the years, and is comprehensively dealt with in Chapter 2.

Suffice to say here, although some criticisms of it are valid, others have proved to be little more than fantasy.

Six P39s were marketed, three for each marque, in general mirroring each other's offering. BSA had the single carburettor A65 Thunderbolt, and the twin carburettor Lightning and Firebird Scrambler, while Triumph's stable consisted of two single carburettor machines – the TR6 Tiger and Trophy – and the twin carburettor T120 Bonneville.

And a much changed, lithe BSA A65L, now looking very 1970s. (Author's archive)

In common with the P34, the engine unit was the only surviving feature from 1970, and, as with all 1971 bikes bar the P30, two sizes of fuel tank were offered. BSA's small American market, 2½ gallon (11.5 litre) tank did wonders for the engine, instantly giving the bike the look

BSA 650cc A65T Thunderbolt. (Author's archive)

of flat track specials raced by the likes of Jim Rice, Dave Aldana, and many others. Its slim proportions, combined with the beautifully-styled side panels that, with the two inner sections, formed the induction plenum chamber, gave all three versions an almost Gazelle-like appearance when compared to the previous year's models.

For the three Triumphs, improvement had less of an impact in this respect as their predecessors were far more

Triumph 650cc TR6C Trophy. (Author's archive)

agile in appearance anyway, and, outwardly, the fuel tank was a virtual clone of the 1970 version, being slightly more bulbous at the front to maintain the same capacity initially reduced by the larger frame backbone indentation.

Somewhat surprisingly, in view of the barrage of vitriol over the years from British journalists, negative comments from the UK's original press tests were few and far between, and neither *Motor Cycle* nor *Motor Cycle News* had anything to say about the raised seat height of their A65 Lightning and T120 Bonneville, measuring 32-inches (81.3cm) and 34-inches (85cm) respectively (although 31½-inches (80.05cm) was actually quoted for the BSA by another journal).

Power plants
BSA A65
The most important change for this series was adoption of a now cast iron-bodied oil pump, which boasted a 30 per cent increase in delivery – both very instrumental in reducing the A65's sintered bronze timing side main bearing's sometimes problematic tendency to wear prematurely. A further change to the lubrication system was a more reliable piston-type pressure relief valve, which dispensed with the former ball bearing setup.

The cylinder head's exhaust ports were slightly more splayed than previously, and the rocker box studs had been enlarged, with a corresponding change to the rocker box itself, which was further modified to accept the new and much improved head-steady bracket.

BSA A70
Leaving the assembly line in late June and during July 1971, the 200 750cc 'A65s' featured major bottom end changes: in the main crankshaft, fly wheels, con-rods, crankcases, and, more obviously, pistons for the enlarged bore size. The bikes, all of which were officially destined for the USA, were built purely for homologation purposes, as many BSA-mounted flat track racers had, since 1969,

been entering AMA Grand National events on bored-out A65s.

Triumph TR6/T120

All three 650 Twins for 1971 featured a modified cylinder head, studs and rocker boxes, deemed necessary due to the problems that Meriden was having fitting the engines into the new P39 frames. The crankshafts were now also fitted with

a different set of fly wheels, with a revised balance factor that some press testers felt was responsible, in conjunction with the frame, for an improvement in vibration levels.

P40 (750cc OHV Triple)

Of the redesigned bikes, BSA's A75 and Triumph T150 3-cylinder 750s (mechanically identical but with the BSA featuring a sloped top end), received the least number of

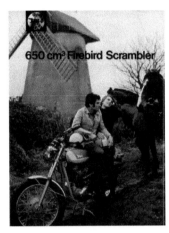

As with the P34 brochure shots, these P39s are from the same source. The temperature was well down, with frost on the grass (left), and centre right, a rather chilly-looking model perched on a Triumph TR6. (Author's archive)

What the press said –

A65 Lightning

"The new front fork has 61/2 inches of travel, and its well-damped action, in conjunction with the Girling-controlled rear springing, gave first-class road-holding.

"Essential on any large, fast machine are powerful, fade-free brakes. On the BSA they were first-class. Housed in conical light-alloy hubs, they were progressive and amply powerful for maximum speed. Repeated hard use failed to produce any sign of fade.

"Frame finish is in an attractive Dove grey.

"In a nutshell, the new-look Lightning blends trendy, up-to-the-minute looks with a big, all-round performance based on good old-fashioned know-how and painstaking development" – Motor Cycle (UK)

TR6 Tiger

"On the road-holding score, the new frame and forks seem to give the bike a more taut feeling ... it has removed some of that wallowing which one encountered on long, fast bends on the earlier frame ... [though] the

rough-cast aluminium fork sliders do little to enhance the appearance of the front end.

"The new brakes? Well, when they're set up correctly, they are superb. A couple of times I made those do-or-die panic stops, and with beautiful, tyre-squawking effort, they heaved the lot to a sharp standstill ... it is precise and progressive.

"Another minor point noticed on the new Tiger 650 was the increased saddle height ... but there are many riders under 5ft 8 inches ... the riding position proved comfortable with adequate room for the pillion passenger." – Motorcycle Mechanics (UK)

T120 Bonneville

"[The petrol tank] is a very attractive shape, looks large but, unfortunately, holds only 23/4 gallons. We were told at the [Colex] show that 4-gallon tanks were available at no extra cost to home market buyers. Is that still so, we wonder?

"[The silencers] are of the reverse megaphone style that looks very noisy! In fact, quite the reverse holds good; indeed, they make a beautiful sound.

"Without doubt the general handling of the Bonneville was absolutely first-class, with the big bars making leisurely riding particularly comfortable. Arriving at a standstill was less comfortable for me as the 32 inch seat height was just too high for both feet to be placed firmly on the ground. The brakes were tremendous, especially the 8 inch twin leading shoe front one. It really was a stopper but was light and pleasant to use.

"As a motorcycle to look at there are few better. This latest model, finished in tiger gold and black, with a welcome absence of unnecessary chrome, is very attractive indeed." – Motorcycle Sport (UK)

T120 Bonneville – "Best Bonnie yet"
"Most people agreed, when the 1971 Triumphs were unveiled five months ago, that the new bikes looked impressive. But how would they go? Were the changes mere fancy window dressing, or would the wholesale redesign work really make the bikes better machines? Set your minds at rest. The most famous Triumph of all, the 650cc Bonneville, is now smoother, stops more effectively, and looks more impressive than ever before.

"The 8 inch diameter front brake is easily capable of controlling the Bonneville's 382lb bulk, yet it offers an unusually high degree of 'feel' in the lever.

"The flashing indicators are best forgotten, for you need a concert pianist's touch to avoid flicking the blade-type switch straight through the neutral position. But otherwise the Lucas cast aluminium control clusters and levers look much tidier than the gadgetry that used to hang over Triumph handlebars." – Motor Cycle News (UK)

T120 Bonneville
"Still functionally British in appearance, Triumphs have sprouted many modern-day innovations and styling trends.

"Gracefully tapered silencers with a gradual upsweep ... and a wide dual seat improves comfort.

"The wheel hubs are very racy in appearance, and house an excellent set of brakes ... even after several hard, high speed applications, the front wheel continued to do its share of stopping the machine.

"Steering geometry felt just right for normal road riding, with a bit of fast swervery thrown in. Gone is the tendency of earlier Bonnevilles towards under steering.

"Other nice touches are rubber-mounted front fender braces, the overall excellent quality of finish (both paint and chrome), and precise handling qualities. This machine is one of Triumph's best." – Cycle World (USA)'

A65 Lightning
"The stylists spared nothing in updating the external appearance of BSA's new line of 650s. The new Lightning looks much better than the Bonneville ... its look is more refined, up-to-date, and the new [ivory] frame and rolling gear is a delightful come-on.

"BSA has now switched to ivory-painted frames, which has the effect of attractively emphasizing and outlining the function of the machine and setting it off from the engine and other parts ... The bike is beautiful and more compact-looking.

"The new layout for electrical components is excellent. Lift the seat, and you find the dual coils, battery, wiring, all in sensible, roomy array.

"Seating is not overly high at 32 1/2 inches; this comes as a pleasant surprise, for the new Bonneville, which has the same frame, has a seat 34 1/2 inches high: overly tall for a rider with short legs.

"The Lucas switches, which we criticized on the new Norton and Triumph Twins for being oddly placed and difficult to operate, are the same on the Lightning." – Cycle World (USA)

A65 Lightning
"The new tank does two things for the Lightning: it makes the bike look longer and racier, and its front end comes to a halt short of the steering head, so as to emphasise the gorgeous front forks ... the beautifully-proportioned headlight is mounted to the triple clamps via bent, grommeted rods, rather than being hung from fork-tube covers with ears. The designers took just as many pains figuring out how to mount the other front-end components, and the results justify the effort.

"Its frame is light gray, which, in theory, is a good idea – it makes the bike look lighter and nimbler – but in practice it doesn't work. Every bit of grime or grease or road tar stands out on that gray frame.

"The motorcycle is tall, but probably not too tall. The 5ft 8 inch rider could straddle it and plant the toes of both feet on the pavement.

"Most of the design changes are good ones, though, and – equally important – BSA quality control seems to have been vastly improved." – Cycle (USA)

changes of all, and were the only models to retain their respective frames. Unlike BSA's Twin downtube frame, Triumph's single tube one was somewhat archaic in construction, with brazed lugs and tubing, and a bolt-on rear section: practices that really belonged back in the 1950s. Besides the new parts common to the whole range, the only other significant changes were to the fuel tanks, side panels, and seats.

The A75, while more usually retaining the previous year's 4½ gallon (20.25 litre) tank for the home and general export markets, featured for the USA the now obsolete 1970 A65 item, and although something of a throwback in shape, its imaginative red and chrome colour scheme gave it a certain flamboyance, in keeping with the bike's status as range leader. For the first time – and without doubt part of the fuel tank's appeal – the impressive looking engine was now shown to full advantage; a strong selling point in the extrovert States. With restyled side panels, and in common with the other models, the bike looked far less bulky and a good deal more agile, which, at 13lb (5.9kg) lighter, it was.

It was a similar tale for the T150 that now wore a 2¾ gallon (12.36 litre) tank, shaped as the Bonneville's, and again with abbreviated dual seat and side panels, the latter having already been fitted to the 1970 US T150s with a similar tank, as part of an update package introduced in recognition of the original bike's unpopular aesthetics, which US sales people soon realised was dramatically affecting sales.

Power plants

The only engine unit change for 1971 was the introduction of an optional, five-speed gearbox, a legacy of the very successful racing Triples. As with the A70, 200 were again built for the purpose of homologation, this time for the Daytona 200 race in March. These were largely assembled during February 1971, and are identified by the engine number prefix A75RV. How many T150 Tridents for 1971 were so equipped is unclear, however.

The Triples of both marques, seen here fitted with small, US-spec fuel tanks. Larger tanks were available as an option. (Author's archive)

What the press said –

BSA A75 Rocket 3
"It's big, it's brutish, it's beautiful. You can say all these things about the new generation Rocket Three and be correct. This is the new 750 Beezer Three, 40 pounds trimmer and a whole lot prettier than the ones that first came from across the Atlantic"... the front brake on the 750, although a bit heavy on pull, is adequate for the machine ... With proper use of the engine's compression and gearbox, the BSA pulls down very well." – Modern Cycle (USA)

Triumph T150 Trident
"The new 750 and 650s have a cleaner, lighter look that doesn't do violence to the time-honoured Triumph shape.

"Gone is the huge Triumph front fender with enormous over-the-fender braces. The new fender is shorter, lighter, and less cumbersome.

"The conical hubs, both front and rear, please the eye ... [but] the 8 inch brake, despite its twin-cam design and ventilation, is no match for the Trident's speed and mass.

"The alloy (handlebar switch) housings have small plastic wing levers, which move up and down. The sharply radiused edges jab and bite your thumbs when used repeatedly within a short time span." – Cycle (USA)

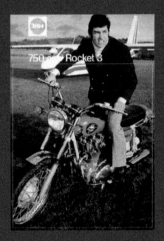

Dissatisfied with the previous Rocket 3 location shots, BSA's Advertising Department set up a further location shoot, shortly before these home/general export brochures were issued. (Author's archive)

Chapter 8

P40/13 Hurricane

The BSA Vetter 3, or Triumph X75 Hurricane, as it was eventually named, in many ways epitomised the image of the new Umberslade Hall-designed bikes, though in a far more radical form. Only an American could have designed such a way-out machine, and probably only a freelancer at that, as he would be free from all the usual constraints inherent in large corporations. For BSA to have stuck as closely to the prototype as it did when it engineered the bike for production, can only be to the credit of some of the people concerned with the project; not least Umberslade's Stephen Mettam, more of which later.

It is worthwhile pointing out here the hypocrisy that is so often prevalent when BSA and Triumph products of the era are discussed. The Vetter 3, with its 2-gallon (9 litre) petrol tank, small seat, and lack of carrying capacity, etc, is impractical as an everyday machine, despite its beauty and uniqueness, making it a true leisure machine, which, of course, it is. A point seemingly missed by many latter-day critics is that the 1971 BSA/Triumph range concept was also that they be predominantly bikes for leisure, which the abundance of publicity material produced clearly portrays.

Concessions such as large fuel tanks, luggage racks, and longer front mudguards were available for the more conservative markets that BSA operated in, but to have ignored the demands made by the financially vital American market would have left both companies, and more so Triumph, with no long-term future worth talking about. Yet, today, as the Vetter 3 rightly enjoys universal acclaim from all quarters, its British-designed counterparts still often attract derisory comment for some of the very same aesthetics that the Triple is venerated for.

Craig Vetter pictured in the latter part of the 1970s, his name, by now, etched into motorcycling history. (Courtesy AMA)

Craig Vetter, for the most part, had been designing and building motorcycle fairings since leaving Illinois University, where he had gained a BFA in industrial design. In 1968, he tried his hand at designing an integrated fuel tank/seat/tail unit for his Suzuki T500, and took it along to that year's Daytona 200 race in the hope of impressing someone enough that they put some design work his way. The plan worked, with BSA's eastern region Sales

Manager, Harry Chaplin, sufficiently inspired by Vetter's innovative work to pass his contact details onto BSA's Vice President, Don Brown.

Brown had taken an instant dislike to the rather odd styling of the new BSA/Triumph 750cc Triples, and suspected the design would be detrimental to sales. As events were to prove, in this he was correct. He had guardedly discussed aspects of the bike with Chaplin, and asked if he could recommend anyone able to carry out motorcycle custom design.

Vetter was duly invited to BSA headquarters at Nutley, New Jersey early in June 1969 for a meeting with Brown, where the pair found that, regardless of the difference in their cultures (Brown a besuited company executive; Vetter something of a hippie), they shared some mutual interests, and respected each other.

Hired, Vetter found himself returning the 1000 miles home on a BSA Rocket 3, which he was to use for the restyling exercise. The financial details of the agreement were a little off-beat: Vetter was reimbursed for materials and any time his assistants spent on the project, but would only be paid for *his* time if the design made it into production. The project was never an official BSA sanction, initiated purely on Brown's say-so, with funds sourced from Nutley's cash float.

Within a couple of weeks, Vetter had studied the rather ungainly Rocket 3 intensely, and made notes on the areas he considered needed improvement – most notably the tank, seat and rear mudguard – and from this it was obvious that the huge side panels which partially enclosed the air filters would go as well. By the beginning of July, Vetter had begun to put together the now-famous integrated tank/side panel/seat unit, painstakingly built from plastic auto putty. After shaping to the required profile, the entire unit was coated in resin to create the finished surface, which, after trying Don Brown's colour preference of yellow, Vetter repainted Hugger Red, a colour used on the recently-introduced Chevrolet Camaro, setting it off with a tapering strip of reflective yellow Scotchlite tape running from the tank top onto each side panel, where the line was continued by the chrome grab rail.

A second strong styling feature to grace the machine was the exhaust system, which had all three downpipes travelling along the lower right-hand side before fanning out into three short megaphones, stacked one on top the other. The top of the engine also came in for some attention by way of lengthened cylinder head fins on each side of the head, achieved by gluing shaped pieces of plexiglass over the existing fins. As with the other changes, the result was impressive, lending the bike a far more macho look than the stock item.

Throughout the design period Vetter had been sending weekly progress reports to Brown, and, when available, explanatory photographs as requested. Initially, Brown had been trying to steer the designer a little with minor criticisms of some of his ideas, though this abruptly ceased when his eyes fell on a photo of the now-painted seat/tank unit. "I realised that Craig was onto something of importance, and backed away from micro-managing the project," he explained.

The first week of September saw conclusion of the restyling, and a study of the photographs within this chapter clearly show that very few existing parts had escaped change. As well as looking considerably lighter, overall appearance was now light years away from that of the cumbersome A75 which had entered the workshop three months earlier.

Beauty from the beast. Vetter's finished model displaying absolutely nothing of its Rocket 3 origins. (Author's archive)

Although the project had been deliberately shrouded in secrecy, BSA Inc President Peter Thornton eventually got wind of it, and, suspecting Brown of having his hand in the till, not unnaturally demanded to see the bike. Vetter delivered the now non-running model to Nutley at the end of October, whereupon Thornton uttered those now famous words: "My god, it's a bloody phallus." He was, presumably, impressed with it.

On Thornton's instructions, it was there and then apparently packed for immediate despatch to the UK for assessment, spending time at Small Heath and Umberslade Hall in the process of making a production-viable version. The precise movements of the prototype are unclear, but it did receive a hike in fork length somewhere along the line. Vetter has recently offered photographic proof that he had lengthened the forks on

Vetter's prototype photographed at Umberslade Hall prior to being dismantled for production assessment. Careful study of the top of the fork stanchions reveals two separate sections, added to increase overall fork length. (Author's archive)

his prototype by using a single extension block in each fork stanchion, yet by the time that it was photographed at Umberslade in early spring 1970, it had gained an additional set of extension blocks.

About this Stephen Mettam says: "I remember that when we dismantled the Ceriani forks there were blocks of wood, like sawn-off broom handles, inserted in the sliders to keep them looking long. The frame guys commented

on incorrect fork angle and trail because the forks were longer than standard. If Craig did not insert these blocks, someone else did. The change did not occur over here."

Once in production two years later, the then Hurricane, as it was eventually named, wore forks that were two inches (5cm) longer than the stock P40 model.

Mettam also played a vital part in ensuring that

The Vetter 3 undergoing photographic scrutiny at the R&D Centre as soon as the bike was unpacked from the States. (Author's archive)

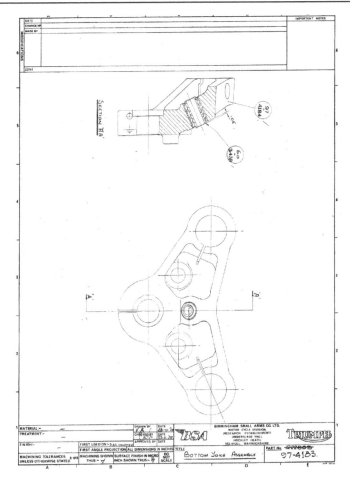

It wasn't only Vetter who had been inspired by US flat-track racing trends. In parallel and without knowledge of his efforts, Umberslade Hall was working along similar lines. (Author's archive)

Dating from November 1970, this Umberslade Hall drawing graphically illustrates how the production version of the bottom fork yoke was stepped in order to adequately brace the extended stanchions. (Courtesy Steve Sewell/SRS)

Vetter's ideas were followed as closely as possible while the prototype was being assessed for production. The production engineers involved were pushing to use an existing fuel tank with a separate fibreglass seat base; thereby, in a stroke, dismissing the most important and eye-catching aspect of Vetter's work. Commendably, BSA's stylist stood fast in defence of retaining the one-piece moulding, as he also did with the fanned silencer arrangement, the latter something his department had coincidentally been working on in parallel as part of a P40 rationalisation/restyling plan for the USA.

So, clearly, it was not only in the States that dissatisfaction with the P40's aesthetics was felt. The exhaust system on both designs had been influenced by the flamboyant layout used by Jim Rice on his three-cylinder flat track BSA.

Mettam confirms that, at Small Heath and Umberslade Hall, the bike was commonly known as the Vetter Chopper 3, and, interestingly, he also states that: "Very few at BSA had any faith in that model. But they were on the wrong side of the Atlantic, too old (brains, anyway) and unimaginative."

By March 1970, the prototype bike had made its way into an internal BSA/Triumph folder, along with details of all the other machines that were to make up the new 1971 range, indicating that BSA was serious about actually producing the bike: the accompanying text is reproduced here:

Special Rocket 3.

The American fairing designer Craig Vetter customised a B.S.A. Rocket 3. The company intends to produce a limited quantity of 500 replicas of this machine.

This "production chopper" uses a slightly modified frame and special fibreglass seat/tank unit.

Ancillaries such as headlamp and instruments are fitted on special mountings.

A new 3 pipe exhaust system will be fitted.

A general very high standard of finish and assembly is required for this machine.

The first official but confidential notification of the Vetter 3's existence. (Author's archive)

The folder, largely descriptive but also featuring either photographs or sketches of prototypes, was limited to 15 copies, and sent to departments such as advertising and costing, in order that they could familiarise themselves with the salient features of the new bikes at the earliest opportunity, because production parts were not yet available.

The number of bikes to be built was decided not by Small Heath, but BSA Inc, which, by now, had seen the Vetter 3's potential as a flagship for the restyled bikes: without doubt they would have complemented each other superbly.

Throughout 1970, a succession of component drawings flowed from the Umberslade Hall drawing office as the process of 'productionising' the bike took place. It's interesting to note that, while these continued through 1971, some minor parts amendments were still being proposed a matter of days before production finally began the following year.

While at Umberslade, a Canadian member of the styling team, Alf Judd, trundled the prototype to the

while Craig Vetter enthusiastically explained the thinking behind the design. A low-key appearance at the US range launch at La Quinta in November 1970, and an early 1971 showing at January's Houston Trade Fair, kept the bike in the eye of the media and public.

In the meantime, back in Britain, the planned production of the P40/13, as it was now designated, had presumably been removed from the 1971 schedule as the extent of the delays getting the rest of the range into production became apparent, and later financial problems emerged.

It wasn't until the end of 1971 that the first production specification Vetter 3 was built at Small Heath, the finished machine bearing BSA fuel tank decals. Built on December 22, and – according to factory records – sent on its way to the USA the same day, the machine's crankcases were

Early 1970, and the Vetter 3 poses in the undergrowth at the rear of Umberslade Hall. (Author's archive)

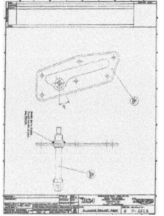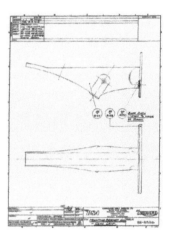

Component drawings for the triple silencer bracket and rear lamp unit, the latter using the longer version from the P34 models, due to the reduced length of the X-75's seat unit. (Courtesy Steve Sewell/SRS)

rear of the Hall's grounds, where he took a handful of atmospheric shots, aided by a smouldering bonfire lit by the estate's ground staff, giving the impression of a light mist. Luckily, some of these images survive today, providing a further glimpse of the Vetter 3 during its six months or so in the UK.

By May the bike was heading back Stateside, where it was due for a pre-arranged Don Brown photo shoot with *Cycle World* magazine – the deal was mutually beneficial, with BSA able to sound out public opinion without actually announcing the bike as a model, and *Cycle World* gaining a best-selling issue, the cover graced by a stunning shot of the bike.

Within the article's text were some rather vague and non-committal comments from BSA Inc's Product Planning Director, Tony Salisbury, about the bike's future,

stamped V75V, the second V denoting fitment of a five-speed gearbox. The bike was subsequently put on display at the 1972 Houston Trade Show, where Vetter, for the first time, saw his labours of 2½ years earlier represented in pre-production form, closely faithful to his vision.

A second, pre-production BSA was put together three weeks later on January 14, 1972; this time sent 'on loan' to Meriden's Development Department, where the successful racing Triples were built. One of these two V75Vs, presumably the latter example, was taken to the MIRA proving ground for thorough testing, where just over 120mph (193kph) was wrung out of the slightly weaving Triple: the combined result of longer front fork stanchions and ribbed tyres thought necessary to enhance the Chopper image.

The two inch (5cm) longer forks were only one part of

a specification that would place the bike in a more exotic sales bracket than that of the Rocket 3 and Trident. Wheel rims were flanged aluminium; the conical hubs and brake plates polished; both components laced with chromium-plated spokes. A pair of specially-cast aluminium fork yokes supported tubular headlamp brackets, and the two clocks were mounted on a 1970, A65-type aluminium bracket, while the rear lamp bracket also received the chrome treatment.

The exotic exhaust system had been reproduced fairly closely to that of the prototype – only the angle and length of the silencers different – though, with forthcoming US noise emission regulations for 1973 around the corner, the system's days were already numbered. The cylinder head was also modified in line with Vetter's thoughts, the fins extending up to three-quarters of an inch (19mm) on each side of the head. The bike's centrepiece – the integrated tank/seat unit – was made in two halves that encased a two-gallon steel fuel tank rather than a single moulding, as Vetter had designed, the resulting central joint disguised by a strip of tape that matched the original styling stripes. Dry weight was down by about 16lb (7.3kg) over that of the T150.

In hindsight, with all that was going on at BSA, it is of little surprise that the world never saw the bike built as a BSA. With the company fighting for survival, a limited edition model that would, because of its specification, be retailing at $295 more than the company's standard 750s was just not on the cards.

With the model aimed squarely at the American market, it made sense to produce it as a Triumph. Most of Meriden's output went there, anyway, and the marque was also more popular than BSA. Even though Triumph's financial position was inextricably linked to that of BSA (and therefore pretty dire), there must have been sufficient confidence in the sales potential of the model from the American end of the company (which, by May 1972, was in the hands of Felix Kalinsky, who took over from interim President Denis McCormack). It was also suggested by BSA Inc Engineering Vice President Pete Colman that building a quantity of V75s would be a solution to the surplus Rocket 3 crankcases and frames that were now largely redundant, as the BSA Triple had either ceased production or was to do so shortly.

TRX75 Hurricane

The first 'production' P40/13 left the Meriden assembly line on September 6, 1972, now badged and named the Triumph X75 Hurricane, and marketed for the 1973 season. No-one seems to know with any certainty whether BSA or Triumph was responsible for the name,

though, in all likelihood, it came from BSA, with its strong link to several previous meteorologically-derived bike names: it's hard to imagine that Triumph would have emulated BSA in this way, given the rivalry between the two marques. It's also rumoured that Kalinsky may have had a hand in the naming, which is feasible, as it was, of course, in his country's market that the majority of sales would occur.

Unlike the T140 and T120 that the Aztec Red X75 would be sharing brochure space with, the Hurricane was still fitted with the now-discontinued, 8-inch (20.3cm) conical hub/brake unit rather than the new single disc, as well as the short wire-mounted mudguard, which certainly fitted the chopper image better than the more staid-looking, pre-1971-type mudguard that Triumph had reverted to for its 1973 models. The hub may well have been chosen as a way of clearing surplus stock.

The first 200 or so Hurricanes confirmed BSA's

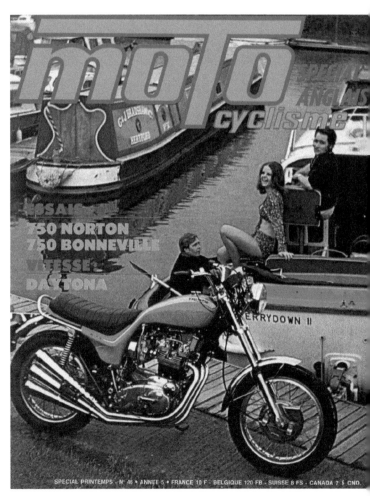

Just one of many worldwide cover slots acquired upon the X75's launch. (Author's archive)

initial intention of building the bikes *as* BSAs, these already having V75 rather than TRX75 stamped on their crankcases. Production continued for approximately four months before ending in January 1973. The exact number of machines built, regardless of what figures have been entered in relevant factory records, is difficult to determine, but somewhere in the region of 1150 would seem to be about the mark. Surprisingly, a number of Hurricanes were built using the standard four-speed gearbox, presumably due to five-speed box availability problems, though it is not known whether these were sold at a lower price.

Once the bikes began to arrive in the USA, staff at Duarte's Technical Centre also picked up on the light front end, and, as a result, put together a fork kit that was shipped out with each bike for the receiving dealer to fit, although it is not clear whether this was optional or mandatory. Front end characteristics were something that most subsequent press road testers also felt obliged to mention, although it was generally accepted that, once the rider had become accustomed to the trait, it ceased to be a concern.

That the bike failed to emerge as a BSA, only adds to the final ignominy.

As in 1971, 1972 saw BSA/Triumph again hold a dealer preview meeting for the following season's models, coinciding with California's Ontario 250 Classic in September. Outside the stadium Julie Mann, journalist and wife of reigning AMA No 1 Dick Mann, poses for the photographers on an early build X75: quite possibly number 647 or 648, both of which were built by the Triumph Experimental Department's Harry Woolridge. (Courtesy FMDG)

Chapter 9

Promotion

Home and general export

Whereas previous campaigns had fluctuated in terms of the amount of advertising material produced for any given year, the Power Set '71 – the bold, collective name of the new bikes for the home/general export market – set a new level as far as British motorcycle manufacturers were concerned, not that there were very many of these still in business by 1970.

As a snapshot of the campaign's scope of the new machines, somewhere in the region of 45 black and white photographs, six brochures (two of them produced in several languages), 21 single-sided, full colour, A4 brochure sheets, and an unknown number of posters (possibly around 24) alone were issued for both marques. In addition to this were many technical and dealer publications; totalling well over 30 items in all. Slightly more obscure dealer promotional material existed – such as the set of print block ink stamps for each BSA model, as pictured on page 87.

The magazine campaign was no less adventurous and operated on two levels: the ads placed by the division's Advertising Department, and the promotional spreads produced by some of the journals.

Several countries had been targeted for increased sales in 1971, with some well-supported motorcycle shows worldwide testament to this objective.

To steer the campaign in the desired direction, the

division had recently (October 1970) signed up with the newly-formed Wasey, Pritchard, Wood and Quadrant ad agency, a subsidiary of US ad giant Interpublic, itself associated with McCain Erickson; the previous employer of BSA Inc's President, Peter Thornton.

Exactly when the November date for the world launch of BSA and Triumph 1971 season motorcycles was determined is not clear, but some highly placed executives must have suspected that the launch was a little premature, given the late delivery of the P39 frame drawings, BSA's difficulty in recruiting skilled

Caron Gardner and Carol Cleveland aboard BSA's new-look A65 Thunderbolt at launch day in West London. (Courtesy VMCC)

Extract from the Power Set press release –

"Two complete ranges of motorcycles, incorporating more changes than in any new season's models in the last 25 years, are announced by the BSA/Triumph Motor Cycle Division for 1971.

"Three years of intensive development work lies behind the 13 basic machines, which include a 350cc double overhead camshaft twin, and the return of the famous BSA Gold Star series.

"The machines have been designed with a new generation of motorcycle owner in mind – the fast-growing fun and leisure market," said a company spokesman, "but potentially they have all the high performance factors which can match anything our competitors can produce, and which have left a long line of BSA/Triumph successes on the tracks of USA and Europe.

"The ranges cover six capacity classes – 175, 250, 350, 500, 650, 750cc – in specifications varying from 'trail' models for cross-country riding, to 'street scramblers' that can be used either on or off the road.

"The new BSA 350cc Fury and its Triumph counterpart the Bandit – available with electric starters and five-speed gearboxes – will be the last of the new models to come off the production lines for '71. They will be in dealer showrooms by the spring.

"Motocross enthusiasts throughout the world will welcome the introduction of the 500cc BSA Victor. This is the latest development of the machine which carried BSA star Jeff Smith MBE to two World Championship titles.

"The BSA Group's Motor Cycle Division is Britain's biggest motorcycle manufacturer, with an annual turnover currently in the order of £30 million. About 90 per cent of the production of its two factories – at Small Heath, Birmingham, and Meriden, near Coventry – goes to well over 100 different export markets."

"With the exception of the 350cc double overhead camshaft models, and the 750cc three-cylinder Rocket 3, all BSA four-stroke machines feature a new spine frame, in which a large diameter top tube carries the engine oil supply. Thus, the weight and space of an orthodox oil tank is saved, and the oil-filled top tube helps to make the frame particularly rigid. Triumph's 650cc twin cylinder models also use similar frames.

"Machines of both ranges now have two-way damped front forks with alloy legs. These incorporate a special 'quick change' feature which enables springs of a different rating to be fitted without stripping the forks.

"With the exception of those fitted to the smaller trail machines, all front brakes are of the twin leading shoe variety. All brakes have been redesigned and use weight-saving conical aluminium hubs.

"New electrical systems which include flashing indicators have been fitted on all models, and a starter motor is an optional extra on the 350cc BSA Fury and Triumph Bandit. Single cylinder machines now have the majority of electrical components housed in an aluminium box. This also acts as a high efficiency heat sink for the zener diode.

"The new 350cc models will be available in road and street scrambler versions from both BSA and Triumph. They will produce 34bhp, have five-speed gearboxes, which is an innovation for both BSA and Triumph production machines, and new sleek and quieter exhaust systems."

labour, and the ongoing problems of the many outside component suppliers, who were themselves bedevilled by the industrial action that was rife within the British manufacturing industry at the time.

West End swank

During the evening of Tuesday, November 10th 1970, the new bikes were dramatically unveiled at London's Royal Lancaster Hotel. Most of the machines on show were pre-production, hand-built bikes, with only the Small Heath-built BSA/Triumph 250cc Singles anywhere close to mass production. Unfortunately, events were to prove that the launch was, in fact, several months too early, with BSA's B50 models the last to leave the production line in quantity during May 1971, and the 350cc models ultimately failing to get even that far.

Prior to this, earlier in the day, record producer Mickie Most, Lord Rollo Denbigh, and actresses Caron Gardner and Carol Cleveland attended a photo session in the hotel with several of the, as yet, unveiled motorcycles. This was followed, later in the afternoon, by a further session with the two ladies posing outside the hotel on an A65T. With the bike moved out of the rain, more photos were taken, this time with Denbigh and Lionel Jofeh. Mickie Most failed to take his place at table for the evening's presentation, due to an unforeseen engagement in the States, which meant he had to leave the UK the same day.

The evening was a sumptuous occasion, organised by the group's Public Relations Officer, Reg Dancer, who had been allocated £15,000 for the event, which, for the main part, was held in the hotel's Nine Elms Suite. Celebrities, dealers, importers, government officials, and press representatives from all over the world (except the USA, which had its own, far more extravagant launch two days later) were invited to the event, together with some of the division's key personnel. As guests assembled in the foyer, bulging racks held black and white press photographs, freely available to all, whilst, additionally, dealers and journalists were presented with a large and impressive folder, packed with details of both new ranges, as well as the revolutionary Ariel 3 Trike which had been launched earlier in the year.

Once inside the suite, and after consuming a handsome meal, the audience was presented with speeches by Eric Turner and Lionel Jofeh. The latter had not quite left the stage when it was engulfed by 30 silver-clad Young Generation dancers, who spent the next six minutes or so dancing, singing, and unveiling the 13 bikes present from the new range. Both song and choreography were written and specially arranged for the event.

The first nine machines, including an Ariel 3, were enclosed within large, purpose-built, spot-lit cabinets situated around the perimeter of the room, and each accompanied by three dancers and a trumpeted fanfare upon opening. Back on stage, a further five bikes were revealed: three from the honeycomb-like pods that formed the stage backdrop, plus the two top-of-the-range 750cc bikes – Triumph's T150 and BSA's A75, both of which glided across the stage, decorated with a brace of dancers.

Following this magnificent performance, the pace was considerably slowed by the popular Irish comedian Dave Allen, who entertained the audience for over an hour with his well-known brand of somewhat controversial humour.

After the show the bikes came in for close scrutiny from many of the guests, with BSA/Triumph executives and sales staff on hand to answer the many and inevitable questions posed. Incidentally, the shape of the evening's cabaret had been decided by nothing more than a flippant remark by Chief Stylist Stephen Mettam, when Reg Dancer had asked some months previously "This is your show, Stephen, what do you want to do after dining?" to which Mettam had replied "Oh, bring on the dancing girls; tell a few risqué jokes."

The previous day, November 9, a related event – a

Triumph's little-changed Daytona 500, captured at the moment of its unveiling. (Courtesy VMCC)

Stand-up comedian Dave Allen, obligatory alcoholic beverage in hand. Stephen Mettam recalls that his repertoire was "very blue." (Courtesy VMCC)

dealer sales incentive seminar – had been held at the nearby Hilton Hotel. The seminar was intended for 70 of the UK's top dealers, each of whom had been placed in one of three divisions relative to their previous year's sales figures, with a series of stepped cash prizes for highest sales achieved: top prize being £1000 and the lowest £100. As with the Lancaster Hotel, a Motoplas display was also in evidence, promoting the range of wares designed for the new models and the Ariel 3.

For the 30 overseas distributors, a special meeting on the morning of launch day was held at the Lancaster Hotel, and delegates received details of the marketing strategy that was so integral to the concept of the new bikes, and watched a film as part of the audio-visual presentation.

Extract from Eric Turner's speech –

"If our expectations for the current year are realized, the ex-works value of our motorcycle exports will be well over nine times that of nine years ago. We are justifiably proud of the fact that we export more than 80% of our output, and one cannot help feeling that if some other industries did only half as well as the motorcycle industry there would be no balance of payments problem. Of course, we would very much like to see a larger home market, and I think we would be helped enormously if

Extract from Lionel Jofeh's speech –

"We set about increasing our engineering strength by supplementing the division's very considerable fund of knowledge and experience through bringing into our operation experienced people from other industries. This has enabled us to rapidly introduce a large number of detailed improvements to our products, to add to customer satisfaction, and also to meet environmental legislation. Any industry battling against a Japanese industry on a worldwide basis needs courage, a strong stomach, and capability of a very high level.

The final bike of the evening is revealed – BSA's E35R 350cc Fury. (Courtesy VMCC)

BSA Service Manager Frank Adderley in conversation with two Dutch trade delegates, following the Tuesday morning overseas seminar. (Courtesy VMCC)

our products, including the little Ariel 3-wheeler, did not suffer from the same iniquitous rate of purchase tax of 36% which applies, for example, to a Rolls-Royce.

"In the richer countries the motorcycle is now, of course, mainly a fun, leisure, sporty, groovy product;, even a symbol of virility and manliness. Since the USA and Canada enjoy the highest standards of living, these are the reasons why North America is by far our largest market. But the disposable income in other parts of the world is rising rapidly also. Indeed, our market research indicates that the rate of growth in these other countries will be even faster than the growth in North America.

"Never before has any motorcycle company in the world unveiled so many new models at one time. They have been designed to make the maximum use of common components, with obvious benefit to the dealer, the customer, and to ourselves, but without jeopardising the separate identities of the BSA and Triumph brands."

"We decided we could do a more efficient job, as well as reduce overheads, if we not only concentrated our resources, but reorganised them to give a better flow pattern and better detailed working arrangements. These improvements, and the resultant greater efficiency, will help offset the extraordinarily high rate of cost inflation from which we, in common with other engineering companies in Great Britain, suffer these days.

"We began by improving our marketing capability in the United States, our biggest single market. We set up a new form of organisation for our operations in the USA, supplementing the considerable capability we had there for many years by the expertise of a number of very competent, seasoned executives, most of them having a background in the US automobile industry. We then began to look at our arrangements in some of the other 150 or so markets in which we operate, and much improved arrangements have been made in South Africa, France, Sweden, and Switzerland – many are represented here tonight."

Royal Lancaster & Hilton Hotel show bikes

Engine/frame number	Model	Despatch dept. entry	Venue
KE00818	B25SS Gold Star	6-11-70	Hilton or Lancaster Hotel
KE00856	B25SS Gold Star	6-11-70	Hilton or Lancaster Hotel
	E35 Fury		Lancaster Hotel
PE01714	B50SS Gold Star	6-11-70	Lancaster Hotel
KE01188	B50T Victor Trail	6-11-70	Hilton Hotel
PE01713	B50MX Victor MX	6-11-70	Lancaster Hotel
NE01014	A65T Thunderbolt	6-11-70	Lancaster Hotel pre-launch
KE00686	A65L Lightning	6-11-70	Lancaster Hotel
KE00246	A65FS Firebird Scrambler	6-11-70	Lancaster Hotel
KE00101	A75R Rocket 3	6-11-70	Lancaster Hotel
NE01658	T25SS Blazer SS	6-11-70	Hilton Hotel
JE00494	T25T Trail Blazer	6-11-70	Lancaster Hotel
	T100R Daytona		Lancaster Hotel
110	T100C Trophy	15-09-70	Lancaster Hotel
2652	TR6R Tiger	28-10-70	Hilton Hotel
2655	TR6C Trophy	28-10-70	Lancaster Hotel
	T120R Bonneville		Lancaster Hotel
	T150 Trident		Lancaster Hotel
	K2 Ariel 3		Lancaster Hotel
	K2 Ariel 3		Hilton Hotel

Of the 22 motorcycles listed on the previous page, those which appear with engine/frame number details were entered as 'on loan' to the Royal Lancaster Hotel in the relevant factory despatch records, even though only 13, plus an Ariel 3, were actually present for the unveiling. The BSA A65T was used for the press photo session during the afternoon, and, as previously mentioned, a second Ariel 3 was displayed in the hotel foyer. It is highly probable that the remaining six machines were delivered to the nearby Hilton Hotel for the linked presentations. Where available, engine/frame numbers and the date the bikes entered the despatch dept. have been included.

The next day the two UK weekly motorcycle newspapers, *Motor Cycle* and *Motor Cycle News*, each donated several pages and cover slots to the new motorcycles, with the totally new DOHC 350 taking precedence over all.

These presentations would have been prepared in co-operation with the BSA Press Office, which had supplied the many photographs and technical information some weeks earlier on a confidential basis. This was also the case with many of the overseas journals, the singular aim being to achieve simultaneous worldwide coverage. Both UK papers featured factual text devoid of opinion, though *Motor Cycle's* Editor craftily managed to air his own thoughts on the new machines indirectly in the following week's issue, by printing a selection of letters from unenthusiastic readers only, thereby creating the thinly veiled illusion that the bikes were not what the British public wanted.

In a similar way to *Motor Cycle* and *Motor Cycle News*, magazines the world over published articles and presentations on the new machines, with the 350s invariably having their own piece in a separate issue. Some of these presentations were particularly comprehensive, and on occasion featured colour photographs, the stand out publication in this respect the French *Motocyclisme*, which, in its Christmas edition, had no fewer than ten pages dedicated to the new models.

Publicity material

Both marques featured in similar fold-out brochures, carrying black and white images of the new models, and it was these that were produced in other languages such as French, German, Italian, etc, first becoming available at the November launch, and each with its own colour-coded price list.

A sheaf of 8½-inch x 6⅝-inch (21.75cm x 16.9cm) black and white photographs were released for dealer and journalists alike; one for each motorcycle (21), supplemented by a further 14 location shots and five featuring technical drawings. A further five or so illustrated various views of some of the bikes, and were sent direct to the media for use in the previously mentioned mid-November articles.

Most of these items could also be found within the large 'Press Information' folder presented to journalists and some dealers at the launch. Within this folder were two more folder booklets – one BSA and one Triumph

– entitled 'The Year of BSA' and 'Power Plan '71' respectively, plus a three-page press release, speech excerpts, retail price lists, and a production schedule.

The Ariel 3 was represented by June's 1970 brochure, and some promotional leaflets. The Year of BSA folder was also present in a slightly different guise, titled 'The 1971 Salesman's Guide,' and featured a diagonally-striped, two-tone colour cover as used on the Press Information folder: a design that was soon utilised on most BSA technical manuals. Content was virtually the same; the principal difference being a page of copy that was, in essence, a pep talk for the salesman about how to sell his BSAs.

Two interesting anomalies within these folder booklets were the appearance of a white A75, also listed as such in the relevant specification page, and Triumph T25 models designated as both T25 and T80 on different pages. T80 had been in use confidentially since at least early 1970, and was originally chosen as a link to Triumph's successful Single, the Tiger 80, from some decades previously. However, after reconsideration (albeit at a very late stage), the T25 designation was considered more relevant to present day potential customers.

April 1971 saw the release of an influx of new colour material; the result of the series of very cold photo shoots in North Wales. Each model now had its own A4, full-colour, double-sided brochure leaflet depicting an atmospheric location shot on the front, together with several smaller pictures, information, and some fine blurb from the Advertising Department for each model. The front cover photograph was in most cases mirrored when reproduced as a series of 33-inch x 23-inch (83.8cm x 58.4cm) posters, although it is not clear whether or not the whole set was printed (but probably so). Extracts from these A4 sheets were used in a series of ads placed in magazines during spring and early summer, and two 'special supplement' issues of *Motor Cycle* and *Motor Cycle News* used material from the full line brochure alongside the newer images. Both Italy and France offered some interesting and colourful ads, initiated by the ad departments of respective importers.

The BSA technical manuals comprising spare parts catalogues, owner's handbooks and dealer-only manuals such as the Data Book and Operations Manual, eventually appeared, carrying the striking, striped cover design previously mentioned. Pink was the primary colour

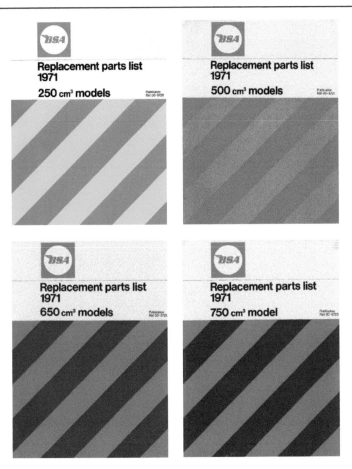

The face of 1971. Variations on the striped covers appeared on most of BSA's many technical manuals, as well as on a handful of Triumph's, albeit with blue as the primary colour. (Author's archive)

Dealer-only ink stamp blocks leaflet. (Author's archive)

The two full-line home/general export brochures that were printed in several different languages, and two striking ads from Italy. (Author's archive)

for this, the second colour varying in accordance with which motorcycle it was relating to. This theme was also adopted by Triumph on a few of its publications, all of which were dealer-only. The decision to introduce these new designs would appear to have come a little late in the day, as September 1970's master price list features a plain cover, as does, for instance, the French Operations Manual. In addition, early owner's handbooks had initially continued to use the same cover layout as the previous years' items.

Ongoing to the new material were BSA and Triumph promotional dealer items introduced during 1970. These were split into two categories – shop decoration and public purchase – and included products such as illuminated signs, desk clocks, overalls, ties, balloons, pens, stickers, etc, all of which carried the logo of the relevant marque.

Olympia Show
In Britain the annual Cycle & Motorcycle Association (CMCA) Show in January was the first major event on the calendar, although, for the first time, was merged with the Camping and Outdoor Leisure Exhibition (Colex). Held over ten days in the Empire Hall at London's Kensington Olympia, and opened by Industry Minister John Eden, the show saw the largest attendance figures (150,000) since 1962, undoubtedly assisted in this by the diversity of showgoers. Somewhat strangely, the company responsible for publicising the event, Trade Exhibitions Ltd, made no mention whatsoever of the motorcycling side of the show in publicity material. Relations between Trade Exhibitions and the CMCA took a further downturn when, in July, the latter was forced to serve Trade Exhibitions with a writ after several requests for the sum of £2196 – commission for selling stands to motorcycle manufacturers – were repeatedly ignored.

Although not officially supported by either factory, beginning five days earlier on Saturday, January 2, the specialist interest Racing and Sporting Show held three miles away in Westminster at the New Horticultural Hall, gave the British public its first view of one of the new machines, with Hampshire scrambler and off-road bike builder Ken Heanes displaying the ex-Lancaster B50MX.

Returning to Olympia, several machines from the two ranges were represented, and, in all likelihood, were the same ones that had appeared at the Lancaster Hotel two months previously. With very few P30s in show condition then, the display Triumph T35SS may have been returned from the US La Quinta Launch, or may indeed have been

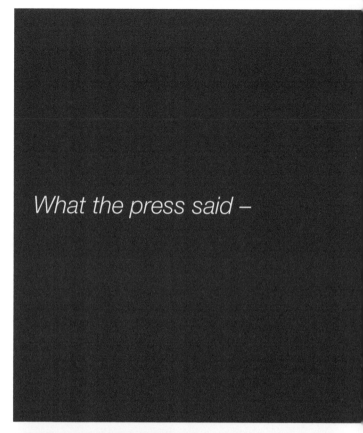

What the press said –

Caron Gardner with a 6-inch (15cm) braked Triumph Blazer SS at Olympia. (Courtesy VMCC)

"The best news at COLEX was the new BSA/Triumph range. After my frequent painful encounters with BSA/ Triumph products over the last few years, I am delighted to report that the new range shows evidence of a complete and carefully considered overhaul. The one bright spot in my recent acquaintance with their marques was a very early Trident – a beauty – would that more like it had been around last year. The restyled – and reworked – Rocket 3 is a vast improvement over the old. All it needs now is an electric starter and perhaps disc brakes. Most of the machines on the two stands were cursed with a sleazy grey finish on the frames. On machine after machine this let down the otherwise well-styled appearance. The frames themselves are of the new spine design, and have less longitudinal compliance than the older designs. Certain features are shared by many of the models – notably the spine frame is almost ubiquitous – and the Lucas flashing indicator units. The 650 Twin is transformed by the new frame and the slim styling. The motor is a rough and brutish unit, providing a great deal of torque and vibration: its best feature is its sheer uncomplaining strength. In the new frame the appearance is vastly improved, the braking is better (the conical brake units are shared by most of the new models), and the whole machine is lower. The new 350 looks a swine to work on, and I was silenced to discover that vertically split crankcases have been retained for a wholly new design. One can only suggest that the greater production precision required is still not considered reasonable at Umberslade Hall.

"The frantic development activity at Umberslade is the reason why the Victor MX has taken such an unconscionable time to appear: it was simply too far down the queue. Now that it is here it really looks the part, and should sell furiously in America. The road- going version desecrates the name of Gold Star, but no doubt we shall overcome this natural disgust engendered by the use of the illustrious name of what must have been one of the most fussy and complex singles to have won the hearts of a generation by its stalwart performance (after suitable incantations had been chanted). Rough, rude and responsive to care, the Goldie in its higher states of tune was – and is – an intractable machine about town, and the new Star will undoubtedly shine here.

"Silencing of all but the 3's is now done at both intake and exhaust, and it will be interesting to see just how effective this has been." – Motorcycle Sport

the same T35 that Carol Cleveland had modelled the previous autumn. Its provenance is not clear, although, for some reason, it was now bereft of side panel decals: very odd for a show bike.

On hand to pose for press shots was actress Caron Gardner, who had a long-standing association with BSA dating back to 1966. As well as the bikes, the BSA and Triumph stands each featured an information desk, free brochures scattered around, and A75 and T120 display engines. The Motoplas accessories stand featured an A65L adorned with many Motoplas products, and of particular interest was a pair of sturdy, tubular-framed, rear-mounted panniers holding two easily removable ABS plastic despatch cases, which appear never have made it onto the market, as was seemingly also the case with the luggage rack fitted to the B50SS present. The latter item – which, with minor dimensional modifications, was intended to be available for 650cc P39 models also – even managed to make its way onto one of Top Gear's (BSA's US accessories subsidiary) flyers, though its subsequent rarity would suggest that it, too, ultimately failed to become a production item.

Further publicity at the show for BSA came via the White Helmets Army Motor Cycle display team, which was manning an indoor trials course for members of the public to try their luck on: one of the bikes in the team was an electrically-powered Victor Trail model.

All of the motorcycle manufacturers present apparently found the combined show worthwhile, with BSA's Export Manager, Wilf Harrison, commenting "We are very pleased with the public response to the new range." Norman Vanhouse, head of UK fleet sales, commented on the, by now, ubiquitous Ariel 3: "We've had constant enquiries, particularly from women and non-motorcycling types, and the majority of them obviously genuine."

Each side of the next big event held across the English Channel in France were two smaller exhibitions, the first of which was the Midlands Bike Show at Black Heath, Birmingham, where several of the new models shared the adjoining stands of C E Copes and Vale Onslow, two big Midlands BSA/Triumph dealers. Taking place between Wednesday 24 and Sunday 28 February, the show pulled in around 6000 visitors.

The British Motorcycle Federation's Woburn Abbey Rally, held on Sunday, May 23, offered another promo opportunity, made all the more relevant by the fact that most UK dealers actually had the majority of models in stock for the first time since they were announced several months previously. How many machines were sent to the

Bedfordshire stately home is unclear, although a B25SS and A75R were present, at least.

France

France, along with South Africa, had been earmarked as potential growth markets due to their economies having recently taken an upward turn. To take maximum advantage of this, the Motor Cycle Division had signed a new deal in May 1970 with the Peugeot Group's subsidiary company, Comptoirs Generaux du Cycle et de l'Industrie Mecanique (CGCIM). Triumph had been handled by GGCIM, for a time anyway, but the new deal's purpose was to give the BSA/Triumph Motor Cycle Division a more prestigious image; Peugeot being the sixth largest public corporation in France. With 200 dealer outlets, CGCIM was planning to import over 2000 bikes for 1971, an increase of over 500 more than 1970's total. With this figure in mind, it's interesting to note that, in an interview conducted in the early months of 1971, CGCIM's Guy Peyron, when asked what the major problem was with importing BSA and Triumph motorcycles, replied along the lines of "I have one problem only, the deliveries. BSA/Triumph export 95% to the USA, Canada and Scandinavia, so I have to wait a long time." One can only imagine the frustration that Monsieur

Peyron experienced as the production delays of the 1971 models eroded potential sales in France.

The new machines were given a generous amount of space in the French motor cycle press, and many presentations were lavish, to say the least. Articles ran to 24 pages, and, as well as including road tests, often featured complete dismantling of the engine concerned for analysis.

The 16-day Foire de Paris held at the Parc des Expositions between Saturday, April 24 and Sunday, May 9 generally mirrored Olympia in its scope, with most of the new bikes sharing a spacious stand. Somewhat disconcertingly, no examples of the P30s were displayed, however.

South Africa

At the same time as the French deal went through, BSA concluded talks with South African distributor Williams Hunt, whose primary business interest was in distribution for a number of engineering companies. Its newly-created subsidiary, AMD (Pty) Ltd, was to handle the majority of BSA/Triumph Southern African exports on an exclusive basis throughout South Africa, South West Africa, and Mozambique. Tied into the planned expansion of this market was a significant increase in dealer outlets: surprisingly, perhaps, South Africa was actually BSA's fourth largest foreign market, outsold only by the USA, Canada, and Australia.

In February – and intended as an additional promotional tool – a pair of works 750cc racing Triples – one BSA, one Triumph – were sent to South Africa with riders Ray Pickrell and Paul Smart to compete in the South African TT at Pietermaritzburg, and the Kyalami Grand Prix. While failing to win either event, Smart managed an impressive second place behind Giacomo Agostini's works MV Agusta at the TT event.

The Rand Easter Show held in Johannesburg, the home of importer AMD, saw the Lancaster B50SS on display after a stint at south east London dealer Harvey Owen, and, presumably the Colex Show. The exact number of machines present is not known, though it is thought that at least three 250cc Singles accompanied the 500 Gold Star.

Italy

The biannual Milan motorcycle show held towards the end of the year was a little awkwardly placed for taking advantage of the 1970 Power Set launch, and by the time that the new BSA/Triumph machines had made their appearance in Italy, the division was already in dire financial straits, as witnessed by the reduced number of show bikes.

From France, possibly the most evocative advert produced for the 1971 campaign. (Author's archive)

In the meantime, Triumph importer Koelliker Autos made strenuous advertising efforts to promote some of the new machines. A series of very colourful, almost psychedelic, cartoon-like ads were specially created by the Italian design house Studio Troisi, and placed in various Italian magazines. Unfortunately, at some stage, the images somehow became transposed, resulting in the motorcycles appearing with front brakes and engines reversed.

BSA ads were far less in evidence – the only one being the A65 Lightning seen earlier in this chapter, presumably by BSA importer SRL Ghe-Ba. That Italy had been identified by the Marketing Department as recently showing positive signs of increased sales for 1971 makes this apparent lack of promotion all the more puzzling.

Once the 1971 Milan Motor Cycle Show rolled around, the models on display were, of course, to 1972 specification. Both importers put on commendable displays, with each marques' stand crowned by a genuine factory racing Triple.

Shows in Belgium, Switzerland, Austria, and Norway, and two in Sweden, also benefited from either factory or importer support.

In the southern hemisphere both New Zealand and Australia held late season shows, the former taking place in August. As with Sweden, Australia also presented two events – in Sydney and Melbourne – in the autumn and a matter of weeks apart, though whether 1971 or 1972 spec machines were displayed is unknown.

Because Italy's Milan Show was held so late in the year, 1972 models were displayed throughout in company with two works racing 750 Triples. (Author's archive)

USA

The American campaign differed in most aspects to the home/general export effort, not least the launch, which was a very different affair altogether. BSA Inc had hired the prestigious Palm Springs, California La Quinta Country Club Hotel for an impressive four-day event, starting on Thursday, November 12. As well as having its own airstrip, the hotel was also renowned for its high profile guests, with the likes of President Eisenhower, Marlene Dietricht, Katherine Hepburn, and Erroll Flynn among its regular patrons. Additionally, its location on the edge of a desert ideally suited the needs of a motorcycle range launch, with space for actually riding the machines, compliments of a half-mile Tarmac track, and the unlimited desert plains that sat beneath part of the barren and inhospitable Santa Rosa mountain range.

Press men from America's top selling motorcycle journals were invited for an all expenses paid stay, which, for an $80 a day venue, was not to be sniffed at. Included with the free lodging was use of all hotel facilities, such as the tennis court, golf course, swimming pool, and horse riding, with all bills picked up by BSA Inc.

As well as the 18 machines on display (including an

BONNEVILLE 650 (TRIUMPH)
TRIDENT 750
avanguardia tecnico-sportiva

BONNEVILLE 650 cc.
campione incontrastato degli ultimi 5 anni,
50 cavalli effettivi,
doppio carburatore e camme gemelle,
telaio a serbatoio d'olio,
motore dotato di tutte
le soluzioni tecniche Triumph '71

TRIDENT 750 cc.
motore a tre cilindri con valvole in testa,
tre carburatori Amal,
60 cavalli effettivi,
nuovi freni, forcella anteriore telescopica,
mozzi conici.

importatore e distributore esclusivo
per tutta Italia

BEPI KOELLIKER
C.so di P.ta Vittoria, 36 - Milano
Tel. 799.244 - 795.560

Concessionari in tutta Italia

One of three groovy ads placed in various Italian journals by Triumph's importer. (Author's archive)

New Triumphs as far as the eye can see! All but the second motorcycle were available for the assembled journalists to ride when they wished. (Author's archive)

Ariel 3), the BSA and Triumph AMA and motocross racing teams were personally represented by Jim Rice, Dave Aldana, Chuck Minert, and Gene Romero, who gave riding demonstrations and talks to the press. BSA Inc's top brass were also present, namely President Peter Thornton, Executive Vice-President Dave Bird, Product Planning Director Tony Salisbury, Market Research Manager Ken Brown, and Engineering Vice-President E W 'Pete' Colman; all available for question-and-answer sessions.

From the British Isles, MD Lionel Jofeh and his wife were in attendance (having left for the US immediately after the Lancaster Hotel event), as well as four members of BSA's Works Motocross team, who were currently in America competing in the first-ever Trans-AMA MX series.

Guests were issued with two very full press kits, BSA's offering comprising 70-plus pages, as well as 11 black and white model photographs. The kit outlined in great detail the new range of machines and the market research that led to their creation, accompanied by several pages of charts illustrating the company's new management structure and dealer regions.

Both BSA and Triumph were allocated a day each, Thursday and Friday respectively, for the launch of their new models. Most of these were dramatically unveiled one-by-one, with either Tony Salisbury for the BSAs or Pete Colman for the Triumphs explaining various technical features. During unveiling on BSA day, the unmistakable roar of large capacity, four-stroke Singles had everyone gazing out into the desert, where Keith Hickman, Dave Nicoll, and John Banks appeared, mirage-like, mounted on three B50 singles. Moments later a lone Ariel 3 Trike

Extract from the La Quinta BSA press release –

Re-engineered BSAs unveiled for 1971
LA QUINTA, CALIFORNIA, November 12, 1970 – with the motorcycle industry still glowing from the biggest sales boom in its history, and with indications that 1971 will be even bigger – BSA unveiled its aggressively re-engineered line of motorcycles for 1971 here today.

Manufactured by the Birmingham Small Arms Company Limited in England, the 1971 line of BSA motorcycles reflects possibly the most far-reaching design and dramatic styling changes since the BSA was first introduced in the United States. Favoured for their engineering based on the British tradition of large, high speed touring machines, BSA motorcycles have been extremely popular in the US for two decades.

Headed by President Peter Thornton, a complete reorganization of the Birmingham Small Arms Company Incorporated (the US subsidiary) in the fall of 1969, resulted in the re-thinking behind the new BSA range.

"We decided in January this year," Mr Thornton said, "to offer a new range of motorcycles based wholly on American market research and American rider preferences." "These machines represent a substantial first for us," he continued, "since BSA will now be selling British engineering with American styling."

The most notable result of BSA's re-engineering is its dramatic styling. With new colors, speed striping, updated electrical equipment, new switch consoles and direction indicators, and matt black exhausts and brake drums, one may be temporarily diverted from BSA's major engineering improvements such as frame design, brakes, and wheels.

Setting a precedent in the motorcycle industry, BSA production machines are now offered with new, racing-type frames that carry the engine lubricating oil – a space- and weight-saving device that has long been popular with professional motorcycle racers. This new feature is now standard equipment throughout the line, with the exception of BSA's largest road machine, the Rocket 3, and the new 350cc models – the Fury and Fury SS.

One sure-fire method to improve balance and handling is to trim weight by the use of alloys, which accept higher stress loadings pound-for-pound than steel. With this in mind, all 1971 BSA forks have aluminium alloy sliders, and the wheels have finned, aluminium alloy brake hubs for reduction of unsprung weight. Combined with their weight- and space-saving frames, BSAs are lighter than ever for 1971.

followed, piloted by twice 500cc MX World Champion Jeff Smith. Whether or not Ariel 3s were ever shipped to the US in quantity is not known, but their scarcity there would indicate not.

Ready or not?

A rather ominous sign, however, was that, whilst every bike in the two ranges was represented, of the four BSA/Triumph DOHC 350s, only one was present, this being a non-running T35SS. Back in the UK the factory test bikes were still experiencing minor problems, and the spectre of a breakdown at the press launch was far too frightening and potentially damaging to contemplate, resulting in this rather halfway measure.

BSA's B50SS. Note the missing top silencer heat shield and the skinny, one-gallon (4.5 litre) motocross fuel tank. (Author's archive)

What the press said –

"For anyone who has cast sad eyes at BSA all these years, as well as worried eyes at Triumph, there's definite reason for rekindled hope. Buyers have a fine year ahead." – Cycle World

"The Birmingham Small Arms Company Incorporated has come of age ... It's become responsive to the needs and demands of the American motorcycle rider ... We think you'll agree once you dig the new BSA and Triumph motorcycles for 1971. That they are different, that they are what seems to be fashionable in this country, that they are colourful, that they are stylish is not subject to debate.
"We did have the chance to ride each one briefly and we generally liked what we rode at the press review of the new models." – Supercycle

"With all new 350cc overhead cam machines and a little three-wheeler also on the list, big billing for 1971 is a full range of Singles patterned on the impressive and exciting Trans-AMA motocross machines." – AMA News

"Triumph/BSA styling and engineering came off the wall with the explosion of a Jai alai ball ... forewarned by rumours of sweeping changes for the new year, the motorcycle press was still obviously taken aback at Palm Springs, California, when the wraps were dramatically whipped off each model, one at a time during a long-lead preview in November."
"The hardware is remarkably well designed and finished – truly exciting."
"... never before have they [BSA] come forth with such an impressive array of varied and fresh machinery." – Motorcycle Sport Quarterly

"Some of the newest and best developed machines to come from the shores of Great Britain in many a year. We were impressed enough to show you what's going to be available for 1971 from BSA and Triumph." – Cycle Guide

"They have not only re-organised their executive structure, but their thinking as well, and their bikes show it. The optimism of the press ran high as each bike was uncovered. The new models were re-designed, utilising many features derived from the company's racing efforts." – Motor Cycle World

La Quinta show bikes

Engine/frame number	Model	Despatch dept. entry	Despatch date
KE01070	B25SS Gold Star	6-11-70	7-11-70
NE01317	B25T Victor Trail	6-11-70	7-11-70
PE01710	B50SS Gold Star	6-11-70	7-11-70
PE01711	B50T Victor Trail	6-11-70	7-11-70
00032	B50MX Victor MX	6-11-70	7-11-70
	A65T Thunderbolt	6-11-70	7-11-70
NE00733	A65L Lightning	6-11-70	7-11-70
NE00742	A65FS Firebird Scrambler	6-11-70	7-11-70
KE00105	A75R Rocket 3	6-11-70	7-11-70
NE01659	T25 SS Blazer SS	6-11-70	7-11-70
JE00585	T25T Trail Blazer	6-11-70	7-11-70
PE00001	E35SS Bandit SS	6-11-70	7-11-70
	T100R Daytona		
	T100C Trophy		
	TR6R Tiger		
	TR6C Trophy		
01516	T120R Bonneville		4-11-70
	T150 Trident		

Listed above, where available, are the engine/frame numbers of the bikes, and the dates that they entered and then left the despatch department of the two factories to La Quinta.

Despatched from Small Heath only a week beforehand, and presumably sent to La Quinta as priority air freight in order to arrive in time, several of the bikes were clearly pre-production in their make-up, and careful inspection reveals some deviation from final specification. Oddities included omission of the upper silencer shields on the B25/B50 road and trail bikes; the B50SS wearing a one-gallon B50MX aluminium fuel tank, albeit painted in the red and black SS colour scheme, and the three A65 models sporting flat-topped seats, which were later altered to incorporate a chamfered edge along their length for production models. The B50MX was not a factory-fresh machine, but almost certainly one on which either American BSA motocross team members, Chuck Minert or Dave Aldana, were racing in the aforementioned Trans-AMA series. With its alloy tank devoid of any striping, the visual link to the other four Singles in the new range was absent, regrettably, therefore reducing the family image a little.

It would appear that the A75, A65L, T150 and T120 were road registered in time for the event, as on one occasion at least Rice and Romero, accompanied by Tony Salisbury and a motorcycle journalist, took to the road for a trip to Palm Springs town centre.

Publicity material
For the North American market a totally separate set of brochures, posters and ads to those of the home/general

The elegant but non-running P30 Triumph Bandit SS, unwittingly pre-empting events as the sun goes down at La Quinta. (Author's archive)

export campaign was produced, though these still largely relied on the same studio shots. Four full-colour brochures were produced: two for each marque. The two full-line ones entitled 'The Power and The Glory' (BSA) and 'Think Big' (Triumph) ran to 16 pages, and each model was featured, and several pages highlighted some of the new engineering innovations. Most of the motorcycles inside looked as though they had been airbrushed to some

Described as the "Crown Prince of the large BSA Twins" in the press release, magazine publisher Shirlee Bagnall plays princess in La Quinta's hot desert. (Author's archive)

extent, lending a slightly surreal appearance, although the overall effect was credible enough. Whether or not the original photographs – with one exception exactly the same as those used in the home/general export material – were actually shot with black and white film is not known, and it's feasible that a second colour studio session – planned specifically for the American brochures – may have failed to materialise.

The second pair of brochures, again, one for each manufacturer, were produced to capitalise on the popularity of trail riding in the USA, which had taken off in recent years, and between them contained the seven single cylinder machines offered for 1971. BSA's brochure, somewhat ironically titled 'The British are Coming,' was an 8-pager, utilising many images from the 'Power and The Glory,' as did Triumph's four-page T25 offering entitled 'Hit the Trail Big' from 'Think Big.'

Early December 1970 saw BSA dealers receive a single sample copy of the Power and The Glory brochure (identified by a white band running across the top), followed up within six weeks by a visit from the Regional District Manager, who, as well as explaining the forthcoming promotional campaign, also supplied a folder entitled 'Dealer Merchandising Guide.' Topics covered included the framework for a television commercial, a 35mm film for showroom use, and ideas for poster displays, brochures, photos, etc. During this same period, a complete promotional package comprising multiple posters, ad blanks based on two brochure images, and a dealer data booklet was also sent to all dealers.

The TV ad came in the form of a 30-second video that

The four American brochures for 1971. Several of the riders on the cover of 'The British Are Coming' are from the division's Styling Department, the first two identified as Rodney Humphries and Stephen Mettam respectively. (Author's archive)

Two of the poster display suggestion pages contained within 1971's Dealer Merchandising Guide. (Courtesy Ed & Arlene McDermott)

simply presented three pre-prepared slides of the new Rocket 3, a Rocket 3 racer, and B50MX, coupled to a commentary. A fourth slide was locally prepared by either the dealer or TV station, as was its audio track, relaying

The British Are Here With A First.
THE WORLD'S FIRST 500cc TRAIL BIKES.

John Banks, champion British Motocross rider, helped BSA develop the features of three, new, powerhouse trail bikes —a Street Scrambler, a Trail, and a Motocross.
All have telescopic front forks, 3-way shocks and double-shoe brakes, to name just a few of the features that make these 1971 BSA trail bikes Britain's best—and our best.

The Power of British Engineering.
The Glory of American Styling.

BSA

DEALER NAME
ADDRESS

Available in three sizes, these ad templates were issued to dealers for use in regional news and motorcycle papers. (Author's archive)

the dealer's name and address. The dialogue, short but to the point, ran as follows –

• The Power of British engineering and the Glory of American styling come together in BSA for 1971
• BSA, the motorcycle that last year won more AMA championship races than any other make
• This year's new models feature a full line of off-the-road bikes, including a competition motocross machine
• See them all now at [dealer name and address]. BSA for '71, the Power and the Glory!

The exact number of posters issued for the American market is a little unclear, though a very large 45-inch x 40-inch (114.3cm x 101.6cm) full-range BSA item, entitled 'The Power And The Glory' was produced, along with two 34-inch x 22-inch (86.3cm x 55.9cm) items, a similarly titled one picturing Jim Rice on a road-racing Rocket 3, and another that was clearly related to 'The British Are Coming' Singles brochure. A fourth offering at 50-inch x 37-inch (127cm x 94cm) was a direct copy of 'The Power And The Glory' brochure cover picture of Mettam riding the A65 Firebird Scrambler.

One can only presume that similar themes were used for Triumph, which had, in recent years, enjoyed a higher profile in the States than BSA.

In addition to these pre-prepared posters, throughout the year BSA Inc released a number of race win-related items, usually presented in either black and white, or red, white and blue, and were produced for both BSA and Triumph.

The 21 black and white model photographs used in the home/general export campaign, while being part of the La Quinta press kit, were also issued to dealers in a larger 9¾-inch x 8-inch (24.7cm x 20.3cm) size, featuring the B25SS and T25SS fitted with the US-spec, 6-inch (15.2) front hub.

Ad campaign
The US market required a larger and more far-reaching campaign than employed in any other country, not surprisingly, due to the number of motorcycles it took from Small Heath and Meriden. Of the top five motorcycling magazines published in America, the two, easily removable off-road brochures were to be found inside many issues, while 'The Power and the Glory' and 'Think Big' brochures were represented by abbreviated versions, sometimes running to ten pages, albeit printed on stock paper. Between the months of January and April 1971, American readers couldn't fail to be aware of the new machines, which, in BSA's case, were often accompanied by the robust slogan 'The Power of British Engineering,

The fact that BSA's motorcycles proved as competitive as the publicity for them had claimed gave the US Ad Department endless scope for related posters. (Author's archive)

Using images taken from the 'Power and the Glory' brochure, this ad was sporadically placed in the latter half of 1971. (Author's archive)

Photographed at autumn 1970's four-day BSA/Triumph launch at La Quinta, AMA No 2 plate holder Jim Rice takes the new Rocket 3 for a spin to accommodate the US motorcycling press. (Author's archive)

the Glory of American Styling,' and for Triumph 'The Big One for 1971.' January and February saw only the off-road 'brochures' featured, and not until March that year did the American public get its first taste of the road bikes, when the full-line ads were placed.

For both marques – and in line with UK assurance about delivery dates – 4-page ads should have been placed in June in the five key magazines (*Cycle, Cycle Guide, Cycle World, Modern Cycle* and *Motorcyclist*) for the four P30 models. However, by the time June arrived, it would appear that BSA Inc had been informed that the bikes were not going to be in the States that summer, resulting in June's ad space remaining either unused or amounting to a single page ad for 650 models only. Subsequent ads for the remainder of the year followed suit, and marked the end of big-time advertising for BSA. During the same period Triumphs ads, also 650s only, were more or less single page in extent, occupying the lower halves of two facing pages.

Shows

Because of its enormous land mass, motorcycle shows in America were generally of a local nature, and more low-key as a result. The earliest significant event of the year was the Houston Trade Show at the end of January 1971, followed by the equally prestigious Motor Cycle Trade Show held at Long Beach, California, though the exact date of the latter is unclear (but probably early spring), as are the number of BSA and Triumph machines present at both events.

1971's stand-out show, because of the publicity it afforded by being sponsored by one of the leading motorcycle publications, was probably the *Cycle World* Motor Cycle show held in Los Angeles between Wednesday 15 and Saturday 18 April. Examples of both BSA and Triumph P39 Twins were supplemented by an E35R making its American public debut, and Craig Vetter's radical and very cool 'Vetter 3,' the reworking of BSA's rather staid and plump pre-1971 750 Rocket 3.

Chapter 10

Competition

As part of the promotional campaign for the new range of motorcycles, and the marketing concepts behind them, the Motor Cycle Division had, for 1971, re-prioritised the racing efforts of the BSA Motocross Team and the BSA/Triumph three-cylinder Road Racers, especially in the United States, the latter outfit having only made its debut the previous year.

The well-established 650cc, A65 engine – enlarged to 750cc mid-season for flat track racing in the USA – was also to play a part in winning the No 1 Plate for BSA and Dick Mann in the American Motorcycle Association (AMA) Grand National Championship.

An unexpected Coupe d'Endurance series trophy win also considerably boosted BSA's image in an area of sport that the company had hitherto shown little interest in: although two races were won outright by 750cc T150s, it was a B50 that actually scored the series win after four rounds.

To legitimise the claims of the Advertising Department's slogans which appeared in the many brochures and advertisements released during the period November 1970 until the opening months of 1972 (when the following year's campaign would commence), it was essential that the machines and their riders proved themselves on the racetracks of the world. That this was largely achieved makes the virtual demise of the BSA group the same year all the more galling.

Part One: Motocross
(250/500 Singles)
BSA's Small Heath-based Competition Department had, in recent years, concentrated its efforts on

motocross racing with great success (the pinnacle being the two World Championship titles gained in 1964 and 1965 on the 420cc predecessor to the B50), and as 1971 approached, the situation was much the same, with the 45bhp B50 Road Racers and A65 sidecar outfits the only other officially-backed racing machines at Armoury Road.

The department – commonly known as the Comp Shop – had been caught up in the massive works reorganisation that had taken place in 1970, though still found itself housed in an outbuilding adjacent to the canal that flanked the north and western sides of the complex,

New signing Andy Roberton, who, after switching from two-strokes, had a remarkably successful debut season on the B50 Victor. (Courtesy Eric Miles)

albeit now situated behind the main office block. Often ridiculed for being small and pokey, bearing in mind that most development work was already carried out at the division's R&D Centre at Umberslade Hall, the 40ft x 40ft (12.24m x 12.24m) workshop provided more than enough space for the fettling and building of race machines.

The department had been managed by Brian Martin since 1958, and personnel involved in the motocross effort were rider and twice world champion Jeff Smith (who, by now, had been given a free hand in the workshop), and mechanics Graham Horne and Norman Hanks, both of whom attended the 1971 Grand Prix series, whilst a third, Fred Barlow, remained UK-bound for the year, working on bikes for the domestic season.

Ridden by BSA employee Bob Heath, the B50 Racers were able to put in some good performances on short circuits, their lightweight, torquey engines very much at home on the twistier courses, though the Road Racer's primary purpose was always as a mobile engine test bed for the motocross bikes.

With a production motocross racing machine back in BSA's range for the first time since the 441cc B44GP had been axed in 1967, it was vitally important to demonstrate to the world the potential of the new 499cc motocrosser (B50MX Victor 500). To help achieve this, BSA hired two of Britain's top scramble riders, Welshman Andy Roberton and Scott Vic Allan, to complement the existing works team of John Banks, Jeff Smith, Keith Hickman, and Dave Nicoll, with all but the latter, Smith and 20-year-old Roberton to contest the 1971 Grand Prix series.

Trans-AMA competition

Prior to this, a perfect opportunity to showcase the scrambles bike's abilities in the USA presented itself in the shape of the first ever Trans-AMA Motocross Series. The objective of this American Motorcycle Association-initiated event was to both promote the sport and educate the enthusiastic but technically inferior American riders in the art of motocross racing, by inviting some of Europe's finest competitors to take part in the series. This thinking

BSA Competition Department boss Brian Martin on 1971's off-road policy – January 1971 –

"Those who accuse BSA of trying to corner the market in scrambles riders are looking no further than our own shores. We have to look at the scene worldwide. With two new trail bikes, plus the production motocross Victor now in the range, BSA have more of a cross-country image than ever before, and it is the job of the competitions side to project that image as forcefully as possible.

"We want to go grand prix motocross racing in a big way, and so we must have riders who are on the ACU grading list, and, therefore, acceptable to foreign organisers. In our favour is that we are now actually producing machines we will be using, a situation we have not been in for several years past. Parts no longer have to be specially hand-made, but are drawn from stock, and so it becomes cheaper to field a motocross team, and we can afford to increase team strength.

"Now, let's look at the 1971 world motocross championships. The main attack will comprise Vic Allan and Keith Hickman, second and third on the current grading list, plus John Banks, who is certain to be accepted on past merit. That leaves us with Dave Nicoll, Andy Roberton, and Jeff Smith.

"We will try to get Dave accepted abroad wherever possible, though I am aiming to have him available for development as an ISDT man, of which more in a moment. Andy Roberton will be our main contender in home events, with the object of tackling the 500cc world championship next season. As for Jeff – well, he has earned his corn

many times over, and he can do whatever he likes.

"Now we come to the ISDT; the reason we are taking an interest this time is that in the 250cc and 500cc trail bike singles, BSA already have what are virtually ISDT models, needing little modification. So this is a promotion exercise, but also an opportunity for us to learn lots of things about the bikes.

"The intention is to mount Jeff on a two-fifty, and Dave and Andy on a five-hundred and slightly bored-out five-hundred. Naturally, the boys are a bit rusty on long-distance trails, so we will start by entering all three in the Welsh Two-day trial, and giving them plenty of opportunity to practice.

"Recently there has been quite a bit of speculation about the appearance in one-day trials of Mick Bowers and his Bantam, and the lightweight 250 I have built myself. However, BSA have no intention at this stage of re-entering the one-day trials field, and both machines are experimental exercises.

"There are many things which one may want to try out on a motorcycle, and it's good to be able to do the trying out in a competitive event. Besides, it is surprising the effort that the competition shop mechanics will put into something, when they realise it is just that little bit different. We have a keen bunch of blokes in the department, and experimental jobs like these give them added interest.

"The fact that this year's ISDT is being held in the Isle of Man is certainly convenient, but has little bearing on BSA's decision to re-enter the scene at this time. We would probably have been making a comeback in any case, to promote the machines we are featuring in the 1971 range. These are aimed at an international rather than home-based market, so the venue is coincidental.

"We will probably be supporting next year's ISDT, too, wherever it may be held, though it is too early yet for any definite policy statement to be made about that. However, now that the firm is taking a renewed interest in the event this would seem likely.

"Instead of suggesting that they might block factory entries of any riders they want for the dealer-backed Trophy team, I feel that the ACU should be doing more to encourage British manufacturers to have a go. Waving a big stick is no way to cement good relations. If a factory enters a team, they are entitled to use their own riders – after all, we feed and train them for the rest of the year – on models of the firm's own choosing.

"So far, of course, there has been no suggestion that the ACU would want to grab Jeff, Andy or Dave for the British Trophy team; speaking as a BSA man, I would be very unhappy if they did.

"Yet, for all that, I sympathise with the ACU's viewpoint. They have six machines which have already performed well in battle, and about which the selectors are fully confident. In their eyes, any bikes which we (or, for that matter, Greeves) may offer, would be unknown quantities.

"But the ACU want to do the best they can for Britain, and so do the manufacturers. It's a matter of getting together to arrive at an amicable compromise, and that is one thing at which Britons are very good."

BSA's Trans-AMA team. Riders from left – Jeff Smith, Chuck Minert, Dave Aldana, Keith Hickman, Dave Nicoll, and John Banks, all astride 250 B25MX machines. (Courtesy AMA)

proved sound, and, by 1978, America had its first AMA MX champion.

Held over eight rounds beginning 11 October, BSA sent over its existing Works team of four to team up with American Motocross veteran Chuck Minert and AMA Championship new-signing, 20-year-old Dave Aldana. With half of the races in the 250cc class, this provided an additional opportunity to showcase the B25MX, eight of which were specially built for the series. Positive results on these smaller bikes would, of course, reflect well on the new B25 road and trail production machines due for the coming season.

It was during this Trans-AMA period that the first run of BSA owner

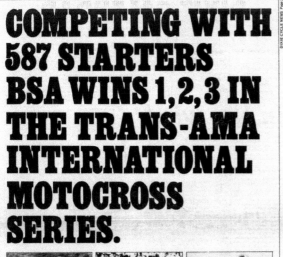

COMPETING WITH 587 STARTERS BSA WINS 1, 2, 3 IN THE TRANS-AMA INTERNATIONAL MOTOCROSS SERIES.

Dave Nicoll — John Banks — Jeff Smith

(DOESN'T THAT TELL YOU SOMETHING ABOUT RELIABILITY?)

At the recent Trans-AMA Motocross series, there were 8 grueling feature races, each with two heats, plus supporting races.

Against a field of 587 starters and about 80 different riders, 4 British BSA entrants finished 61 out of 64 starts (with no mechanical failures) and came in 1, 2, 3.

The winning BSA riders in that 1, 2, 3 order were Dave Nicoll, John Banks and Jeff Smith. Quite a tribute to their skill and stamina—and to the rock-like reliability of BSA engineering.

Shouldn't you consider that 4-stroke reliability before you buy your next bike?

Not only did BSA win the 8-round competition outright, it also had just one DNF throughout the series. (Author's archive)

handbooks was printed. Surprisingly, within the Singles version, the B25MX was listed alongside the other five models. As if this wasn't curious enough, the bike also found its way into the 1971 Lucas components catalogue, sufficient evidence to suggest that BSA had, perhaps, seriously considered it as a production machine.

Although Jeff Smith had recently won the 1970 BBC Grandstand 250cc trophy, and had also achieved third place in the British 250 Championship on a B25MX that was fitted out with a super-light titanium frame and engine parts, it was accepted that in more standard form, the bikes were simply not competitive in top flight competition against the dominant two-strokes. Nevertheless, in the hands of very experienced Works riders, and aided by weaker opposition, the Trans-AMA Series gave the 250s a slightly illusory boost of image.

Also in their favour was the absence, early on, of Belgian 250 World Champion Joel Robert on his ultra-light

John Banks powering on to an overall third at Newbury's 1971 Fox & Hounds scramble. (Courtesy Eric Miles)

250 Suzuki. With Robert contesting only the last half of the series (although winning all of his races), Nicoll, Banks, and Smith were able to amass a greater points tally, giving BSA the first three places as well as the team win.

Back in the UK, and to further promote the new trail bikes, BSA entered one 250 and two 500s in the Welsh Two Day Trial as a warm-up for September's ISDT. This again proved an outstanding success, with Andy Roberton winning the event on a Works B50T; the combined points of the three riders enough to take the manufacturer's title as well. To BSA's credit, it was acknowledged at the time as the toughest ever Welsh Trial to have taken place, further enhancing the company's reputation.

With the established riders back from the States by mid-December, the UK domestic races were again contested by BSA's 'Stars,' beginning with domination of the BBC Grandstand New Year Trophy on January 2, where BSA convincingly won the 250, 500, and Unlimited races. This set the pattern for the remainder of the season up until July, when Works support was abruptly withdrawn, with headlines such as 'The BSA steamroller' and 'BSA dominate screens again' having been commonplace, week in, week out.

Hawkstone drama

The first round of the British Championship was a dramatic one for BSA No 1 John Banks, where poor reliability and bitter determination became intertwined and played their part in this tale. Banks, Allan, and Hickman were all riding updated B50 motocrossers, the Hawkstone park meeting being something of a test run for the Italian Grand Prix three weeks later, where they were to compete.

The first race passed without incident, with Banks taking the win, Allan third, Roberton fifth, and Hickman sixth.

The new bikes were fitted with the staggered head and cylinder finning taken from the 250MX bikes; electron crankcases; lighter frames; the slim, one-gallon production fuel tanks which, up until now, had only been used sporadically (Chief Stylist Stephen Mettam had asked Comp. Shop boss Brian Martin to use them to publicise the production models), and, pertinent to this tale, a new type of battery for the ignition system, plus thinner rear brake operating rods.

The first sign of trouble came during the second race when Banks' brake rod broke after the first couple of laps, leaving him disadvantaged practically from the off. Nevertheless leading for much of the race, but struggling to make many of the corners, he was eventually passed by Roberton on a fast downhill section, where he had been unable to use the remaining front brake with much purpose. As if this was not enough, the engine then started to misfire before cutting out completely in the latter stages of the final lap. Lucas, who supplied the new batteries, had assured BSA that these would last for six racing hours, though, evidently, this was not the case, with Vic Allan's battery already having succumbed several laps earlier.

As Banks' bike finally rolled to a halt, he knew he was only about 800 yards (731m) short of the chequered flag. With much encouragement from the crowd, he dismounted and pushed the stricken BSA to the finish line, whereupon he collapsed, totally exhausted, but claiming third place, Hickman by now having also passed him. The trio of BSA riders had long since lapped all the other competitors, hence Banks having enough time to reach the finish, despite difficult going on the sandy ground. This heroic effort was justly rewarded with Banks now leading the championship.

By the beginning of July, with only two more meetings to contest, Banks was enjoying a 12-point lead, and at this juncture in the series, Roberton was placed second, Nicoll fifth, and Hickman sixth. Eight days later, to the disbelief of all, Divisional Chief Engineer Mike Nedham was saddled with the unpleasant job of telling Brian Martin that his MX team was to be disbanded, a casualty of the cuts deemed necessary after BSA's financial problems were made public. Hickman, Nicoll and Allan were allowed to keep their Works B50s as compensation for severance of their contracts, though now without full Works support.

Banks went on to win the British Championship,

albeit Husqvarna-mounted (as was Roberton), despite an MZ test ride earlier in the season, and that company's apparent keenness to sign him.

Grand Prix maladies

The Grand Prix series yielded a rather different story, unfortunately, with an unusually high number of retirements, many of which apparently ignition-related, although, more recently, Jeff Smith has admitted that the Lucas auto electric company had sometimes been made a convenient scapegoat.

The bad luck continued at April's Italian GP, with Vic Allan crashing heavily, breaking his leg: an injury that was to put him out of racing for the remainder of the season. By the end of June, matters were beginning to look up a little for John Banks, who managed a pair of third places in the East German GP, and, two weeks later at Farleigh Castle for the British round, a ninth and a third, although this all became rather academic for BSA the following day, when the Competition Shop's racing activities ceased for good.

However, within five weeks, signs of life were again detected, as Brian Martin and Jeff Smith supervised a new venture aimed at converting the department's assets into much-needed funds: namely, a total rebuild of the remaining Works bikes in order to sell them. The machines involved were four B50 and two B25 motocrossers, as well as the three bikes earmarked for the ISDT challenge – a B25 and two B50s. Additional to this was the sale of the department's complete inventory of spares, plus a venture intended to make available frames and fork units, and, in time, offer complete conversion kits.

Speaking at the time, Marketing Director Peter Deverall offered some hopeful comments regarding BSA's future in motocross racing "… if we are to

Dave Nicoll wearing his Trans-AMA shirt, and ripping it up at a national scramble in the early months of 1971. (Courtesy Eric Miles)

maintain certain activities, they will have to raise a bit of money. In producing special equipment, the Competition Department becomes a profit centre within the company – I like to think that the door was not completely closed by our recent decision to pull out, and that we might get back into competition."

Alas, all such hopes were, of course, in vain, as BSA failed to achieve the necessary financial wherewithal.

Part Two: 1971 Coupe d'Endurance (500 Singles)

Due, in all probability, to persuasive pressure from BSA shareholder and endurance racing team owner Mike Tomkinson, BSA agreed to partially and unofficially support an effort on the FIMs 1971 Coupe d'Endurance, regarded as the pinnacle of success in the endurance racing world. Tomkinson, one half of the motor garage partnership he had set up with his friend and ex-grass track champion Colin Mead in post-war 1940s, had also previously raced, although it was as an endurance team boss that he would find most success.

It was sometime during the mid- to late-1950s that Tomkinson first prepared and entered a machine in a 24-hour race: the bike in question a 500cc Velocette Venom; the venue Barcelona's Montjuic Park in Spain. The venture boded well for the future with Tomkinson's two riders, Howard German and Stan Dibben, bringing home the single cylinder four-stroke in second place in its class.

BSA Victor

By the late 1960s Tomkinson had begun using a BSA B44 Victor Roadster, a transition to BSA that made good sense as the Mead & Tomkinson garages were already BSA agents, and the Small Heath Competition Shop facilities were made available to Tomkinson. During these years with the 441cc single, the best result achieved was a sixth place at Barcelona in 1968.

From this B44 period came an interesting problem, the solution to which was passed on to the BSA factory. Again at Montjuic, though this time in 1970, the Victor had blown its left-hand crankshaft seal, flooding the primary chaincase with oil. While investigating the problem in the pits, Tomkinson noticed how the oil was also being drawn back into the crankcase as the piston started its upward stroke. A drain hole was drilled into the lower part of the crankcase to prevent the chaincase from flooding again, and the bike continued the race without further problem in this respect.

Within a few months, some of the Works Motocross B50s competing in the American Trans-AMA competition were fitted with a similar system which omitted the crankshaft seal, had either one or two holes in the

Early days with BSAs. 1967's Barcelona B44 Victor Roadster entry being tested by racer and journalist Alan Peck. (Author's archive)

crankcase, and carried a large bore breather pipe from the top of the chaincase. This system, in turn, was adopted in 1971 by the production B50 machines.

With BSA's forthcoming series of B50 bikes (Gold Star SS, Victor Trail, and Motocross) all having enlarged versions of the B44 engine, which, as well as featuring an incredibly tough, three-bearing crankshaft assembly, and a higher delivery, distortion-free cast iron oil pump, now tied in with the new, lighter cycle parts; Tomkinson felt that the B50 stood a good chance in the forthcoming series. The 1971 Coupe d'Endurance was made up of four long-distance events, the first a 500 mile (804km) daylight race at Thruxton circuit in England, followed by 24-hour races in Spain, Belgium, and France.

Speaking shortly after the Thruxton race, Mike Tomkinson gave the following succinct statement, which was guaranteed to ruffle a few traditional feathers –

"The BSA Victor could have won if it had held together. The Gold Stars are much better than the Victors. People who disagree and say the new Goldies aren't worth the name, are living in a dream world."

Part of the attraction of these long- distance races is that the machines entered were, by and large, production-line models with modifications allowed within a certain framework, although as Tomkinson was to discover as time went on, many teams interpreted the guidelines in a rather loose fashion, which tended to move the machines away from the 'production' bike ethos. However, if the man on the street sees a machine very similar to the one he can purchase at his local motorcycle shop winning a punishing endurance race, this can surely only be good for the bike's reputation and subsequent sales.

With the first race taking place in May, and BSA's B50 models still not ready for production (coincidentally, it was to be this month also that B50 mass production finally commenced), the factory supplied Tomkinson with two unnumbered B50 engines and a pair of B25SS models, (one blue – registered UVJ 1J, and one red – registered UVJ 2J) which, apart from the B25 frame numbers stamped onto the prop stand bracket (although these were removed as part of the lightening procedure), were identical to the forthcoming 500cc versions (this being acceptable to both the ACU and FIM). Rather amusingly, the side panels carrying the 250 Gold Star decals were retained throughout the season, prompting raised eyebrows from casual observers.

Engine performance modifications were surprisingly limited – essentially, just a ported inlet tract and the 32mm Amal concentric carburettor and camshaft from the production B50MX machine. In the interests of reliability – the epitome of endurance racing – the two engines were treated to stronger valve springs, a Nimonic 80 exhaust valve, welded-in clutch cush drive rubbers, manual ignition advance (to compensate for wear during the 24 hours), and a revised breathing system that had been modified in such a way that it now served as the gearbox breather as well.

Cycle part changes were limited to alloy wheel rims, a Victor-type rear hub (in order to fit a small enough rear sprocket), rear-set footrests, a small gusset plate welded above the swinging arm pivot (presumably done on the advice of BSA, which, during March, was to implement a similar modification to production frames), and, from the second race on, the front 8-inch (20.3cm) twin leading shoe brake was converted to hydraulic operation, not necessarily to improve the brake, but to reduce rider fatigue by reducing lever pressure. Additional to these changes were the usual concessions, such as large capacity fuel tanks, racing seat, ace bars, etc, and for continental races, twin headlamps.

Conflicting regulations between Britain's ACU and governing bodies of continental events resulted in the British race being contested using the two machines fitted with a 'production' box silencer, although this had probably been subjected to internal modification, as the MX cam is reluctant to work properly with a standard road silencer. At European circuits, Tomkinson was permitted to use a custom-made, megaphone-type of silencer, reminiscent of the B50MX's item. Even though it allowed a similar power

output to the box silencer, unlike the production version, it didn't disintegrate over the duration of a race.

Top speed of these endurance B50s varied from an impressive 115 to 120mph (185 to 193kph), depending on gearing used.

A fine study of one of Tomkinson's endurance B50s, seen here at Le Mans in September. This is the blue bike (UVJ 1J), although it now has a different frame from that which it started the Coupe d'Endurance series with. Note the discarded box silencer and the replacement megaphone fitted to the bike, with the word 'Red' painted on it. (Courtesy Thierry Bourguet)

The races

The first of the four races took place on May 8 at Thruxton, the UK airfield circuit, and was witness to a convincing class win by one of Tomkinson's B50s. Having signed up two pairs of riders to contest each event (excepting Belgium, where only the one bike was entered), at the Hampshire track Clive Brown and BSA jig and tool drawing office employee Nigel Rollason (UVJ 2J) – who were to race at all four meetings on the same bike – were paired alongside Joe Thornton and Michael Taylor. The former pair took the lead in the 500cc class, and eventually finished 7 laps ahead of the second-placed Suzuki 500cc Titan, in what proved to be a problem-free 500 miles (809km). Overall position was eighth, with the second bike (UVJ 1J) coming in at twentieth.

Almost two months later the second race was held over the weekend of July 3/4 at the Spanish Montjuic Park circuit near Barcelona, with Brown/Rollason this time racing with the BSA Comp Shop's B50 Works riders, Bob Heath and Tony Melody.

Once again, Brown and Rollason stole the headlines by not only taking the class win for a second time, but also finishing second overall, sandwiched between a pair of 750 Works Laverdas. The second B50 failed to finish after crashing in the early hours of the morning, six hours into the race.

August 28/29 witnessed something that had many critics of the new B50SS Gold Star eating humble pie, which must have delighted Mike Tomkinson. Travelling to the Zolder circuit near Liége in Belgium, Brown and Rollason pulled off an outright race win. Even though two laps had been lost during the night whilst the number plate lamp was repaired, the pair still managed to finish ten miles ahead of a Belgian-ridden 750 BMW. The 24-hour race followed a slightly different format to the usual non-stop event, in that after six and 18 hours, the race was suspended, and each machine was subjected to a timed lap of the course.

The final event of the Coupe d'Endurance was held in France at the famous Le Mans circuit over the wet weekend of September 11/12, Tomkinson entering two bikes with the return of Heath and Melody. Why only a single B50 had been present at Zolder two weeks earlier is not clear, although the fact that UVJ 1J now had a different frame – easily identified by the factory-fitted gusset plates – could be part of the answer, plus the fact that Tony Melody was partnering Zolder's third-placed 750 Norton Commando. While not quite achieving the success of the previous race, after having led the 500cc class with less than an hour's racing to go, the B50 of Brown and Rollason lost the position due to a front brake problem, having to settle for a class second and eighth overall. The B50 of Heath and Melody was forced into retirement when Melody suffered a broken leg after colliding with another competitor who had been pushing his bike.

So, with the four races completed and the points tallied, Brown and Rollason topped the table with 36 points, followed by an Italian Works Laverda on 30, and the Norton 750 of Douglas Cash and (in a bizarre conflict of interest) Tony Melody. Tomkinson and his riders had achieved something that very few would have thought possible in 1971 – winning the Coupe d'Endurance on a single cylinder, OHV, 500cc four-stroke, that was not so very different from the production B50SS.

Nigel Rollason staring somewhat blankly at a damp Le Mans track in company with mechanic Patrick Tomkinson (left). (Courtesy Dominique Bresson)

UVJ 2J, the Coupe d'Endurance-winning B50, seen here at Le Mans in September with its sister bike just visible behind. The guy in the green T-shirt is Chris Tomkinson, youngest son of team boss Mike Tomkinson, and next to him is older brother Patrick. (Courtesy Jean Paul Bayer)

Brown and Rolllason – Coupe d'Endurance Championship results

Country	Date	Race venue	Points
Great Britain	8 May	Thruxton 500	3
Spain	3-4 July	Montjuic 24-hours, Barcelona	12
Belgium	28-29 Aug	Zolder-24-hours, Liége	15
France	11-12 Sept	Le Mans-Bol d-Or	6
Total points scored			36

The epitome of flat-track racing. BSA's Jim Rice with full opposite lock applied. (Courtesy mahonyphotos.com)

Part Three: flat and short track (250 Singles/650/750 Twins)

The mainstay of motorcycle racing in the United States during the late 1960s/early 1970s was the American Motorcycle Association's (AMA) Grand National Championship (GNC), a series combining the two vastly differing disciplines of flat track and road racing. However, by the 1970s, flat track had become something of a poor relation to road racing, where participation by the world's top motorcycle manufacturers, and the exotic and expensive machinery involved guaranteed its popularity with the American race-going public and media, although it was still flat track that mainly comprised the GNC series.

At this time, this form of racing was undoubtedly one of the most spectacular throughout the world in which to compete and watch. The combination of very fast, beautiful-sounding parallel and Vee-twins with brutish good looks, allied to the flamboyant personalities of many of the riders both on and off the track made for a compelling spectacle, as the bikes were thrown into the corners of the oval dirt tracks in a lurid sideways manner.

The 1970 season involved, on average, a staggering 70,000 road miles covered between venues, due, in part, to poor geographical planning that necessitated, for

instance, a trip from the east of the country to the west side, and then back east for the next event! At season's end an influential body of competitors successfully lobbied the sports governing body about this matter, resulting in a revised itinerary, sensibly comprising 21 races rather than the previous 31.

On this subject 1970 AMA Championship winner Gene Romero offered the following thoughts prior to the start of the 1971 GNC. "All your time is spent travelling or working – it's a round-the-clock thing. Your chance of injury is greater, but your chance of making money is less on an overall basis. You're not as alert for 31 races as you'd be for 21. Guys get hurt, it's a poor show and people aren't impressed. The bikes are under par because if something breaks you have to improvise – there's not enough time to do all the work."

Also new for the 1971 season was the rider numbering system. Previously, a rider generally held onto a particular race number for several years if he wanted to, but, for 1971, each rider's number would denote his final finishing position in the previous year's Grand National series: hence Triumph's Gene Romero wearing the No 1 plate, BSA's Jim Rice No 2, etc, for the whole of the 1971 season. This actually made good sense, as each rider's standing and recent form could now be gauged at a glance, although Triumph's Gary Nixon did plead with photographer Dan Mahony not to take his picture with his current rating of No 10!

The reduced race calendar consisted of seven road races (Daytona, Loudon, Ontario, etc) and 14 dirt track events, the latter on either quarter, half or one mile

Gene Romero's 1971 250cc short-track racer. Note the fat, 4-inch (10cm) front tyre. (Courtesy mahonyphotos.com)

BSA COMPETITION GUIDE

"BUILDING A BSA SHORT-TRACKER"

B25 Short-Track racer builder's guide –

Eager to push sales of the BSA and Triumph 250s, BSA Inc put together a 16-page booklet entitled 'BSA Competition Guide – Building a BSA Short-Tracker,' which was sent to dealers, though was presumably also available to the private racer.

Everything within was based on the actual tuning preparations used for the BSA team bikes, with engine work being particularly thorough. Reliability measures such as bonding the cylinder liner to the barrel and fitting a steel carrillo con-rod featured as strongly as the power tuning modifications, which included a 12:1 piston, hot camshaft, the use of larger valves and the fitment of a supplementary breather pipe to name but a few. Every conceivable gear ratio configuration was listed, as were the addresses for suppliers of everything required to build a bike from scratch.

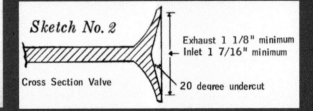

Sketch No. 2

Exhaust 1 1/8" minimum
Inlet 1 7/16" minimum

Cross Section Valve   20 degree undercut

(0.4/0.8/1.6km) tracks, with TT courses featuring left- and right-hand corners, plus jumps. Race length varied from five to 30 miles (8km to 48km). The short quarter mile (0.4km) tracks, sometimes in indoor arenas, had BSA and Triumph teams competing on 250cc B25/T25-engined machines, tuned to give around 30bhp. However, they were still a little uncompetitive against the 250cc two-strokes, and did not find too much favour with their riders, who, until the 1971 season, had been free to compete on 250s from any factory. Regardless, they still managed to achieve some good results, primarily due to their riders' abilities.

Prior to 1971 the number of points on offer at these races had been significantly less than those at road races, thereby putting the short track dirt specialists at serious disadvantage in the harvesting of points for the GNC, although – again for 1971 – this deficiency had been satisfactorily amended. Prize money for the season varied from $7500 at the dirt track of Terre Haute to $53,100 at the final race of the year in Ontario.

For the 1971 season, American riders were now, for the first time, on year-long contracts, ensuring that even in the event of injury, they would still be retained by BSA, rather than given the elbow as was normal practice. This policy was also aimed at trying to keep the mostly young riders loyal to their teams, as it was not unusual for some riders to be employed by rival manufacturers to contest some of the smaller capacity classes. Annual salaries ranged from $4200 for the rookies to over $8000 for top guys like AMA No 1 plate holder Gene Romero, and 1970 Daytona 200 winner Dick Mann.

After years of allowing the home produced, side-valve KR750 Harley Davidson – with its less efficient combustion chambers inherent in engines with this valve configuration – to run in flat track events with a 100cc advantage over all other marques, in 1969 the AMA amended the ruling by permitting every one to use 750cc engines, regardless of configuration. This benefited non-Harley road racers in particular as, prior to this, they had been restricted to a 500cc limit.

In response to the ruling, BSA/Triumph put together several 750 flat track Triples for the mile tracks, though both teams abandoned these after a few races, as they proved too wide, and were significantly heavier than the 650cc parallel Twins which, in tuned form, were pushing out a similar power output, anyway. With the Triples unsuitable, Triumph built just over 200 750cc 'T120' engines during the 1970 season, purely for homologation purposes (Triumph had a racing 750 Twin since 1968), and these, when tuned correctly, were capable of in excess of 70bhp. All Triumph-mounted competitors were now able to bore out their machines to 750ccs if so

Possibly the first A75 flat track racer built, seen here outside the workshop of BSA's US HQ at Nutley, New Jersey, in summer 1969. (Courtesy VMCC)

Dave Aldana between races, with crash damage from a previous heat. Note the fitment of an oil cooler, necessary for some of the longer races. (Courtesy mahonyphotos.com)

desired, putting them on a par, capacity-wise, with the Harley Davidson XR750s, one of which had won the GNC title in 1969. BSA was slower off the mark in this respect, and not until late June 1971 did its 200 A70 750cc Twins leave the production line.

As part of the investment in the 1971 racing programme, each race on the calendar was attended by an enormous company truck, which was, in reality, a mobile machine shop that also carried numerous spare parts to cover any eventuality during the gruelling, nine-month series. One benefit for riders was that it eliminated certain practices that had occurred in 1970, such as Gene Romero having to not only source spares mid-season, but also fit his own tyres, and then balance the wheels.

Track surface

There's a little more to the make-up of tracks than might at first be thought. Surfaces vary considerably, and what are known as 'cushion tracks' have very tractable surfaces that cover the entire track width, and are topped with lime, sand or clay: races held on these tracks are probably the most exciting to spectate. With traction available on all parts of the track, the racing line is not necessarily the fastest way around a course, and some riders are able to successfully perform the exciting move of 'squaring off.' Taking a much wider angle into the corners, a rider will 'jag' his bike across in a sudden turn, and hopefully dive up the inside of his target, passing him on the bend's exit.

Circuits with a harder surface are usually known as 'groove tracks,' and tend to follow more conventional racing practices, with the groove denoting the racing line that forms during practice sessions and qualifying heats (though it was not unknown for potholes to appear, making for increased excitement from the spectactors' point of view). While the groove (which varies in width at different tracks) will be the shortest route around the track, some of the more powerful machines are able to take a wider line on the bends, and pull off a passing manoeuvre.

A variation of this track condition generally found on the hardest surfaces is the 'blue groove,' its name derived from the bluish-black tyre deposits on the tracks. Traction in the blue groove is not too good, although if a rider strays from it onto the unridden part of the track, he will struggle even more for drive. As a consequence, blue groove tracks usually follow the pattern of a road race, with all the riders sticking rigidly to the racing line for much of the event. To pass is difficult, and only with the right combination of rider skill and experience, and careful gearing and tyre selection can this be consistently achieved.

Tyres

Each track could easily demand a different type of tyre tread, such was the variety of surface type and condition, which often changed as the meeting progressed. Altering the pattern by cutting parts of the tread block was a big part of race preparation, and some riders were apt to experiment in the quest for ultimate traction, whilst others often had their own tried-and-tested 'cuts.'

Jim Rice, flat track supremo with trademark sunglasses, and blade in hand altering the tread pattern of his rear tyre. (Courtesy AMA)

The most popular tyres were fat 4.00 (10cm) (front and rear) Pirelli Universals, the Avon Track Racer, and Dunlop's K70 Gold Seal studded tyre (the latter fitted to all 250, 500 and 650cc BSA/Triumph road bikes for 1971, providing a further useful sales link between racing and showroom motorcycles).

Unique machines

The flat track machines were a distinctive and unique breed, the only motorcycles that, apart from their engines, had little connection with the respective factories, and even then these were often heavily modified with 'trick' tuning components in the quest for ultimate power.

Gene Romero on the make up of two typical tracks at the conclusion of the 1970 GNC –

Houston Astrodome Short track

"The whole thing is a giant fiasco; every man in the country is there; officials are blowing whistles, people are running up and down. It's a good show but there's no time to practice. You get there early in the morning to practice, then you qualify right after – one shot. Three hours time off and then race. So you really race twice in one day – four times in two days and you're worn out. They must have 200 riders between the Amateurs and Experts – that big if not bigger. It's the first race, the Astrodome, and it's a big deal. Being centralised it draws from everywhere – all the guys from the south, from California, from the Midwest – everybody that's a racer is there, plus all the guys who think they're racers. The pits are outside and there's this block-long line for practice. You practice for five laps, then back out and get in line again. You're lucky if you get two practices in."

Sante Fe Speedway 25 Lap TT

"It's different than any other TT going. The first corner is kinda like the end of a bowling alley, where if one pin falls, most of the rest do too. It's a tight track, hard to pass, and the jump is designed wrong. It catapults you. There's no way to go over the jump and land correctly and make time. It's dry and slick, with spots that are a bit damp – not a grease type of wetness – but it's a kind of a hard track to gear for. From a spectators standpoint it could be improved, and from a riders standpoint too. With that bottleneck at the end of the straightaway you could get through."

Having signed to BSA just the previous year, the flamboyant Aldana made a big impact in 1970, finishing the season as AMA No 3.
(Courtesy mahonyphotos.com)

Reliability only mattered for the length of each meeting, as parts earmarked as potential fatigue items could be changed as a matter of course between events.

Frames were more often than not fabricated specifically for the job by specialists such as Sonic Weld, Swanson, and Trackmaster, and 'o-i-f' was the rule rather than the exception. Each frame kit was tailor-made for a variety of power plants, and the most popular finish on the chrome molybdenum tubing was nickel plating, lending the frames an exotic look. Swinging arm length varied depending on which type of track the bikes were racing on, and the most popular front fork units were either Spanish Betors or Italian Cerianis. Flanged alloy rims circled either small hubs without brakes, or at the other extreme for the very fast TT dirt courses, triple discs. Fuel tanks and seat/number plate units were also produced in a variety of styles.

While 1970's championship had been a great success for BSA Inc, with either BSAs or Triumphs taking the first five places, and Gene Romero becoming AMA No 1, 1971 was far more satisfying for the BSA marque in general, the GNC ending with BSA bikes in first place (Dick Mann), third (Jim Rice), and fourth (Dave Aldana); the deposed Romero claiming second place. BSA riders managed five race wins (four for Dick Mann), all in road racing, while Triumph achieved the same number on dirt tracks; Romero winning three of these.

By the end of the season everything was to change, and most contracts were curtailed, leaving only Dick Mann and Gene Romero with factory support for 1972. Development work came to a virtual standstill, and it's no surprise that neither marque achieved an AMA No 1 plate again. Mann, who finished the 1972 season in sixth, managed to take two national dirt races, as did the now-private BSA runner, Jim Rice, ending the season in seventh place. For Romero, dogged by unreliability, there was just the one dirt win. Privateers Gary Scott and John Hateley helped keep Triumph's name in the headlines with two and one Grand National wins respectively, but the glory days for both marques were, sadly, at an end.

BSA Motor Cycle Division domination illustrated from right to left – Current No 1 Romero, 2 Rice, 3 Aldana, and 4 Mann (bike only). (Courtesy mahonyphotos.com)

Part Four: 1971 Daytona 200
(750 Triples)

Peter Thornton's prophecy in January 1971, that the BSA/Triumph Works triple cylinder, 750cc racing bikes would win that year's Daytona 200 race, was neither bravado or flippant comment, but born of a genuine belief in the machines and the calibre of riders who would be piloting them. By entering a total of ten BSA and Triumph Triples (three more than in 1970's race), plus organising a massive spares back-up programme, the maxim 'Commit the resources – you get results' was clearly in Thornton's mind. BSA Inc booked two entire floors of the Plaza Hotel, equating to over 50 rooms, for the Speed Week, to accommodate personnel involved (top brass from the UK at both board and factory levels; mechanics; trade and press representatives, etc, as well as three armed policemen, who guarded the bikes 24 hours a day to prevent anything untoward). In addition, the racetrack was leased on the first Saturday of the week for extended test sessions. This year's Daytona 200, the 12th since the raceway opened in 1959, was also the richest to date, with a total of $33,000 prize money.

Of the ten 750s (all prepared at Meriden's race shop), six were, in essence, the same machines that had contested the previous year's race, while four totally new ones were shipped over from Meriden's Competition Department at the beginning of March, ensuring adequate time for a final shakedown in the Californian heat. The 'new' Triples, consisting of a pair of BSA A75s, and two T150 Triumphs, had been substantially improved

over the previous year's versions (though some of these received updated parts, including the front end), and were earmarked for the riders who BSA Inc considered had the best chance of winning.

Commonly known as 'low boys,' the bikes' main features were a $1\frac{7}{8}$-inch (4.8cm) lower frontal area (hence the name), courtesy of a redesigned version of the 1970 Triple's racing frame, built by Britain's specialist frame builder, Rob North, that now also had a revised steering head angle. Additionally, the bikes wore shorter fork stanchions, and had three Lockheed callipered disc brakes – the front pair mounted on a wider pair of forks that did not require the alloy fork brace that all Fontana double-sided brake machines were fitted with. Because of the extra width, a pair of specially-fabricated fork yokes had to be used on each bike.

The engines featured modified and more efficient combustion chambers, due to adoption of Squish cylinder heads, which, in conjunction with the pistons, now gave a compression ratio of up to 12.5:1. In the interest of reliability, the rockers and pushrods had been revised, resulting in components that were heavier but more robust than before; also in this area, the geometry of the rocker arms changed slightly, for the same reason, the tips of the valve stems now having a little less stress to cope with. These engine modifications, while modest (Divisional Chief Engineer Mike Nedham's comment was simply "The basis was so right last year") pushed peak power output to 84/85bhp.

The new, three-piece fairings were appreciably more 'slippery' than those of the 1970 bikes, with the division's Umberslade Hall R&D team able to achieve a 5 per cent reduction in drag factor, aided by the wind tunnel at the MIRA research and testing ground. These fairings were easily identified by their frontal slot, which diverted air flow direct to the re-sited oil cooler. Fuel tanks also featured two filler caps: one to aid expulsion of air from the tank while the rapidly pumped in petroleum entered the other, making it possible to replenish the 5-gallon (24.6 litre) tanks in 6 to 8 seconds. At the time the BSA/Triumph Triples were regarded as the most elaborate and expensive motorcycles ever seen at Daytona.

Complementing the two American teams comprising Dick Mann (low boy), Jim Rice, Dave Aldana, Don Emde (BSA), Gene Romero (low boy), Gary Nixon, Don Castro, and Tom Rockwood (Triumph), BSA Inc once again signed up nine times World Champion Mike Hailwood, riding a BSA, and fellow Englishman Paul Smart on a Triumph. Hailwood had already ridden for BSA as a one-off at 1970's Daytona race, though had retired from second place with engine problems after completing under 30 miles (48km) .

Speed Week

Major problems were relatively few during practice sessions early in the week, with Jim Rice's engine throwing a con-rod; in addition to which – rather fortuitously, as it turned out – Hailwood parted company with his BSA at 100mph (161kph) after a braking error, necessitating some repair work, during which one of the mechanics noticed that the bike's swinging arm was two inches (5cm) shorter than

it should have been. A correctly dimensioned one was immediately despatched from Meriden via air freight, and Hailwood was back on the track within two days, on a bike that he now felt handled considerably better.

On the first day of running the Florida heat played havoc with the carburetion of all ten bikes: fuel aeration causing misfires and engine cut-outs. A minor modification to the fairing eliminated the hot air around the carburettors by allowing cool air to flow past this area.

Most of the American riders stuck to the Goodyear racing tyres they were familiar with; only Dick Mann switching to the Dunlop versions used by Hailwood and Smart. Although clearly better suited to the handling characteristics of the Triples, part of the reluctance to change was apparently due to the sponsorship deals between riders and Goodyear already in place.

The final qualifying session saw Triumph's Paul Smart emulate his performance in the final practice session, posting the fastest lap and claiming pole position. Split

Following a one-year lay-off from motorcycle racing, Mike Hailwood was back at Daytona for 1971. (Author's archive)

Triumph's Daytona team consisting of, from left to right, Gene Romero, Don Castro, Tommy Rockwood, Gary Nixon and Paul Smart, the two low-boys at either end. (Author's archive)

Left to right – Floyd Emde, 1948 Daytona 200 winner, son Don, and his mechanic, Mack Kambayashi. (Courtesy Don Emde)

A gloveless Gene Romero during Daytona Speed Week, who went on to take second place in the race. (Courtesy AMA)

by the Harley Davidson XR 750s of Cal Rayborn and Mark Brelsford, fourth and fifth grid places were taken by Don Emde and Mike Hailwood, with Jim Rice closing the top ten. Smart's consistent blistering pace and obvious confidence were, undoubtedly, the result of having only just returned from South Africa with his T150, after spending part of the winter racing there with BSA Works rider Ray Pickrell, and being as one with his machine. No other Daytona team member had ridden a Triple in anger since the 1970 season terminated in October.

Under starter's orders
As the flag man signalled the start to the 97 race competitors, Honda 750/4 privateer Gary Fisher immediately made up several places from the second row to take the lead from pole man Paul Smart before the first bend was encountered. With the deposed Triumph rider and Hailwood constantly pushing hard for the next 8 laps, an ever-increasing gap with the rest of the field was the result, achieved, incredibly, by the trio consistently topping Smart's qualifying lap speed by five miles an hour.

During the ninth lap, as Dick Mann closed on the tail of the leaders, Fisher's Honda pulled off the track, its cam chain broken; the same weak link which had put out all other 750/4s – bar Dick Mann's winning Honda – from the 1970 race. This placed Smart in the lead, still hounded by the two BSAs, though within a lap it was Hailwood's turn for mechanical misfortune when his three-cylinder engine suffered a broken valve tip, leaving Smart and Mann to exchange positions a few times before settling down to a marginally slower pace. In spite of Hailwood's retirement, good news for the BSA/Triumph equipe soon came as top ten runners and rivals Cal Rayborn (H-D), Jody Nicholas (Suzuki), and Kel Carruthers (Yamaha) found themselves visiting the pit lane, elevating Gene Romero and Don Emde to third and fourth places respectively.

With both Smart and Mann having completed refuelling pit stops on the 27th lap, Smart was enjoying an extended lead approaching half a minute over the BSA rider, who, after over-running a bend and taking to the grass, ran into a pylon, which resulted in a damaged rear brake pedal that took vital seconds to rectify.

With only 12 laps remaining – and Smart looking as though he would continue his domination of the week's

BSA/Triumph Press Officer David Lloyd's 1971 Daytona 200 impressions –

"Motor Cycle City – not a name to be found on the map, but first-timers view of Daytona Beach, Florida, scene of the fabulous Daytona 200, one of the world's most significant motor cycle events.

"Fabulous is not too strong a word; almost perfect weather (at least while I was there); and motorcycles everywhere. Two-wheelers so exotic that the big multi-cylinder European and Japanese models were mundane in comparison. Chromium plated, chopperised, decorated – and everyone, it seemed, parading the length of the beach under my bedroom window every night.

"As race week built up towards Sunday afternoon and the big race, so the crowds began to roll in. Bikes and cars everywhere; crowds, dust and HEAT. When the woman in the drug store opposite the Plaza Hotel, headquarters of the BSA/Triumph contingent, persuaded me to buy a sun resistant golf cap, she knew what she was talking about.

"The approach of the weekend brought activity to a furious pitch in the track-side lockups rented by BSA Inc.'s president, Mr Peter Thornton. I couldn't help wondering how the British contingent, headed by Triumph's Doug Hele, felt about working under those armed policemen, present to see that not too many secrets were given away?

"By Thursday, months of hard work on the six American-prepared machines and the four new British models seemed to have paid off. Britain's Paul Smart had taken his Triumph Trident to first place in the speed trials, at more than 150mph – and seven other BSA and Triumph riders were listed in the first twenty of the 100-strong field.

"Everyone knows, though, that Doug Hele is the eternal pessimist. The speed trials and the opportunity they gave to see what the opposition could do provoked him into

even more concentrated efforts behind the scenes.

"For others not so involved in the mechanics of the machines, there was time for a brief look at the surroundings. The multiplicity of neon signs, the never-ending queues of traffic at virtually every hour of the day and night, and souvenir shops – dozens of them!

"None of this could disguise the kindness of the Americans, and their insistence that they should do everything possible to help. Nowhere was this better demonstrated than at the track on race day, when the record crowd of 38,000 cheered Britain's Paul Smart and Mike Hailwood on their Triumph and BSA triples. One was left with the distinct impression that the crowds were just as disappointed as these two riders when they were obliged to retire, after one or other of them had been leading the American racers a fine dance for the best part of 49 laps."

activities – a slowing bike with a telltale smoking exhaust enabled Mann to regain much of the time he had lost. Smart pitted and reappeared with a new set of plugs, but to little avail as the engine would now only fire on two cylinders. Two laps later the Triumph came to a halt, its centre piston blown as the result, it was thought, of a high compression ratio of over 12.5:1: his being the only triple to run with it.

The remaining 40 miles (64km) were covered without incident for the trio of American-ridden Triples, with Mann taking the chequered flag, followed by Romero and Emde, making an unprecedented 1-2-3 for BSA Inc's racing team.

Exposure

The knock-on effect of the win – and, indeed, the top three placings – was, as Thornton often said, worldwide publicity at no charge. Magazines, and not only motorcycle publications, gave BSA cover slots and features, as well as reviewed the event itself. Sparkplug producer Champion, which had supplied the team's plugs, placed related ads in the top American motorcycle journals, as did Bates Leathers and Bell crash helmets, all eager to be associated with the success of the Triples.

In America, BSA was quick to produce a 34-inch x 22-inch (86.3cm x 55.9cm), black and white poster entitled 'BSA Takes Daytona,' and adverts for the following year's models also revolved around Mann and the win. By the beginning of August, a six minute long, 16mm film comprising race highlights was made available to dealers to either loan or purchase for film shows.

And in Britain 'A great victory deserves a great free offer, so here it is,' was the slogan included in an ad

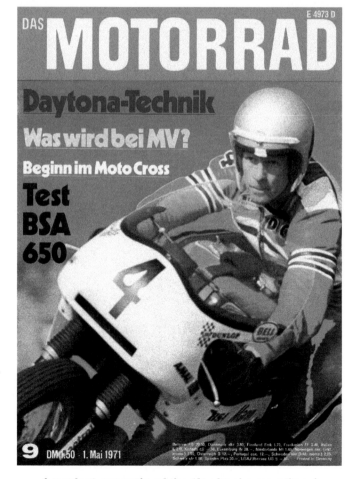

A perfect example of the 'for free' promotional exposure that comes with success. (Author's archive)

for a 33-inch x 21-inch (83.8cm x 53.3cm) art poster featuring Dick Mann. The scheme, run in conjunction with the weekly *Motor Cycle* newspaper, required only that participants cut out the picture of the poster, and present it to any BSA/Triumph dealer in exchange for the genuine item. The offer ran from mid-July until the end of August.

Both emanating from BSA's Advertising Department, the top poster wasn't issued until summer 1971, while the second item was used to promote the April Anglo-American Match Race Series. (Author's archive)

To help promote the series, BSA marketed a commemorative package made up of a poster and two stickers. (Author's archive)

Anglo-American Match Race Series, 1971 (750 Triples)

The Match Race Series, although originally conceived in 1970, was the perfect vehicle for continuing to publicise the impressive Daytona success, in addition to which, this would be the first time that a 750cc race series had been run in the UK. The sight and sound of ten BSA/Triumph Triples racing against one another was something to experience, and enthralled the many race-goers (55-60,000) at the three meetings held over the 1971 Easter weekend. To actually have present six of BSA's/Triumph's American Works riders was indeed inspirational.

The idea for the series was put to BSA/Triumph Marketing Director Peter Deverall by Peter Thornton while he was in London in January. Thinking behind the series had been fuelled by the question of which country had the best riders – America or Britain? – although, understandably, conclusions were, and still are, difficult to draw, due to the very different nature of the US's AMA championship races and the type of racing that British racers carved a living from.

BSA found a keen promoter in Chris Lowe, the Motor Circuit Development racetrack-owning boss, and it was he who agreed to provide most of the finance for the series. Lowe had the foresight to realise the attraction that the American team would have for UK crowds, especially as the two British manufacturers were to contest the USA's prestigious Daytona 200 mile race in March, with a predictably good measure of coverage in the British motorcycle press if they won. So, with his Easter Bank Holiday schedule already in place, Lowe simply added two more races in April to each of the three meetings – at Brands Hatch, Mallory Park, and Oulton Park – and put up prize money totalling £5000.

Although it did not detract from its success, and the enjoyment of all involved, including spectators, the series was always a very one-sided affair, with the mainly young and therefore relatively inexperienced American riders finding English circuits, and the unpredictable weather conditions, very alien, compared to the more mature members of the UK team (except 22-year-old Tony Jefferies), who knew the tracks inside out. Additionally, whilst UK riders were equipped with 1971 versions of the racing Triples that had contested the Daytona race, only two of the 'American' bikes were to this same specification; the rest of the US team, in theory, having to ride 1970 hub-braked machines (although at various times between Daytona Speed Week and the Match races, both Aldana's and Emde's BSAs and Castro's Triumph were upgraded with Lockheed discs, leaving only Jim Rice to compete in every race with the Fontana brake).

A further note on the lack of parity between American and UK machines is illustrated by the fact that the former retained the large Daytona fuel tanks and seat tail units, while UK riders were equipped with the smaller, short circuit items, thereby further improving overall performance. In general, the British team used the superior 1971 fairings, although, somewhat confusingly, several races had UK team captain Percy Tait riding with the 1970 fairing, and Don Castro rode T150s with both types fitted.

Several times during the series the handling deficiencies of the 1970 specification bikes became apparent, the machines often appearing to 'squirm' out of slow corners under hard acceleration, though even this apparently did little to thwart the racing instincts of the visitors, all of whom endeared themselves to everyone with their enthusiasm for racing.

What did favour the Americans was that each race was to be a clutch start, rather than the more traditional British dead engine push start. For clarity, all ten riders used the same race numbers for the six races.

Carol Cleveland flys the flag(s). Match Race Series advertisement from *Motor Cycle*. (Author's archive)

The Americans are here

Initially, the current US AMA No 1 plate holder, Triumph's Gene Romero, was to be part of the team, but upon reflection decided that the risk of injuring himself in the Match Race Series – and thereore being unable to defend his No 1 plate – was more important. Also, race fee comparisons were given as further reason for quitting the series. However, Romero did eventually travel to England, where he attended the press conference and spectated at the races, but a reported recent leg injury precluded him from competing, in any case. His 'low boy' T150 was allocated to fellow Triumph rider Don Castro, although, a little confusingly, Castro apparently rode two bikes: the different fairings being the clue here.

Disaster struck again when 30-year-old team captain Gary Nixon, twice AMA Champion and fourth place man at 1970's Mallory Park 'Race of the Year,' was sidelined by injury. Although the first rider to be announced for the American team, Nixon's appointment became doubtful when he broke a leg while racing in mid-February in the States. Having competed in the Daytona 200 race without ill effect, he was given the green light for the Match races, but, unfortunately, at a practice session at Brands Hatch two days before the first race, he crashed, sustaining a wrist fracture that put him out of the competition, thereby depriving the team of an experienced racer and leader, and leaving 37-year-old Dick Mann as the only member with a good knowledge of circuit racing.

This did, however, resolve one problem ... With six riders, one of them was always going to have to be reserve – either permanently or on a rotational basis – as

The US team posing with Dick Mann's Daytona-winning A75 at the press conference. (Author's archive)

the series was based around five riders per team. With Nixon out of the running, Mann, Castro, Emde, Rice, and Aldana would be able to start all six races.

The American team, including mechanics Dick Lytell (Triumph) and Lloyd Bulmer (BSA), along with Team Manager Danny Macias, arrived at London airport on Thursday, April 1, and were driven to the Royal Lancaster Hotel, where they were booked for the duration of their visit; the tab picked up by BSA. The following day a press conference was held at this venue, with all riders from both teams present, and in the company of two of the Triples that were taking part in the races: Gene Romero's T150 and Dick Mann's Daytona-winning A75; the only two 'low boys,' remember, that the American team possessed.

The resulting various press photographs of the two teams illustrated an interesting difference between the two camps in accepted dress code. While both wore team blazers – light blue for the Americans and dark blue for British riders – here, the formality ended, as both Dave Aldana and Don Castro wore pretty way-out striped trousers, the latter, along with Gary Nixon, also sporting large ties based on a Stars and Stripes theme. In many ways, their dress sense perfectly reflected their flamboyant dirt track riding style.

The BSA/Triumph Press Department, headed by ex-

The culprits return to the scene of the crime! In first place Jim Rice, second Dick Mann, and third Don Castro. (Author's archive)

Birmingham motoring journalist David Lloyd, knowing well the publicity value of pretty girls, had Paul Smart's fiancé, Maggie Sheene (sister of the then Yamaha racer Barry Sheene), attending the conference, adding to the glamour of the occasion.

Pre-race appointments

In the period between Friday's press conference and the first race at Brands Hatch a week later, the six Americans found themselves with a busy daytime itinerary, beginning on Saturday at Oulton Park for the first practice session of the week. However, before starting, three of them – Dick Mann, Don Castro, and driver Jim Rice – did several laps of the circuit in their hired Ford Zephyr, until Rice overcooked it on one of the corners and rolled the car. The guys climbed out, righted the car, and then set out on foot to start the practice session proper.

An unfortunate consequence of this incident occurred shortly afterward, when BSA-mounted Dave Aldana dropped his bike, after finding some of the oil on the track dropped by the Ford, although, thankfully, neither bike nor rider suffered much damage. Likewise, Triumph's Tony Jefferies also had an off, the only casualty, fortunately, the bike's fuel tank.

Sunday was presumably a day off, whilst Monday brought the second practice session, this time at Leicestershire's Mallory Park circuit, accompanied by rain showers; two days later it was Brands Hatch for the final pre-series practice where, as previously mentioned, Gary Nixon fell and put himself out of the series. It was also here that a new problem with the three-cylinder engines materialised, resulting in at least two very premature big end bearing failures. The cause? The thick, monograde oil that was used was not circulating properly due to Kent's cold weather conditions, prompting the factory to eventually enlarge the diameter of the production engine's oilways.

Either on the Tuesday or Thursday the US team again travelled to the Midlands, and was given guided tours of both the Small Heath and Meriden factories.

The races
Brands Hatch

Starting on a damp, but drying track – a legacy of that morning's rain (which, odd though it may sound, was indeed fortunate for the visitors; three of whom had never raced on a wet circuit before) – Ray Pickrell took the lead, which he maintained until the chequered flag dropped 12 laps later. The start apparently took Paul Smart by surprise, as he was still adjusting his crash helmet as the flag dropped! Throughout the race, John Cooper was noticeably off the pace, put down to the crash he had suffered shortly before on his 350 Yamsel, and came in at tenth. Top-placed US rider was Dick Mann in third place.

On the damp Brands Hatch grid, Triumph mechanic Dick Lytell chats to Don Castro. (Courtesy Mortons)

The second race was also without incident, and again saw Pickrell take an early lead, which he held until the finish, as well as equalling Phil Read's standing short circuit lap record. Once more an American rider claimed third place, this time Don Castro, on the absent Gene Romero's T150, ahead of Dick Mann.

1st race (12 laps)

1st	R Pickrell (BSA)
2nd	P Smart (Triumph)
3rd	D Mann (BSA)
Points	UK – 30
	USA – 25
Fastest lap	R Pickrell 56.2s/79.43mph

2nd race (12 laps)

1st	R Pickrell (BSA)
2nd	P Smart (Triumph)
3rd	D Castro (Triumph)
Points	UK – 31
	USA – 24
Fastest lap	D Mann 58.2s/76.70mph

Total points	UK – 61
	USA – 49

1st race (11 laps)

1st	R Pickrell (BSA)
2nd	J Cooper (BSA)
3rd	D Mann (BSA)
Points	UK – 26
	USA – 23
Fastest lap	R Pickrell & P Smart 53.6s/90.67mph

2nd race (11 laps)

1st	P Smart (Triumph)
2nd	R Pickrell (BSA)
3rd	J Cooper (BSA)
Points	UK – 27
	USA – 25
Fastest lap	J Cooper 52s/93.46mph

Total points	UK – 53
	USA – 48

Mallory Park

Although Don Castro took the lead in the first race, this didn't last long, as after hitting oil on a long, sweeping bend during the first lap, he immediately lost several places, allowing through four of the British riders. However, by mid-distance, both Tait and Smart had slid off at the circuit's hairpin on successive laps, the latter breaking a finger. Before race end, Castro had also pulled out with a broken con-rod, denying the visitors a third and fourth place finish, and allowing Jefferies to take fourth behind Mann, with Pickrell picking up his third-in-a-row series win.

Race two was down to nine starters, as Jefferies had wrecked his T150 an hour or so earlier in the 'unlimited' race final. Once again, Triumph factory test rider Percy Tait retired, this time with undefined engine problems, leaving Smart the win, and thereby depriving Pickrell of his fourth win in a row. Now more on song with second place in the first race and third in this, John Cooper also matched the circuit's lap record set by Mike Hailwood four years previously on a six-cylinder 250 Works Honda.

The official race programme from the mid-series meeting at Mallory Park. (Author's archive)

Oulton Park

The following day at the final meeting of the series, the penultimate race was again witness to a fast start by some of the American riders, with Emde and Castro initially claiming the two lead places, only to be passed by Paul Smart before the first lap was complete. As the race progressed, two more home riders, Cooper and Pickrell, followed Smart through, with Mann now sitting in fourth position, where he finished. As the race was winding up, the final lap saw Castro drop his Triumph as he made his way out of a bend, but never say die: he remounted to come home in tenth place.

The sixth and last race of the weekend again saw an American rider, this time Dick Mann, take the lead

Ray Pickrell, points leader at mid-stage of the series, pictured at the Mallory Park meeting. (Courtesy Mortons)

from the start line, until eventual winner Paul Smart cleared him on the second lap. Mann was able to maintain second place, keeping Cooper and Pickrell behind him for the remaining three laps. A late error robbed Ray Pickrell of the highest points tally of the series, when on the last lap he dropped his machine after a braking error.

The highest American series score was the 46 points held by the very experienced, not to be underestimated BSA, rider Dick Mann, only two points behind joint leaders Pickrell and Smart.

1st race (5 laps)

1st	P Smart (Triumph)
2nd	R Pickrell (BSA)
3rd	J Cooper (BSA)
Points	UK – 38
	USA – 17
Fastest lap	P Smart 1m42.3s/92.72mph

2nd race (5 laps)

1st	P Smart (Triumph)
2nd	D Mann (BSA)
3rd	J Cooper (BSA)
Points	UK – 31
	USA – 23
Fastest lap	P Smart 1m48.2s/91.8mph
Total points	UK – 69
	USA – 40

Even though the British motorcycle press made much of the 46-point margin over the visitors that the UK team finished with, contrary to the image that this may conjure up, there was never a British procession top five finish, and only at Oulton Park did this nearly happen, with Dick Mann again spoiling it for the Brits. It's feasible, of course, that, at this final stage, the remaining American riders, knowing that the Match Race Series was already lost, had one eye on the more lucrative racing season to come, back home in America.

These Mallory Park photographs offer a fine comparison of the two types of Triples in the series. Don Castro on a 1970 'Daytona' spec T150, albeit with retro fitted disc brakes and forward mounted callipers, while Paul Smart pilots the short circuit spec 'low boy.' Note the vent in the side of the 'letterbox' fairing, which worked in conjunction with the frontal slot to supply a constant flow of cooling air.
(Courtesy Geoff James)

MV-beater

Between the Match races and the season's finale at Ontario, BSA's recent find in John Cooper was to pay dividends with two high profile victories in the UK. On both occasions, September's 'race of the year' at Mallory Park and Brands Hatch's 'race of the south' in October, Cooper beat the Works MV Augusta of World Champion Giacomo Agostini to the chequered flag, as well as setting a new lap record at Brands.

Critics have often claimed that the BSA wins were not as spectacular as they appeared, due, in the main, to the capacity advantage of 250cc that the British 750 enjoyed over the MV. However, while the racing BSA/Triumph Triples were derived from a pushrod road bike,

the three-cylinder 500cc MV was a purpose-built race engine featuring double overhead cams driving four valves per cylinder, and lightweight engine casings. Power output was approximately the same, and by September 1971, Agostini had already gathered six 500cc world titles on it.

Ontario Motor Speedway
(750 Triples)

Touted as the world's richest race, with $96,000 prize money, October's Champion sparkplug-sponsored 'Ontario 250 Classic' was to be the last sensational win for BSA in 1971, although – unlike at Daytona seven months previously – the bikes were not considered favourites (this distinction going to the three-cylinder, two-stroke, 500cc Kawasakis, and in particular the French Canadian Yvon du Hamel. The Kawasakis had been fast enough at Daytona, but let down by handling that was not up to the mark: this now, had largely been rectified.

The circuit, situated 40 miles (64km) east of Los Angeles, California, had only opened in September 1970, and cost over $35 million to build from scratch, featuring an arena capacity of 140,000, and parking for 45,500 vehicles. Its main track, designed with Formula One motor racing in mind, ran to 3.4 miles (5.4km), while within this perimeter there was also a 2.5mile (4km) oval track and a drag strip. Facilities were top grade, but failure to secure any F1 business – coupled with a hard line from the venture's financiers over rental – saw the venue close a mere ten years later.

Spearheading the BSA/Triumph effort, two new Triples had been prepared at Meriden – one for John Cooper and the other for Gary Nixon – to compete alongside Gene Romero's and Dick Mann's Daytona low boys, while Castro, Rockwood, Rice and Emde continued with their, by now, variously modified 1970 Threes.

The grid comprised one hundred competitors for an event split into two halves, with a 45-minute break in between. The first race quickly settled, with Nixon and du Hamel repeatedly dicing for the lead, the Kawasaki faster down the main straight but the Triumph often regaining the advantage on the twisty infield section. AMA No 1 Romero had been running in fourth until a spill; the resulting damage putting him way down the field to eventually finish in 41st. Taking everyone by surprise, Nixon and Cooper failed to make a refuelling stop after Doug Hele had calculated that the two bikes could complete the race distance on just a single tank. The gamble paid off, and Nixon beat the refuelled du Hamel over the line by a margin of 7 seconds, followed by Cooper in third, and Dick Mann in sixth.

The second race again saw Nixon getting off the start line well and into the lead, followed by Cooper and

du Hamel, though all was soon to change early on in the second lap when Nixon and several other riders hit oil (resulting in all but Cooper and the 350cc Yamaha rider, Kelvin Carruthers, going down), thereby promoting the latter two to race leaders. At one stage Romero passed both and held the lead for 13 laps until a throttle cable problem spoiled his chances of victory.

As the race progressed, Carruthers eventually began to pull away from Cooper, although, with the race drawing to a close, it dawned on the Australian that the scheduled fuel stop would probably hand the win to Cooper, so he decided to press on regardless.

From the 1972 home/general export BSA brochure, a shot of John 'Moon Eyes' Cooper at September's Race of the Year. The brochure may have only featured four bikes, but racing versions of all of them were victorious in many areas of competition during 1971. (Author's archive)

At the start of the final lap, all was looking well for Carruthers, who had by now drawn out a 100-yard (91m) gap over the second-placed English BSA rider (and, as it turned out, had no reason to worry about fuel). Cooper had been under the misapprehension that there were still two or three laps remaining, due to watching the circuit's inaccurate lap counter as he was no longer receiving signals from his pit. Only when Cooper saw the last lap flag being waved did the true situation become clear, whereupon he proceeded to ride like the devil, eventually taking his engine through the gears up to 10,000rpm, incredibly, crossing the finish line six inches ahead of a dumbstruck Carruthers ("I looked over and saw another wheel!"). Jim Rice took third, Romero eighth, and Castro ninth.

Cooper's first and third places gave him overall race victory – the first time he had competed in America and the first time that a British rider won a major AMA event. From a relatively unknown international rider, Cooper's 1971 successes on the racing A75 deservedly elevated him to celebrity status within the sport.

It was at Ontario that the now well-known episode of a fellow competitor demanding to purchase Cooper's winning BSA for $2500 occurred. There was nothing illegal in this – and it was actually an AMA ruling, implemented to discourage factories from entering motorcycles that were full of expensive trick components. Hele was apparently oblivious to the rule, and totally bemused by the arguments that broke out, as mechanic Steve Brown planted himself on the bike to prevent its removal. The guy making the claim, fellow competitor Bob Bailey, had done all his homework, and legally, BSA was bound to let him have the machine: a horrifying prospect, as the value of the BSA was put at near to £10,000! Persuasive talks between Bailey, Hele, US team manager Danny Macias, and the AMA eventually resulted in Bailey settling for Tony Jefferies' Trident instead, on the grounds that he would find it 'impossible' to source parts for Cooper's 'special' bike.

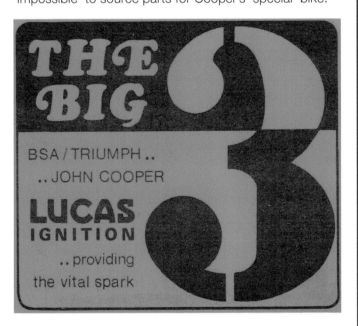

Lucas was just one of several suppliers keen to be associated with the dominating Triples during 1971.
(Author's archive)

Doug Hele reflecting in 1971 on the development of the racing Triples –

"It was a moment of some decision. We had the success of racing the 650 Bonneville Twin behind us, and it was a question of whether the 'Three' was as good or better? It looked good, even with increased weight; it was clear that we could achieve high power having 75-80bhp from the start! A new racing frame had been made for the 650, so we had Rob North build a similar one to accommodate 80 horsepower.

"It soon went round the factory that we had a fairly competitive motorcycle – and Percy Tait proved it by averaging 157mph at Elvington late that year [October 1969]. This compared favourably against his speed of 142mph on a 750 – yes, a 750 Twin in 1968.

"We knew we had sufficient power: it was a question of reliability and handling. A major problem was that an error crept into the frame geometry! The head angle should have been 62 degrees, but it came out at 65, totally upsetting the handling. I was able to change this to 64, but it was not enough.

"[The combustion chamber] was a better design than the standard 500, anyway. However, with the standard head and domed pistons, we found that 12:1 [compression ratio] was too high. The engine was sensitive to ignition timing, and was not being controlled accurately enough at high rpm, causing piston burning.

"Another improvement came from running three exhausts into one megaphone. The problem with this was [how] to evolve a collection-box which provided equal emergence for all three cylinders.

"The nimonic valves specially fitted for racing gave trouble by flaking the coatings on the stem ends. We cured this by using standard valves perfectly satisfactorily. Oddly enough, Hailwood's bike at Daytona this year was stopped through a faulty valve. It was a one-off failure that has never repeated itself."

Chapter 11

USA

Restructure

Although BSA had owned the Triumph Engineering Company since 1951, it wasn't until 1966 that the first signs of rationalisation between BSA Company Inc of North America and Triumph Motors occurred, signalled by BSA buying out the previously independent west coast Johnson Motors Incorporated, and moving the administration centres of the two companies into purpose-built premises in Duarte.

The four distributors – BSA Western, BSA Incorporated East, Triumph Corporation (Tri-Cor), and Johnson Motors – were further amalgamated in 1969 into a new parent company known as the Birmingham Small Arms Company Incorporated (BSA Inc), under the leadership of new president Peter Thornton, who had joined BSA in September that year. Paving the way for the reorganisation were five days of meetings held at Small

Heath and Meriden, attended by five American executives – Earl Miller, Don Brown, Pete Colman, Bill Jacob, and Jeff Hope – as well as several UK Sales, Marketing, Export, and Advertising personnel. The agenda under discussion was marketing strategy and future product specification.

Meetings of this nature were, in the 1960s, very necessary, as Chief Stylist Mettam explains regarding his own jurisdiction –

"Each year a score or more BSA and Triumph top management or key personnel from the USA west and east coast bases visited Birmingham to discuss problems, and plan future campaigns and models. Communication was not so easy 40 years ago: international telephone calls were expensive, and not often indulged, and we usually needed to phone the telephone exchange to book ahead; dialling calls did not happen for years. Internet and email wasn't even science fiction. Telex we had, but it required typing at a very set rhythm – a slow and regular rate for a typist; fast and full of gaps for me – so best typed into punched tape by a typist, then fed into the telex machine. Tele-printers we had but they were slow – say one hour to scan and transmit a drawing – a very expensive telephone call. Grand meetings comprising not always the same persons, lasted for a week in Small Heath's grand

One of the Anglo-American meetings held in mid-1970 that were concerned with the forthcoming reorganisation of the North American setup. In the foreground are Eric Turner and Lionel Jofeh. (Courtesy VMCC)

boardroom (the Chairman had another more compact boardroom). In parallel, or after each day's big meetings, were many smaller discussion groups (often as few as two people) to sort out things; some of these guys stayed for another week. It was productive."

The above mentioned changes saw the previous four distribution companies reduced to just two, BSA Motorcycles Inc and Triumph Motorcycles Inc, which were to share distribution centres at Duarte in California, serving the west, and in the east the ex-Tri-Cor headquarters at Baltimore, Maryland. The distribution warehouse managers were Al Martin and Frank Benson respectively (the former having previously worked for both Johnson Motors and BSA), while the department was headed by Distribution Director Jim Brown. By early 1970 BSA New Jersey HQ had transferred from Nutley to new premises some six or seven miles distant at Verona, and besides Peter Thornton, also housed some of the newly-created departments.

The reorganisation, largely implemented to obviate duplication of activities common to both BSA and Triumph, and improve administration and marketing, brought with it a totally new management structure that comprised both existing personnel and many new faces who had backgrounds in the US automotive industry. Six separate departments came about: Distribution, Engineering, Sales, Treasury, Market Research, and Marketing & Product Planning. Financially, and as hoped, the amalgamation paid dividends, returning a 15 per cent annual saving on administration costs alone.

Engineering
As part of the restructure, a fully-equipped technical centre was created at Duarte, overseen by Triumph stalwart and now Vice President of Engineering Pete Colman, whose commitment to the job was beyond question, making him the ideal choice. The centre was managed by Bob Tyron, while Danny Macias was appointed Race Chief.

Macias was already a successful and respected engine tuner in his own right, and now controlled a race department that employed four BSA and Triumph mechanics in a fully fitted out tuning shop, which included port-flow equipment and a dynamometer. In common with the division's R&D establishment at Umberslade Hall in the UK, the centre also had access to a wind tunnel for aerodynamic work, and ideas/test results were freely exchanged between the two departments for confirmation and analysis. Replacing the four service shops of the now defunct distribution companies, the centre handled many aspects connected to the two marques' operations, including setting up training centres, and exploring and implementing new and existing service techniques.

Engineering Vice-President Pete Colman.
(Author's archive)

Sales
The Sales Department was placed in the hands of ex-Ford Marketing Manager David Bird, brought in, in early 1970, as a replacement for Don Brown, whose personal differences with Peter Thornton had become totally irreconcilable, leading to Brown resigning from his post after only around three months. It was, of course, Don Brown who initiated and subsequently acted as go-between during the 'Vetter 3' project: the radical restyling of a BSA A75 by freelance designer Craig Vetter.

Whereas previously the whole country had been served by two sales and service departments, the reorganisation saw a much improved network, the US now divided into five regions with offices in Baltimore, Atlanta, Detroit, Denver, and Duarte. Each region boasted its own service manager whose district managers (ranging from two to four, depending on area and dealer numbers), would theoretically work in harness with dealers to resolve any service problems. The emphasis was on service managers visiting dealers – totalling around 1500 for both marques – in person. By way of back-up, each region also had a Sales Administrator, who acted as something of a troubleshooter; again, for the dealers' benefit.

From the beginning of 1971, a harder line was taken with dealers who proved tardy or errant in settling their credit bills with BSA Inc. As the nationwide reorganisation was set in motion, it was discovered that, under existing

Eastern Regional Sales Manager Harry Chaplin pictured at the Nutley HQ in 1969. (Courtesy VMCC)

credit policy, BSA was left with in excess of $1,000,000 worth of non-collectable or written-off debt at the end of the 1970 financial year, which had resulted in some BSA dealers being struck off. Added to this, a number of Triumph warranty claims in the eastern region were found to be up to six months old, and still not acted on. New guidelines placed the entire dealer credit system under the control of J P King, a qualified Credit Manager, aided by two divisional level managers working out of Verona as part of the Treasury Department, now headed by J H Heiny. The old credit department based at Duarte ceased operation.

Regional Sales Managers, District and Service Managers were urged to conduct far more thorough financial background checks on dealers applying for spare parts credit, and, once approved, if said dealer subsequently defaulted, enforce newly-introduced interest penalties, as well as carry out an inquiry (also part of the new rules), and if the dealer was deemed at fault, suspend credit immediately and replace with a cash-on-delivery system.

There was a similar policy for delivery of motorcycles on credit, which had, in the recent past, been abused by some dealers. Once the policy was in place, dealers were given 15 days to settle their account, or risk a 10 per cent interest charge on the outstanding amount. Along similar lines to the spares credit policy, penalties for defaulting were withdrawal of 'open account' facilities, and/or cessation of motorcycle deliveries.

Such was the disarray of the previous administration that some of the more unscrupulous dealers who had defaulted on new motorcycle payments were able to deceive BSA about what they actually had on their premises. To rectify this, the previously mentioned sales personnel were instructed to visit each of the dealers, and make a detailed inventory of all stock, with a view to repossessing that not paid for. All motorcycles were to be carefully checked, along with serial numbers. Representatives were told not to leave the premises until monies owing were paid or an agreement of repossession had been reached. A 19-point report sheet had to be completed, which then laid out all the facts, and the condition of the bike(s) in question: ie whether it had perhaps been used as a demonstrator, had parts missing, was still crated, etc.

A memo laying out in full all of the credit policy details was sent to relevant districts, and it's worth quoting the last paragraph, which clearly spells out the intention behind the reorganisation of credit facilities.

"Remember … dealers must be made to realize that we cannot and will not tolerate an out of trust situation, as it is an act of fraud and violates our trust in the dealer. We must receive settlement per our terms. The success of our credit policy is dependent upon you, the District Manager, as you are the liaison between sales and credit, and it is through you that our success will be determined."

Financing for the credit system had also undergone change, resulting in responsibility for dealer loans lifted from BSA Inc, via arrangements with US finance house Commercial Credit Corporation (CCC). In monetary terms this equated to several million dollars in the early months of each year's selling season. Through CCC, a hire purchase scheme was also made available, providing instant credit to potential customers in the showroom, which, in light of the bike boom currently sweeping the States, was considered an absolutely vital tool to aid sales, and at a stroke removed one of the problems cited by Group Chairman Eric Turner, during the 1969 crisis.

One rather peculiar decision - and probably detrimental in terms of sales – was to discontinue the 500-mile (809km) free service on all 1971 models, although dealers were urged to encourage new owners to bring their machines to them for this service, but pay for it themselves. Common sense eventually prevailed, however, and for 1972 models the free service was reinstated.

Marketing/advertising

The departments of Product Planning and Market Research would have worked together to a degree as their spheres of interest overlapped, with Marketing – a small department, principally consisting of Manager of Market Research & Sales Analysis Ken Brown, and Market Analyst R Russell – feeding Planning the results of its forecasts, such as consumer trends and sales predictions.

Under the title of Director of Market & Product Planning, Tony Salisbury was in charge of Product Planning, whose area sometimes entailed collusion with the Styling Department based at Umberslade Hall for decisions concerning projected models. Salisbury, although an American, had, prior to his BSA appointment, worked for the Rootes car factory in Coventry, England. During his time in the UK, he had made some good friends, and had become something of an Anglophile; subsequent visits to Britain on BSA business saw him happily lengthening his stay if circumstances permitted. He was afforded two assistants in Planning: fellow American J Salluzzo, and Jack Redmond, an English guy who handled much of the liaison between the two countries, though he was always on the payroll of BSA Inc.

Advertising was also attached to Salisbury's department, with ex-auto industry advertising executive Philip Michel appointed the position of Advertising Manager quite late in the day during September 1970. By May the following year, Michel had hired two assistants: ex-Vanderbilt Automotive Centre James Brooke, whose duties with BSA/Triumph took in show and exhibition supervision, as well as handling the public relations side of the enormous racing effort, and Thomas McCann, who had recently been a Merchandising Account Executive in New York, and was now charged with overseeing the department's finances and dealing with BSA Inc's ad agency, E E Spitzer. The appointments may have had two purposes – firstly, capitalise on the success of the BSA/Triumph racing teams on both tarmac and dirt, and, secondly, aid the sales push that was shortly to commence in an effort to shift much of the late – and therefore unsold – stock that was arriving in vast quantities from Britain.

Contraband!

"The Triumph Corporation Sales Vice-President at Baltimore was a great Anglophile. He lived out in the country in what Americans call an 'English-style house,' and when I visited there he proudly showed me his MGTF. He used to shoot (he was American!), and wanted a BSA-made Martini 9mm rifle; he did not want to pay import duty or have the fuss of customs clearance to import firearms.

"Al Cave, BSA Production Manager, packed one into a bike crate for free. Every machine, after testing, had its front wheel and mudguard removed, and forks compressed fully and the 'middle lug' strapped to the wheel spindle. This minimum-size bike was located on the base of a crate, crate sides nailed up round it, front wheel and mudguard inserted and top nailed on. This one had a carefully-wrapped Martini as well. Next stop the warehouse, then by rail with thousands of others to the docks.

"In the USA, when the ship docked and was unloaded, customs always selected at random three crates to open and check contents. The Triumph import agent had to be there and a senior Triumph employee. The Sales Vice-President had the number of the crate in which the rifle was hidden. As luck would have it this was one of the three chosen! This poor guy was terrified. He could, of course, deny all knowledge, but the whole shipment would have been impounded whilst customs checked every crate: a lot of expense and lost time, and investigation, etc. Two crates were opened and it was getting near end of work time. The customs guy said: "Those two are okay, these checks with Triumph always are; don't bother with the third crate."

The above tale from Stephen Mettam illustrates well the personal cooperation and goodwill that existed between the British and American organisations.

Key Marketing & Advertising Department personnel: from left – Advertising Manager Philip Michel, Product Planner Jack Redmond, and Product Planning Director Tony Salisbury. (Author's archive)

Extract from Denis McCormack's press release of September 28, 1971 –

"I suppose that the best way to correct misstatements made by those who have to rely on rumours or on guessing is for those who are in a position to know the facts, from time to time to make factual statements or press releases.

"As has previously been pointed out, the affairs of the famous BSA/Triumph brands in the USA are in the hands of the US parent company – Birmingham Small Arms Company Incorporated – whose corporate headquarters are in Verona, NJ, and whole main operating centres are at Baltimore, Maryland and Duarte, California.

"A change in top management of the BSA/Triumph/Top Gear companies, and of the US parent company recently became effective, and Denis McCormack became President of all US operations. Based on over 20 years' successful experience in the distribution of British motorcycles in the US, and aided by highly experienced, and well known management and enthusiastic motorcycling personnel that have been reassembled, we are now well through the first phase of revised policies leading to efficiency, economy, and the restoration of goodwill and loyalty. Our house is in very good order and we are able to launch, on our traditional annual date, (commencing in California on October 14 and on through to October 26 at Baltimore) our full 1972 sales program.

"Immediately afterwards, and strictly on schedule, 1972-improved BSA and Triumph models will be available to dealers, and will shortly thus be on display in dealer showrooms throughout the country.

"The demand for our products has never been greater. The supply situation – which was so inadequate during the 1971 season – has now been remedied. Substantial stocks of 1972 models are already in our warehouses, and we are off to an energetic and enthusiastic start toward what is believed will be, in many ways, a record year for BSA/Triumph.

"My suggestion, thus, to those who may have recently lost some confidence, is that very shortly now – perhaps around mid-November – go visit your BSA/Triumph dealer. Look at our new products in their shiny finished state, and with their many improved features. Plan to ride one of these great machines for 1972, and be assured of dealer backing, and parts and service attention to which these fine products are entitled."

This press release was sent out to all US BSA and Triumph dealers in an attempt to reassure them that the company was again on an even keel, which, in essence, was true.

The looming storm

During early February 1971, Verona issued a bulletin to dealers which gave estimated delivery dates for models (though these were split into two categories). The first category listed the earliest delivery dates, which were short on quantity, leaving some dealers without a product to sell, while the second set of dates ranged from four to six weeks later, depending on model, all of which were available to all dealers. The relevant part of the memo is reproduced here:

Model	Initial Availability	Subsequent Availability
A75-Rocket 3	April 10	April 24
A75V	March 13	March 13
A65L-Lightning	February 13	March 13
A65T-Thunderbolt	February 20	February 27
A65F-Firebird	April 10	May 22
B50MX	May 15	June 26
B50S	April 17	April 24
B50T	May 22	May 29
350 (all types)	July	July
B25T	Available	February 8
B25SS	Available	February 8

Not until February 1971 did BSA dealers receive this revised notification of projected model delivery dates, although – for the B50s – this was still hopelessly optimistic. (Author's archive)

By April, however, a problem other than late deliveries began to impact on BSA Inc. Many dealers were, understandably, refusing to accept their back order quotas, in most cases having already sent customers away on a different brand of motorcycle. In response, BSA reacted by initially cancelling all back orders from May, honouring them only once reconfirmed verbally.

With the end of spring came the realisation that BSA Inc was going to be stuck with a lot of unsold stock, now entering the States thick and fast. Ken Brown's Market Research Department set up what was called a 'sales contest' for the five regional managers to implement in their respective areas. Each region was allocated a certain number of motorcycles to sell via the dealers over a 7-week period beginning June 1. The 'prize' for those regions achieving sales targets was either a $2000 bonus or

$2000 worth of merchandise to be shared amongst district managers. To underline the seriousness of the situation, a memo forbade regional sales staff to take vacations prior to the beginning of August, stating that "... if we are to maximise sales, a maximum effort will be needed."

The same month the massive US dealer network also became involved in shifting stock. Since mid-May, all BSA models had reverted to black-painted frames because of negative feedback from many BSA dealers. Contrary to the general opinion of US motorcycling press, the dove grey-framed bikes were considered liabilities, and from the end of June, dealers were given what was termed a 'promotion allowance' of $100 – excitingly entitled 'BSA 650 Twin Firecracker Special' – against the cost of any grey-framed A65 models: in effect, getting the bikes for $100 cheaper than cost price, so urgent was the need to shift the backlog. Dealers were advised to use the $100 cost-saving to either repaint the frames themselves and reduce the showroom retail price, or simply pocket the money.

The Advertising Department placed advertisements in many non-motor cycling magazines in an effort to further assist sales, though rather hampering this objective was CCC pulling out, in early summer, of the dealer funding and hire purchase agreement that had been established with BSA Inc the previous year.

However, one welcome boost came in the unlikely form of a US government-imposed 10 per cent surtax on imports, announced on August 14, from which all BSA and Triumph models currently in stock were exempt, therefore giving dealers a certain sales advantage with the large quantities (in excess of 10,000 at one point) of late-delivered 1971 models sat in distribution warehouses and dealer showrooms. Compounding the situation was a fluctuating spares supply problem which sometimes meant that customers' bikes were laid up for weeks on end awaiting parts.

Rickman tie-up

It was during the summer that BSA announced a deal with Rickman Engineering, with BSA Inc the sole US distributor of the two-stroke-engined Rickman 125, and 250 MX and 125 enduro machines. The arrangement entailed the Rickman brothers' company exporting 6000 machines to America for the 1972 season, and the small capacity strokers sharing floor space with the larger BSA models throughout BSA Inc's nationwide dealer network. The first year value of the bikes in question was approximately £1 million.

The official statement by Executive Vice-President David Bird read as follows: "... it is our intention initially to distribute three models in the United States market

– 125cc Enduro, 125cc Motocross, 250cc Motocross. Additional products to this highly competitive and quality range will be introduced at a later date. It is our intention that these products give our BSA dealers highly competitive models in sectors of the market where BSA does not compete."

It was undoubtedly a good marketing stopgap, which, up to a point, addressed BSA's lack of small capacity two-stroke machines.

All change

Prior to this, in mid-June, Peter Thornton 'resigned' his position, and was replaced by ex-Tri-Cor President Denis McCormack. McCormack, British by birth, had controlled Tri-Cor for 17 years until his retirement in 1964, though he – until 1969, at least – was a director of Triumph and BSA Marketing Services. Somewhat worryingly, according to Pete Colman, McCormack had a deep dislike of BSA, which was to manifest itself in the virtual disappearance of BSA the following year. Revealing the depth of these almost obsessional convictions, Colman also felt that, while in retirement, McCormack would have been thinking about how to finish BSA, even though by this time he was only on the fringe of the industry.

With the ear of BSA's bankers, and the investigating consultants who were desperately looking for solutions to the group's dire financial problems, with relish McCormack set about advising the end of BSA as a motorcycle manufacturer: sadly, the relevant bodies listened, agreed, and acted accordingly.

This spiteful and shortsighted action didn't surprise anyone who knew the man. As is often the case with such personal obsessions, the repercussions were far-reaching, and in 1972 some US dealers found themselves without any product to sell. In addition, BSA Inc and BSA's parent company lost millions as a direct result of BSA's demise; not to mention the thousands of jobs (BSA and outside suppliers) that disappeared in the UK.

Peter Thornton – hero or villain?

Even though BSA Inc President Peter Thornton has since been heavily criticized by both press and some ex-colleagues for his often extravagant expenditure of BSA funds on racing and publicity events, it cannot be denied that the subsequent motorcycle press coverage derived from, for instance, the La Quinta launch was invaluable. 1970's racing and advertising programme had generated just under an estimated $1.5 million worth of free editorial coverage, and following La Quinta, most of the magazines gave the new bikes showcase features and several cover slots with, incidentally, much praise and little criticism.

BSA Inc President Peter Thornton. (Author's archive)

Thornton's $1,000,000 (£400,000-plus) racing budget for the 1971 season is also often used against him, but the reasoning behind it was undoubtedly sound. To give BSA/Triumph an advantage on the showroom floor – where their motorcycles were more expensively priced than those of leading Japanese manufacturers – a string of racing successes was vital, and this was, in fact, achieved by BSA winning both the prestigious Daytona 200 race and the AMA No 1 plate that year.

It is also well known that Thornton, holder of a Bachelor of Science degree from Massachusetts Institute of Technology, was not the easiest person to work for, often rubbing people up the wrong way, with his automotive industry advertising background not helping matters either. He also alienated himself to many of the 'motorcyclists' already employed in the BSA and Triumph setups when, under the directive of the UK parent company, he oversaw the merger of the administration centres of the two marques. However, he did correctly identify that their images desperately needed to be brought up-to-date, and especially so BSA, as market share had been rapidly declining, in the main, due to the Japanese motorcycle invasion headed by Honda. And it was he who was the driving force behind the concept of bikes styled for the oh-so-important American market.

By mid-May 1971 the decision to sack Thornton had been taken, though he was given the face-saving option of resignation – which he took, along with a $400,000 payoff – albeit with no official explanation for his departure. Press reports connected it to the Motor Cycle Division's failure to supply enough bikes to meet demand in America which, ironically, Thornton, by his lavish expenditure, had partially created. On the face of it, his dismissal seems a little unfair: the factory's failure to produce the bikes on time was hardly Thornton's fault. However, the truth was a little different, and instances of several previous indiscretions came to the notice of Jofeh at Small Heath. The final and rather damming misdemeanour to come to light was that Thornton had actually got the job at BSA by bribing 'someone' to lose the files of all of the other applicants – worse still was the fact that he had been hired by BSA to find a suitable candidate for this position!

Top Gear

As part of BSA's growth plan for the 1970s, a foray into the lucrative motorcycle accessories market was considered a vital step in the USA (the market for 1970 had been worth around £160,000,000 in sales nationwide). To this end, it was announced in January 1971 that another subsidiary of BSA Inc had been set up, entitled Top Gear Accessories Inc, which would operate through the existing dealer network. The company was to be run by A B Porter until Peter Thornton's exit during the summer, when Tony Salisbury (already a director) took over, his previous Product Planning Department apparently dissolved in the shake up instigated by McCormack's arrival.

Products ranged from leather riding suits, gloves, boots, lightweight riding jackets, luggage racks, etc, to tools, control cables, batteries, chains, tyres, and lubricants: just about everything, in fact. These were either supplied by Motoplas, BSA's UK accessories subsidiary, or bought in from outside manufacturers (more so clothing, which, in some cases, was specifically designed for Top Gear).

Much to the envy of rivals, being a part of BSA Inc, Top Gear was able to benefit from the prestige and popularity of some of the top AMA riders promoting its wares, with the likes of Dave Aldana, Gene Romero, Jim Rice, etc, privately and professionally wearing various Top Gear garments. With justification the brochure was able to boast "Our board of experts – the men who helped us design our products and test them – are some of the champion motorcycle riders of the US." During its inaugural year Top Gear had the most perfect product endorsement possible with Romero 1970's AMA No 1, and, later in the year, the plate transferring to BSA's Dick Mann.

Surviving the demise of BSA, Top Gear was still trading in 1973, although, presumably, the company was wound up or sold to a competitor as the corrosive

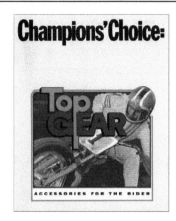

Top Gear's full colour 1971 brochure, which included profiles of BSA/ Triumph AMA team members. (Author's archive)

As well as motorcycle accessories, Top Gear supplied a comprehensive range of clothing, ranging from T-shirts to one-piece leather racing suits. (Author's archive)

Bellstone Cycle's poster-clad showroom in the summer of 1971, with Paul Sutherland and Ed McDermott: two of the three proprietors. (Courtesy Ed & Arlene McDermott)

effects of the Meriden 'sit-in' slowly destroyed the fledgling Norton Villiers Triumph Company.

Dealers view

During 1971 Pittsfield Massachusetts residents Ed and Arlene McDermott, then aged 28 and 26 respectively, along with Paul Sutherland (Arlene's brother), took the decision to become BSA dealers, and, accordingly, bought a local dealership, Bellstone Cycle, as a going concern. The business had, up until then, been run as little more than a part-time hobby by its previous owner, thereby requiring some serious work and commitment to transform it into a full-time endeavour, illustrated by Bellstone's new trading hours which saw the shop open at 10am and close 12 hours later at 10pm.

Enduro racer Ed burnt the candle at both ends, working in the shop during the day, and welding at night for the General Electric Co, while, for two years, brother-in-law Paul did a stint in the shop from 6pm till 10pm after his own day job as an engineer in Albany, NY. Ed doubled up as salesman and mechanic, while Arlene handled book-keeping duties and the spares side of things. Prior to this Ed had been working evenings and weekends for a local Kawasaki dealer.

Far from being just another job, the duo were genuinely into the bikes they sold, and all that this entailed. Building B25 short-track racers was just one aspect of the specialist tuning that Bellstone offered, and the now-popular sport of motocross accounted for much additional workshop time. Any problems with spares procurement

Ed and Arlene McDermott in the year they became BSA dealers. (Courtesy Ed & Arlene McDermott)

was usually resolved by ringing around some of the larger dealers, who were generally happy to help out.

With the exception of the 650cc twins, the new bikes made a good impression on Bellstone: the B25 and B50s "… very nice. We sold many 250 and 500 Singles;" the A75 Rocket 3 "… awesome," and the E35 Fury "… couldn't wait to get it, but it never came. It would have been wonderful." However, the dove grey frames were not liked, and Ed also felt that the A65s would have looked better fitted with the previous year's chrome teardrop petrol tank, much like the new A75 – which is interesting because, from the beginning of 1972, BSA Inc modified a limited number of these tanks for fitment to the P39 650s as what it termed a 'sales aid,' though these were supplied unpainted, and it was left to the dealer to finish them at his cost.

Highlighting the gaping hole in BSA's marketing strategy – the lack of small capacity bikes – Bellstone also sold 50-125cc italjet-engined Indian motorcycles. BSA resolved this issue to some extent with the Rickman deal announced in August: "… the Rickmans gave our sales a big boost – we sold lots of them. They were all blue 125cc at first – MX and Enduro – we loved them! They were priced very high in the beginning, but the company realized we were having a problem with them not being priced competitively, and they allowed us to begin selling them for like $795 – they sold like hotcakes then."

Upon receiving their first B50MX, so enthusiastic was Ed that he loaded it onto his pick-up and drove to a nearby short-track competition at Electric City Raceway in Duanesburg, NY, intending to race it there and then. Frustratingly, he was told he didn't have the valid entry documentation, so could not participate. However, overhearing this conversation, Steve Boyd, a young rider from New York, asked if Ed and Arlene would allow him to enter the bike instead. Before Ed had finished explaining the B50's protracted starting procedure, Boyd had employed his own method, which entailed simply reversing the bike to find the back end of the compression stroke, then just lurching forward, whereupon the 500cc single fired up, leaving all onlookers stunned … and yes, he did go on to win the race!

"This experience ignited a real interest in the B50MX, not only with us, but with anyone who saw or heard about its performance that day. As luck would have it, Ed's brother, Bob McDermott, was willing to try racing that motorcycle to represent our shop in an effort to further promote the popularity of this bike, and increase sales for us. Bob was a big, strong, 18-year-old man, eager

to compete, and he became one of the best Big Bore competitors in New England and New York. The B50MX became a force to be reckoned with!" recalls Arlene.

During the latter part of the year, Ed attended one of the 5-day BSA service schools held at Baltimore, where mechanics were able to familiarise themselves with official techniques required to service and repair the 1971/1972 models. All BSA dealers were invited to attend the free tutorial, with board and lodgings at the individual's expense.

Mid-October saw the 1972 models displayed to US dealers for the first time via two separate shows, catering for both eastern and western regions, with Triumph holding separate events. The west coast show was cleverly timed to coincide with the Ontario 250-mile (404km) race (which, of course, BSA won), while a week later east coast dealers attended an impressive two-day show at a huge conference centre in Towson, the suburb of Baltimore where the east coast BSA/Triumph distribution centre was sited. In stark contrast to the previous year, orders could be placed and bikes actually ridden away on the day. Arlene: "It was spectacular! Each bike was presented with fanfare, lights, music, etc. We were just two young kids from Pittsfield, Massachusetts, and I can tell you we were impressed and took it all in! Hung on to every word that was said and both remember it quite well. Our lives were very tied up in this venture – probably even more than some of the people owning much larger dealerships! Boy, if you don't think we felt like we were very important – let me tell you! They treated us like royalty!"

While wandering around the nearby Baltimore warehouse that day, Ed came across one of the rare 750cc A70 Twins wearing a US-spec Rocket 3 tank, painted in the A75's 1972 colour scheme of chrome and burgundy. Whether or not this was a BSA initiative is not clear, but was also something that Umberslade Hall's Styling Department had been playing around with, albeit on a 650. The combination of the old tank and 750cc would, the McDermott's believed, have been a winner in the States: "… we could have sold them like crazy," says Arlene today.

As BSA's financial bubble burst, Ed and Arlene felt that official statements issued to dealers from US HQ at Verona failed to paint the full picture: "Rumours were flying, and over here it was hard to find things out – we were scared, we had worked so hard and were afraid

Using an 18bhp Zundap two-stroke engine, the quality-built Rickman 125 Enduro was very popular in the States. The nickel-plated frame was in a similar vein to the planned mock titanium silver finish that BSA's Styling Department had planned to use on 1971 BSAs. (Author's archive)

BSA Motorcycle Corporation • P.O. Box 6790 • Baltimore, Maryland 21204 • (301) 252-3400

October 13, 1971

Mr. BSA Dealer

. . . . 1972 BSA Models are in!

1972	LIGHTNING	Firebird red
1972	THUNDERBOLT	Etruscan bronze
1972	VICTOR MX	Hi-violet/polished alloy
1972	VICTOR TRAIL	Flambordeaux/polish alloy - chrome fenders
1972	VICTOR GOLD STAR	Hi-violet
1972	ROCKET 3 (4 speed)	Burgundy/chrome

We can start shipping on October 25 ----

Or you can pick them up at our Dealer Meeting in Baltimore on October 25th and 26th.

Things look real good for BSA in 1972. Mr. McCormack has just returned from England with the 1972 prices finalized. New colors, black frames, polished forks, new seat, all add up to a BSA Profit-Picture for you in '72!

Have you mailed your reservation form in for our Dealer Meeting on October 25th and 26th?

If not - - - do so right away. (We have lunches and banquets to plan!)

We also attach an order form for 1972 models. Use this form for units you desire shipped beginning October 25th. (You already have your order form for Pick Up at the Dealer Meeting.)

We look forward to seeing you in Baltimore on October 25th.

Cordially,

BSA MOTORCYCLE CORPORATION

Harry P. Chaplin
Eastern Sales Manager

Business as usual. Production-wise, everything was on schedule for the 1972 model year, though the range of models had diminished drastically, with the smallest capacity motorcycle now being 500cc. (Author's archive)

of losing it all. We even subscribed to a special British bike paper hoping to find out that way. We mostly found out from other BSA dealers we had made friends with. It was a fairly tight group as we worried and held our breath waiting for news – when we heard something we sometimes let each other know."

One effect of the seasonal demand that is so much a feature of bike sales in the States saw the new venture up against the wall within the first year. With the CCC pulling the plug on the dealer credit scheme, Bellstone was forced to seek alternative finance for seven new BSAs; in this case the Transamerica Finance Company. Quite aware they were buying out of season, the trio did not foresee problems, as they knew they would sell the bikes the following spring.

However, being new to the business – as well as possibly a little naive – they did not notice the small print on the finance contract, which stipulated they repay 10 per cent of the amount borrowed after three months, and the remaining 90 per cent after six months. The first repayment was just about managed, but the second proved way out of reach. Arlene's parents had recently retired, and had sold their house to hit the road for a while; a combination of good luck and kindness meant they were in a position to help. Come the spring the debt was repaid as each bike was sold – and a valuable lesson had been learned.

Once BSA was finally wound up in the US, BSA Inc tried to establish its dealers as Triumph agents, in an attempt to maintain as many businesses as possible. Bellstone Cycle felt it was fairly treated in this transition, and, in addition, acquired the stock from Pittsfield's Triumph dealer who had decided to call it a day.

An unforeseen benefit of becoming a Triumph agent materialised late in 1972, when stock of the limited edition TRX75 Hurricane model began to arrive in the States. Because of the relatively small number built, each dealer was allocated a single example only, and Ed and Arlene still have theirs to this day, having opted to hold on to the Triple rather than sell it. Far from being a static showroom exhibit or a sunny Sunday cruiser, the Hurricane was no stranger to the drag strip, where, at one time, it ran the national record.

Arlene sums up how BSA bikes were generally perceived in the States then –

"The shops with Japanese franchises were tough competition – we had to work extra hard with our British bike business … But BSA had an image and it was not wimpy … we sold a man's motorcycle to men!"

Parked in Armoury Road, a 1972-spec A65L looking pretty, wearing 1970's A65 fuel tank. It is not known whether this mock-up was prompted by US dealer feedback, or simply the need to shift the thousands of A65s stockpiled in the States by any means possible. (Author's archive)

Chapter 12

Into the abyss

First cracks

Thursday, May 27, 1971 was the day that the cork popped out of the BSA bottle, by virtue of the shareholders' interim report, which laid bare the poor prospects of the Motor Cycle Division's finances for 1970/1971, with some of the group's subsidiary companies also having a poor year, though for different and unrelated reasons. BSA shares plummeted accordingly from 71p to 42½p, which, in monetary terms, translated to almost £5 million sliced off the value of the company's shares.

Prior to the report's publication, board-level memoranda dating from the beginning of the year highlighted some of the events leading to the disastrous situation BSA now found itself facing.
• January 27 – revised forecast of necessary banking overdraft limit of £4 million from Barclays Bank, and a further £10 million sourced from the American banks was advised
• February 17 – Managing Director Lionel Jofeh submitted his fiscal reappraisal report, which predicted a reduction in profits for 1970/1971 from £1.9 million to £1.1 million
• April 28 – Lionel Jofeh reported that production levels at Small Heath were lower than required due in the main to a failure to recruit enough skilled labour
• May 26 – profits for April were reported as just £36,000; somewhat lower than the previous prediction of £826,000 mentioned in Jofeh's February report. At this point the Board decided to bring in the company's own auditors, Cooper Bros & Co, to assess BSA's financial position and future prospects, and as part of this investigation, two of Cooper's accountants sat in on all subsequent board meetings until the report had been completed

Four weeks later the future of the premises used for BSA board meetings, BSA House, was also under consideration, as several enquiries about leasehold availability were received. Whether the Board had made it known that the

BSA House photographed in the 1950s.
(Author's archive)

Interim report 1970-1971 –

"It is now clear that the results of the Motor Cycle Division for the current financial year to 31st July 1971 will be extremely disappointing.

"In 1968-69 we took the decision to design and develop what is probably the most comprehensive range of new models ever undertaken at one time, in order to enhance our reputation for quality, styling and performance. This policy involved heavy development and tooling expenditure, much reorganisation expense of an exceptional nature, and a degree of financial risk, but it was an inevitable decision if we were firstly to maintain and secondly to increase our share of world markets.

"From a technical point of view, there is evidence that this policy has achieved substantial success. The new models have been well received by the trade, orders have been at a much higher level than ever before, and our machines have won major international racing events.

"Unfortunately, trading results this year cannot now match these technical achievements. The production programme was expected to be in full swing some months ago, but has been gravely delayed for a variety of reasons. In addition to the usual pre-production problems, major shortfalls have been caused by almost continuous component shortages and defects, strikes, and, not least, by a surprising inability to recruit the necessary additional labour to meet our planned output. Moreover, the division has had to bear very heavy increases in costs of labour and materials, particularly in recent months, which cannot be passed on to our customers, 85% or more of whom are abroad, late in the season.

"Consequently, production and sales for the year as a whole will fall far below expectations and, because of the earlier problems, a substantial loss on the year's operations is inevitable, even though production is now running at a level 50% higher than ever previously achieved.

"The new, wholly-owned subsidiary in the USA recently formed to sell accessories for the motorcyclist and his machine is expected to make a growing contribution to group profits from next year onwards."

lease was available, or interested parties were acting on the news of BSA's imminent crisis, is not known.

At June's board meeting on the 23rd, Jofeh had the unenviable task of reporting that further losses were imminent, due to a production figure that was lower than he had calculated some weeks previously, the shortfall caused by a paucity of castings from outside suppliers. The group's financial loss was estimated at £1,842,600.

Within a few weeks the Board had decided that Jofeh had to go, as ultimate responsibility for the production failures lay with him; his mutually agreed departure was publicly announced early in July. Over the years Jofeh's £35,518 'golden handshake' has been regarded with derision, though the reason behind stemmed from sound legal advice. On studying the case, BSA's lawyers recommended that, rather than straight dismissal – which could well result in Jofeh issuing a lawsuit, the outcome of which would not necessarily favour BSA – the company should make a deal. In addition to the £35,000 payout, Jofeh was also able to buy his BSA-owned Berkswell residence at a knock-down price.

The first tangible sign of the financial turmoil that BSA now faced was an economy drive, declared on Thursday, July 8. Initially, the majority of competition activity ceased, beginning with the announcement at the start of the following week about the closure of the Small Heath Competition Shop. In addition, many of the division's motorcycles were subject to an immediate price increase, varying from £44 for the 750cc machines to a massive £81 for Triumph's 650cc T120.

Four days later, the investment company Vision Enterprises launched a £5.5 million bid for a majority shareholding in the motorcycle and engineering sectors of the group, thereby increasing the current share price of 39½p to 55p, though the bid would only be validated once the man behind the company, Midlands entrepreneur Dr Daniel McDonald, had satisfied himself that BSA's financial position was not too precarious. At this stage Vision Enterprises already held 300,000 shares in the company, and the initial statement from co-director Anthony Beaumont-Dark, acting for McDonald, that: "We want to build up BSA, not carve it up. Dr McDonald is working on new ideas which might be put into BSA in the domestic product sphere," was received with caution by the Board of Directors, McDonald's previous connection with the manufacture of record players no doubt uppermost in their minds. Not unreasonably, the Board asked for more details about these proposed products before commenting further.

Before any further moves from either side, the Board insisted that the accountants, Cooper Bros, should complete their investigations. The Canadian snowmobile company Bombardier, which was planning on expanding into motorcycle production, also expressed an initial interest in BSA, though there is little evidence of any serious follow-up enquiries. Events were moving quickly,

Vision Enterprises statement, Monday, July 12 –

"The Board of Vision Enterprises Ltd, a company controlled by Dr D M McDonald, announced that it has approached the board of the Birmingham Small Arms Company Ltd, to indicate that, subject to Vision being satisfied with the present financial position of BSA, Vision intends to make a cash offer for not less than 50% and not more than 60% of the Ordinary stock of BSA at a price of 55p per share. The offer would thus take the basic form of being for 60% of each Ordinary stockholders' holding."

Lionel Jofeh astride a 650cc Thunderbolt at the Royal Lancaster. Besides divisional work, Jofeh also represented group interests, and from January 1971 was the CMCA's President. (Courtesy VMCC)

however, and by the end of the week, 850 redundancies had been announced, 400 of which were Small Heath production workers, the remainder taken from as far afield as Triumph's Meriden plant and the R&D centre at Umberslade Hall, though a proportion of this number would naturally be taken up by pending retirements. Trade union and management representatives held several discussions on how to minimise job losses, and a partial solution was arrived at in the case of production staff. At a mass meeting – and in what was undoubtedly a heartening display of solidarity – the majority present agreed to these proposals, which entailed all of Small Heath's production workers, some 3500, switching to short-time working, forfeiting their annual production bonus and becoming more flexible as a labour force. With these assurances in place a reduction in the number of redundancies was achieved, resulting in slightly more acceptable job losses of 130 production workers at Small

Lionel Jofeh –

Appointed by BSA Chairman Eric Turner in February 1967 to replace Harry Sturgeon as the group's Managing Director, Marcus Lionel Jofeh had caused waves before he had even accepted the position. Fellow director John Rowe had at the time urged Turner to fill the post from the British motor industry, as the operations of the two spheres were very similar with obvious advantages, and from a confidential letter he wrote to BSA's auditor, Cooper Bros, during the dying days of BSA in 1972, it is clear that he did not endorse Turner's choice. In response to criticisms that he should have appointed from within the division, Eric Turner went on record as saying that although there were several candidates of sufficient stature and ability within the division, by recruiting from outside, any potential personal animosity between internal candidates would be avoided.

By the mid-1960s – and always known as Lionel – Jofeh had risen to the top of the aircraft precision instrument design and manufacturing company Sperry Gyroscope Ltd, holding both the position of Managing Director and Chairman. Such was his standing within certain circles that the end of the previous decade saw him bestowed with an OBE.

There is little doubt, though, that whilst at BSA Jofeh was universally unpopular, largely due to some rather negative and remote personality traits. Variously described by many colleagues as arrogant, unfeeling, vain and unapproachable, he would not accept any criticism of himself or his decisions, and always believed himself correct in every matter he concerned himself with. However, regardless of this, some, although not actually having any sympathy for him, do believe that he was at all times acting in what he thought were the best interests of the division, however misguided many of his actions were felt – and indeed proved – to be. An example of the way he dealt with people and situations is related here by the division's Chief Stylist, Stephen Mettam –

"He surrounded himself with 'yes men' and disregarded or re-located (or sacked) anyone who told him what he did not want to hear. One guy senior to myself (not my boss) who had known Jofeh for years prior to joining BSA, was present when I presented to L J some design changes that were required to make the Rocket 3 more acceptable to the US west coast market. L J had weeks before already told me what he thought should be done. I was a biker and I was a designer, and I had spoken/ written to BSA personnel on the west coast. I think I knew what the problem was and what was needed. I knew what could be done in a hurry without spending much money. Lack of time and money were part of the equation. I presented the 'solution' as if it satisfied what were L J's requirements. He listened, no-one present disagreed, L J departed, not looking very happy. The aforementioned 'senior guy' took me to one side and said 'Lionel Jofeh is no fool; he knew you were not telling him what he wanted to hear. If you ever try that again, he will be certain to remove you'."

Jofeh's mutually agreed resignation in July 1971 was ultimately precipitated by the series of delays and financial deficits which had greatly escalated during the first part of the year. Each report he submitted to the parent board painted a blacker picture, month by month, and regardless of the many contributory factors to production delays outside of his control, overall responsibility for the catastrophic situation was undoubtedly Jofeh's, so it was only right that he 'resign.'

It is indeed ironic that while he was away in the USA at the end of June personally dismissing American BSA President Peter Thornton, Finance Director Laurie Beeson, in Jofeh's absence, delved into the Motor Cycle Division's finances to discover the most devastating figures yet – a shortfall of over £750,000 in Jofeh's previously forecast profit for the month of April. One board meeting later, Jofeh followed in Thornton's footsteps.

Heath, 200 at Meriden, and 56 employees at Umberslade Hall.

As July came to a close, Cooper Bros accountants, aided by financial advisors Lazard Brothers & Co Ltd, issued their findings, which, in short, estimated that BSA's Motor Cycle Division had lost approximately £3,300,000 in the last financial year, prompting Beaumont-Dark to comment that "… the size of the loss has come as a surprise." The accountants also recommended reorganising the management structure, and appointing a 'high calibre' managing director, whilst, on a positive note, stating that providing these and other measures in the pipeline were carried out, BSA *could* still survive, albeit with a reduced manufacturing profile.

By early August, while Vision Enterprises was evaluating BSA Motor Cycles Incorporated in the USA, the American newspaper *Motor Cycle Weekly* ran reports that motorcycle manufacturers Honda and Puch were involved in a takeover bid for BSA, and went on to announce that BSA steel supplier, Tube Investments, was also interested. BSA parried the reports by stating that no approaches had been received from any of the companies mentioned, and it would now appear that the report was based on little more than rumour, as nothing concrete ever materialised.

The following week Vision Enterprises withdrew its provisional bid; having gathered all the facts, it had found the BSA group to be "a slightly different horse from what we had thought when we first set about it," an obvious reference to the depth of the financial quagmire BSA was in.

So, with outside funds apparently unforthcoming, the group fell back on survival plans that had been drawn up in the interim. Birtley Engineering, a subsidiary that designed and built equipment for the coal industry, was sold to the Canadian company Great West Steel Industries Ltd for £254,000, though Birtley's Director, John Rowe, insisted that the business had been searching for a competent buyer for in excess of a year, and the sale was totally unconnected with BSA's current plight.

After unsuccessfully trying for approximately 18 months to offload the largely empty Redditch factory by way of a long-term lease, BSA was forced to sell the premises outright, and found a buyer in car component manufacturer Quinton Hazel Ltd, which generated in excess of £1 million for the beleaguered company.

The third big sale involved the group's holding in Alfred Herbert, the original equipment and machine tool supplier to the auto industry, which harvested £1,750,000; another much-needed sum of money.

On October 7 a lengthy statement from Eric Turner which outlined the course of events from July brought the devastating news that consultants Cooper Bros, in light of the £15 million needed to pay off American banks and subsidise the group until 1972 models began to bring in revenue the following spring, advised that the enormous Small Heath plant cease motorcycle production by the end of 1971, transferring manufacture to Meriden, where, to the horror of both factories, a reduced range of BSAs would be built alongside Triumphs. The influence

Chairman Eric Turner's statement to all group employees, September 1971 –

"I realise that virtually all our employees must be wondering about the present position of the company. Inevitably, rumours of all kinds run rife in these times, most of them based on highly speculative and uninformed comment. I would therefore urge you all to discount these until an authoritative board statement can be made.

"The parent board is in the process of finalising its plans with its bankers and others to improve the company's cash position, and to restore reasonable profitability. Naturally, you will be told what these plans are as soon as possible, since I recognise the need to remove present doubts and uncertainties.

"In the meantime, the directors have been greatly assisted by the continuing support, and, indeed, forbearance of suppliers, customers and stockholders, as well as employees. This faith in BSA is very much in line with the traditional co-operation which has successfully carried the company through other difficult times in its long history."

of the new BSA Inc President, Dennis McCormack, was a contributory factor in this. Three-quarters of the Small Heath complex was to be sold off, leaving the remaining 25 per cent to build engines, produce motorcycle components, handle spares, and begin general engineering work on a sub-contract basis. Up to 3000 redundancies were slated, but it was claimed that such drastic measures would ensure BSA's survival as a motorcycle manufacturer, providing 1972 sales predictions were accurate.

The contract engineering branch was run separately to the motorcycle activities, and BSA Manufacturing Director Ken Strangward was placed in control of the operation, set up in the 'new' buildings at the front of the complex. All of the computer-controlled assembly equipment installed during the latter half of the previous decade, at a cost of just under £1 million, was removed and reportedly sold for scrap, though this is a little difficult to believe. With these measures in place, and a £10 million overdraft from Barclays Bank, BSA still had to find £5 million.

Turner's statement went on to announce two new appointments at board level, with ex-QC and Labour Member of Parliament Lord Shawcross, already a BSA director, agreeing to take over as Chairman from Eric Turner on a temporary basis during November, and Chief Executive Brian Eustace, who had distinguished himself as Plant Manager at Guest Keen & Nettlefold's factory in India, where he successfully brought several industrial disputes to a close, strengthening the company's fortunes.

A further asset disposal was announced in mid-October when BSA put up for sale its £2.1 million share in the central heating pump company Sealed Motor Construction, acquired two years previously, as part of a deal involving BSA Harford.

Two weeks later the first redundancies were actually issued to 870 employees, all of whom had been employed by BSA for less than 12 months. Even though they were officially given four weeks' notice and received a month's pay, their redundancy was actually to start the following week. Company trade unions, eager to save jobs, urged the employees involved to refuse the redundancy terms, and carry on working, following the conclusion of a meeting where 4000 workers backed the rebellion. A Small Heath union delegation also met with Trade Minister John Eden, who, as a result, discussed with Lord Shawcross the possibility of delaying termination of the remaining 2130 jobs.

Regardless, the following week the bottom irrevocably fell out of any hopes of job salvation, when BSA announced that an estimated £8.5 million was required in order for the Motor Cycle Division to continue. The unions

pressed for an all-out strike, but workers could see the writing on the wall, and in the resulting ballot, the union motion was comprehensively defeated by a ratio of 9:1.

On Monday, November 1 an Extraordinary General Meeting approved restructuring plans, and an increase in the borrowing limit to £15 million. Non-executive directors Samuel Roberts and Harry West, along with Finance Director Laurie Beeson, offered their resignations in light of the call for a fresh board, and, in the case of the first two, pressure from stockholders. These were all accepted once replacements had been finalised, with Beeson's position being filled by David Probert, who had previously been at accountants Cooper Bros, and a part of the BSA investigation team. By this time many of the redundancies had taken effect, with around 2200 jobs having disappeared – the division's R&D Centre at Umberslade Hall was now left with just 83 staff, most of whom would soon be transferred to Meriden.

During the last week of November, in what was an ill-timed and bloody-minded move, over 100 tool setters, paid some £8-12 a week less than their counterparts at Meriden, walked out on unofficial strike. Inevitably, workers not involved with the industrial action were also affected, resulting in BSA having to lay off 500 machine operators. Within a week the strike was off.

The GKN company also briefly made the headlines in late November when it was rumoured to have an interest in acquiring the two BSA engineering concerns, Sintered Components and Foundries.

Mid-December saw two more high profile personalities named as board members. Bert Hopwood was elevated from his divisional post of Deputy Managing Director to Group Executive Director and Design Adviser, while Dick Fenton, who was both Chairman and a director of London motorcycle dealer Harvey Owen, and Owen Bros' parent company, Naylor & Root, joined as a non-executive director. Of the original 1971 board, only John Rowe, John Hatch and R Danielson remained.

As it turned out, planned assembly of BSA's P34 500 Singles and the P40 750 Triple (the BSA P39s were discontinued) at Meriden failed to materialise, resulting in Small Heath-built BSA models continuing to be assembled well into 1972, apparently ceasing in April. However, this cut-off date would seem not to take into account either the 1973 specification B50MX or the subsequent 'badge-engineered' Triumph version known as the TR5MX Avenger, production records confirming that assembly of these off-road models had ceased by August 1973. Rather bizarrely, all of the TR5MXs did make one visit to the Meriden factory – to have the Triumph logo applied to the fuel tank – before returning to Small Heath for despatch.

The last BSAs ever built: the US-only 1973 spec B50MX, that boasted its own brochure and is seen here being assembled in the 'new' building. (Courtesy VMCC)

The End

In early May 1972, BSA announced that, by the end of the financial year in July, it was on target to break even, the half-yearly deficit having been considerably less than half of that in the same period of the previous year due to good profits on the current range. Unfortunately, this optimism was a little premature, and by November, Lord Shawcross admitted that the company was still in the red, despite having achieved a further decrease in deficit. Two reasons cited as hindering recovery were the recent devaluation of the dollar, which accounted for a £300,000 loss, and an additional £674,000 in bank interest charges.

It was at this stage that the British government became involved after BSA asked for financial assistance, although initial reaction was restricted to simply conducting a worldwide survey into the demand for British-built motorcycles.

In conclusion to this final chapter in BSA's history, by November, talks with the Department of Trade & Industry (DTI) and Norton Villiers, whose participation had, by now, become a prerequisite for government aid, were proceeding along lines which indicated to some of BSA's board members that BSA was being pushed to the point where it would no longer be making motorcycles. Following a meeting with the DTI, a report issued by bankers Kleinwort & Benson Ltd (whose speciality was in the field of business mergers), laid out some hard to swallow conditions, which had to be met if BSA wanted any survival plan to have a chance of fruition.

The two major points of the report were that BSA's four remaining, non-motorcycle subsidiary companies Metal Components (itself comprising several companies), Birtley Manufacturing, BSA Guns, and Harford Heating, had to be sold to Norton Villiers' parent company, Manganese Bronze Holdings. Even though all four were profitable concerns with good financial futures, the sale price was set at a paltry £3.5million by the audit company hired by either the DTI or MBH.

Secondly, from the early days of discussion the DTI insisted that MBH and Norton Villiers boss Dennis Poore be a part of the management structure, until it actually became a stipulation that for the aid plan to succeed, Poore be installed as Chairman of the new company. In short, if BSA did not agree to these and the other proposals, it would be forced to call in the receiver. This last point, not too far short of a threat, prompted both David Probert and John Rowe to write in protest to Kleinwort & Benson, though, in reality, there was little option but to agree with these rather severe requirements.

For its part the DTI initially proposed that a totally new factory be built, complete with new plant and equipment – the idea being that if the government was to help the British motorcycle industry, it should be in the shape of a long-term investment rather than a short sighted bail-out, and, provisionally, government funds were to be spent thus –

Buildings	£2.5 million
Plant	£8 million
New models	£1.5 million per model

However – and presumably after reconsideration – within a few months the total sum had been reduced to £4.8 million, thereby ending such grandiose plans for good.

In March 1973, MBH finally put forward a takeover bid for BSA which, if accepted, would leave Poore in charge of a £20 million motorcycle company to be known as 'Norton Villiers Triumph' (NVT), clearly spelling the end for BSA as a manufacturer of motorcycles. Within a day of BSA's Chairman, Lord Shawcross, receiving the bid (but before he could put it to the board), a stock exchange tip-off on March 14, in conjunction with illegal stock market practices by broker Ralph Clarke, resulted in BSA's share price plummeting to 4¾p, prompting Lord Shawcross to request that BSA be suspended from further stock exchange dealings. Clarke's actions had reduced the value of BSA as a company by over £2 million, and even though he was banned from the stock exchange for two years, neither he nor his company, Chapman & Rowe, would reveal the identity of the client he was acting for. As well as Clarke's ban, the subsequent enquiry also censured Chapman & Rowe for discreditable conduct, although the damage was done – and irreversible.

With BSA's back well and truly against the wall – and the company in an even weaker financial position – the board had little alternative but to accept the MBH takeover, even though some members still argued vehemently against the merger, regardless of the only alternative – bankruptcy.

Although by August 1973 BSA was to all intents and purposes dead, a final twist was to emerge a month later when NVT Chairman Dennis Poore announced that Meriden would close down early in 1974, and Triumph and some Norton production would transfer to Small Heath, primarily because the site was so much larger than that at Meriden. Additionally, to be rid of much of the militant and highly paid Triumph workforce would also be a welcome bonus. It was, of course, this very militancy that indirectly destroyed any chance of a long-term British motorcycle industry. The villain? The Meriden Co-operative.

Jeff Smith MBE – October 1971 –

"A fact that I could wish was fiction was the virtual closing of the BSA factory at Small Heath. I refer to BSA motor cycles, other activities will continue but the assembly of BSA motor cycles at Small Heath is to cease by the end of the year.

"Mismanagement of BSA has been so gross that in a world of expanding motor cycle sales the group has somehow contrived, year by year, to lose ground in every market. In an effort to regain lost ground the higher management embarked on a programme of modernisation for the interior of the Small Heath factory.

"This was to arrange the capability of motorcycle production which could be classed as the best in Europe. Motor cycles were to pour from the assembly line at the rate of one every two minutes. Millions were put into modernisation, market research and product planning on a vast scale. Eventually, the new concept appeared in pre-production form, and was eagerly applauded by the motor cycling press.

"The advertising campaign went wonderfully well in America; the factory was assured of work for years. Then the bubble burst, as suddenly as bubbles do, and within six months the astonishing state of affairs became brutally apparent. This profligate management had shored up its edifice by borrowing, borrowing, borrowing, to the tune of £10 million.

"Now hopelessly swamped by financial and production problems, the right course we are assured, is to make 3000 people redundant and cease assembly at Small Health, which, despite the enormous expense in re-equipment, is now variously described as 'a huddle of sheds' or 'antiquated buildings.'

"This was obviously not the case when sanctions were given to spend the money on them less than two years ago. Like me they have suddenly grown old! From the catastrophe following the drastic surgery suggested, it appears that Triumph will be saved, but almost certainly, within a year, BSA will disappear from the market or at best merely replace a nameplate on a few Meriden products.

"Meanwhile, the captain and the king depart from the tumbling BSA structure wiser, perhaps, in many things but, one suspects, still uncomprehending in the ways of motor cycles and men."

The sad sight that met the eyes of visitors to Armoury Road in 1977. (Courtesy VMCC)

Also from Veloce Publishing –

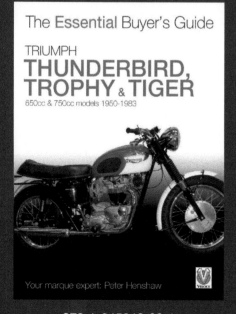
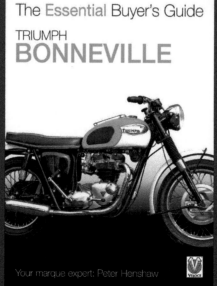
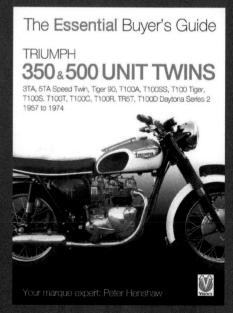

PETER HENSHAW

THE

BSA
BANTAM
BIBLE

ALL MODELS 1948-1971

THE definitive book of the BSA Bantam, a simple commuter bike that thousands learnt to ride on. The book includes year-by-year specifications, colour schemes and engine/frame numbers. Also contains a guide to buying a secondhand Bantam and details of Bantam clubs and specialists.
The essential Bantam companion!

ISBN: 978-1-787111-36-3
Hardback • 25x20.7cm • 160 pages • 167 colour and b&w pictures

For prices and more info on Veloce titles, visit our website at www.veloce.co.uk • email: info@veloce.co.uk
• Tel: +44(0)1305 260068

Also from Veloce Publishing –

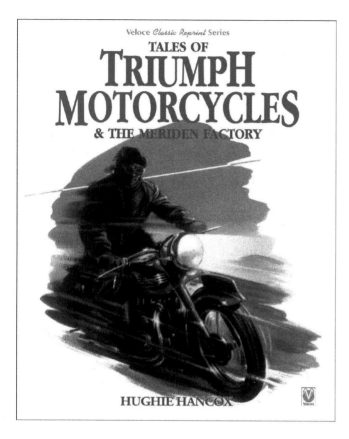

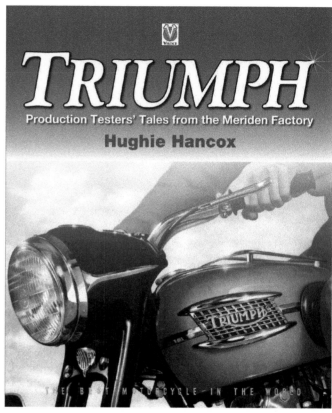

Hughie worked at Triumph from 1954 until its closure in 1974. Here's the story of his life in the famous Meriden factory; of many adventures with Triumph motorcycles & Triumph people. Records the fascinating history of a great marque.

ISBN: 978-1-787115-49-1
Paperback • 25x20.7cm
• 144 pages

The story of one worker's time on the Triumph Production Testing team from 1960 to 1962, packed with amusing anecdotes about the obstacles and adventures associated with a tester's daily life. With guides to fixing problems still found on the 1960s models, this is an intimate and useful account of one of Britain's most famous factories.

ISBN: 978-1-845844-41-7
Paperback • 25x20.7cm• 160 pages
• 183 colour and b&w pictures

For prices and more info on Veloce titles, visit our website at www.veloce.co.uk • email: info@veloce.co.uk • Tel: +44(0)1305 260068

Index